ESSENTIAL SQL
ON SQL SERVER®
2008

SIKHA SAHA BAGUI, EdD
UNIVERSITY OF WEST FLORIDA

RICHARD WALSH EARP, PhD
PROFESSOR EMERITUS, UNIVERSITY OF WEST FLORIDA

JONES AND BARTLETT PUBLISHERS
Sudbury, Massachusetts
BOSTON   TORONTO   LONDON   SINGAPORE

World Headquarters

Jones and Bartlett Publishers	Jones and Bartlett Publishers	Jones and Bartlett Publishers
40 Tall Pine Drive	Canada	International
Sudbury, MA 01776	6339 Ormindale Way	Barb House, Barb Mews
978-443-5000	Mississauga, Ontario L5V 1J2	London W6 7PA
info@jbpub.com	Canada	United Kingdom
www.jbpub.com		

Jones and Bartlett's books and products are available through most bookstores and online booksellers. To contact Jones and Bartlett Publishers directly, call 800-832-0034, fax 978-443-8000, or visit our website, www.jbpub.com.

Substantial discounts on bulk quantities of Jones and Bartlett's publications are available to corporations, professional associations, and other qualified organizations. For details and specific discount information, contact the special sales department at Jones and Bartlett via the above contact information or send an email to specialsales@jbpub.com.

Production Credits
Publisher: David Pallai
Acquisitions Editor: Timothy McEvoy
Editorial Assistant: Melissa Potter
Associate Production Editor: Tiffany Sliter
Associate Marketing Manager: Lindsay Ruggiero
V.P., Manufacturing and Inventory Control: Therese Connell
Composition: Northeast Compositors, Inc.
Cover Design: Scott Moden
Cover Image: © Denis Babenko/ShutterStock, Inc.
Printing and Binding: Malloy, Inc.
Cover Printing: Malloy, Inc.

Library of Congress Cataloging-in-Publication Data
Bagui, Sikha, 1964-
  Essential SQL on SQL server 2008 / Sikha Saha Bagui and Richard Walsh Earp.
    p. cm.
  Includes indexes.
  ISBN-13: 978-0-7637-8138-5 (pbk.)
  ISBN-10: 0-7637-8138-X
  1. SQL (Computer program language) 2. SQL server. 3. Database design. 4. Database management. I. Earp, Richard, 1940- II. Title.
  QA76.73.S67B27 2010
  005.75'85—dc22
                          2009033348

6048
Printed in the United States of America
13 12 11 10 09   10 9 8 7 6 5 4 3 2 1

Dedicated to my father, Santosh Saha, and mother, Ranu Saha,
and
my husband, Subhash Bagui
and
my sons, Sumon and Sudip
and
my brother, Pradeep, and nieces, Priyashi, and Piyali
S.B.

Dedicated to my wife, Brenda,
and
my children, Beryl, Rich, Gen, and Mary Jo
R.E.

Contents

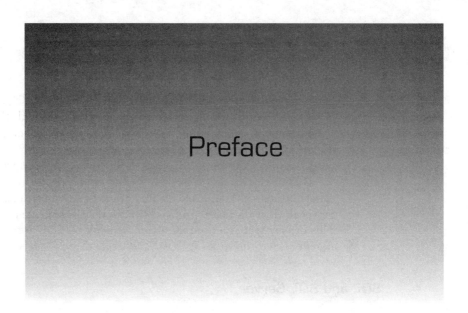

Preface

Why This Book?

SQL Server® database software is one of the most powerful database engines used today. Microsoft's latest release of SQL Server, SQL Server® 2008, is a comprehensive database platform that provides secure and reliable storage for both relational and structured data, enabling one to build and manage high-performance data applications. SQL Server 2008's close integration with Microsoft® Visual Studio® development system, Microsoft® Office® system, and a suite of new development tools sets it apart from previous versions and from other database engines. This system allows one to build, debug, and operate applications faster than ever before.

SQL Server 2008 can be installed on small machines using the Microsoft® Windows® operating system as well as large servers. In recent years, the computer industry has seen a dramatic increase in the popularity of relational databases and multiuser databases, and there is a great need for application developers and people who can write SQL code efficiently and correctly for relational and multiuser databases. This book focuses on SQL programming using SQL Server 2008—a relational and multiuser database. The book is aimed at students who wish to learn SQL using Microsoft's SQL Server 2008, and is expected to be used by schools and SQL training organizations, as well as by database and IT professionals who are actively working with SQL Server 2008.

This book is mainly intended to be a systematic learning guide to learn SQL using SQL Server 2008. The book starts with very simple SQL concepts, and slowly builds into more complex query development. The purpose of this book is to present every topic, concept, and idea with examples of code and output. Exercises have also been included so the user gains proficiency in SQL using SQL Server. The best approach to using this book efficiently is to read with SQL Server open and active. As the book is read, it will be advantageous to actually work through the examples.

If the book is being used for a beginning database course, students can do the exercises over the course of one semester at a pace of one chapter per week. The exercises are found at the ends of the respective chapters.

Due to the dramatic increase in the popularity of relational and multiuser databases, many schools and training organizations are using SQL Server in their database courses to teach database principles and concepts. This has generated a need for a concise book on SQL Server programming: *Essential SQL on SQL Server® 2008.*

SQL and SQL Server

SQL (Structured Query Language) is a standard language used for querying, updating, and managing relational databases, and lately SQL has become the de facto standard "language" for accessing relational databases. SQL is not really a language so much as it is a database query tool. In this book, we concentrate on learning SQL using SQL Server 2008.

SQL allows us to define a relational database by creating and modifying tables (in this sense, SQL is a data definition language, or DDL). SQL also allows us to tell SQL Server which information we want to select (retrieve), insert, update, or delete. That is, SQL also allows us to query the relational database in a flexible way, as well as change the stored data (in this sense, SQL is a data manipulation language, or DML).

This book is targeted at SQL Server users on the Windows operating system, but is easily adaptable to other platforms.

Audience and Coverage

This book can be used as a standalone exercise to learn SQL using SQL Server 2008. It can also be used to supplement a theoretical database text in an introductory databases class. This book does not assume any prior database knowledge.

This book consists of 11 chapters. Chapter 1 introduces the user to SQL Server 2008, explaining how to open SQL Server, load the database, and view and perform simple table manipulations. Chapter 1 also covers how and where to enter a SQL query, how to customize SQL Server 2008's settings, and how to connect to other databases. Chapter 2 introduces the user to some beginning SQL commands in SQL Server. Chapter 3 discusses creating, populating, altering, and deleting tables, as relational databases are built on the idea of tabular data. Chapter 4 introduces and covers all types of joins, which are a common database mechanism for combining tables. Chapter 5 covers SQL Server 2008's functions. Chapter 6 discusses query development as well as the use of views and other derived structures. Chapter 7 covers simple set operations. Chapters 8, 9, and 10 cover subqueries, aggregate functions, and correlated subqueries. Chapter 11 addresses indexes and constraints that can be added to tables in SQL Server 2008.

Appendix 1 describes the `Student_course` database and other tables that are used throughout the book. Appendix 2 contains the script that loads the `Student_course` database. A glossary of important commands and functions has also been provided.

This book is complete enough for beginning SQL users to get an overview of what SQL Server entails and how to use SQL. There are even many SQL programmers who have based their employment on this material. This book gives the user a very good feel for what SQL is, and how it is used in SQL Server.

—Sikha Bagui and Richard Earp

Supplements For Instructors

Instructors may download an answer file (in PDF format) for all review questions and exercises found in this book from the catalog page noted below. Instructors are asked to fill out a course questionnaire prior to receiving approval for the download.

http://www.jbpub.com/catalog/9780763781385/

Acknowledgments

Our special thanks to Tim McEvoy and the incredible staff at Jones and Bartlett Publishers for their hard work putting this book together.

We would also like to thank President Judy Bense and Provost Chula King for their inspiration, encouragement, and true leadership qualities, and Dean Jane Halonen for her continuing support.

Our sincere appreciation also goes to Dr. Leo TerHaar, chair of the Computer Science Department, for his advice, guidance, and support through the completion of this book, as well as Dr. Norman Wilde and Dr. Ed Rodgers for their continuing encouragement. And, last but not least, we would like to thank our fellow faculty members and Diana Walker for their continuous support.

chapter

1

Starting Microsoft® SQL Server® 2008

Topics covered in this chapter

In this chapter, you will learn about the basic workings of Microsoft® SQL Server® 2008 and SQL Server 2008's Management Studio. You will learn how to create a database, view the objects and default tables in a database, use the query editor, activate the database in different ways, and create tables in the database using a load script. The load script is available at `http://www.cs.uwf.edu/~sbagui`. When run from SQL Server, the load script creates the `Student_course` database that is used throughout this text. At this point, copy the load script, *SQLServer2008_load.sql*, by right-clicking on the script on the website, selecting **Save Target As**, and saving it to your working directory.

You will also learn how to view and modify a table design; delete a table and a database; type, parse, execute, and save a query; display results in different forms; stop execution of a query; and print a query and its results. The final section of this chapter discusses customizing SQL Server 2008's settings.

1.1 Starting Microsoft® SQL Server® 2008 and SQL Server Management Studio

In this section, we will show you how to start Microsoft SQL Server 2008 and open up SQL Server 2008's Management Studio.

From the **Start** menu, go to **All Programs**, select **Microsoft SQL Server 2008,** and then select **SQL Server Management Studio**, as shown in Figure 1.1.

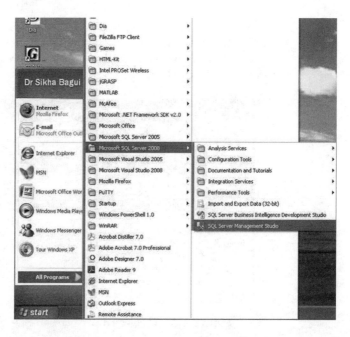

Figure 1.1 Opening Microsoft SQL Server 2008 and SQL Server Management Studio

You will see the dialog box shown in Figure 1.2. This dialog box will allow you to connect to Microsoft SQL Server 2008. To connect to a server other than the default, **enter** the appropriate **Server type** and **Server name**, and select **Windows Authentication**. Then click **Connect**.

Figure 1.2   Connecting to Microsoft SQL Server 2008

You will now be connected to the server that you indicated, and you will see the image shown in Figure 1.3. Figure 1.3 is the **Microsoft SQL Server Management Studio** screen that we will be using throughout the rest of the book.

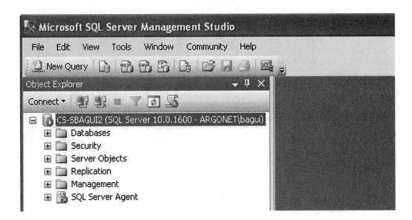

Figure 1.3   Connected to Microsoft SQL Server 2008's server

The Microsoft SQL Server Management Studio screen contains the **Object Explorer** on the left portion of the screen. The Object Explorer provides a hierarchical view of objects. For example, you can drill down into a database, table, column, or other object, as we will soon show you.

1.2   Creating a Database in Microsoft® SQL Server® 2008

Before we begin to work with Microsoft SQL Server 2008, we will create a database. To create a database, right-click on **Databases** and select **New Database**... as shown in Figure 1.4.

Figure 1.4   Creating a new database

You will see the screen shown in Figure 1.5. We will create a database called Student_course, type **Student_course** as the **Database name**. You may leave the **Owner** as <**default**> for now, as shown in Figure 1.5, and click **OK**. You will see the screen shown in Figure 1.6.

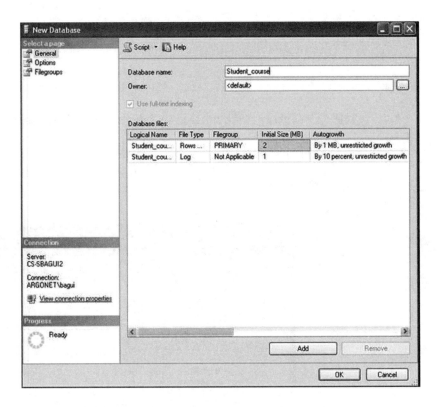

Figure 1.5 Typing in the database name

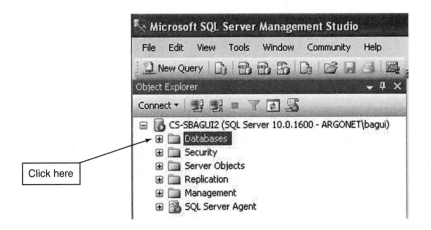

Figure 1.6 Viewing the databases

The Student_course database has now been created. As shown in Figure 1.6, you may now expand the databases node by clicking on the + sign beside **Databases** in the Object Explorer (on the left side of your screen). You will also see the **Student_course** database node under **Databases**, as shown in Figure 1.7.

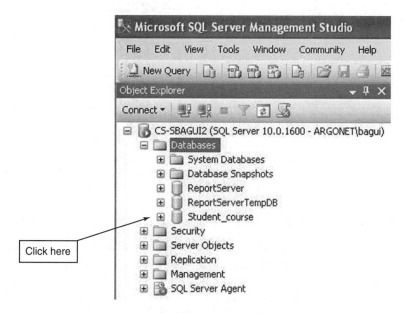

Figure 1.7   The Student_course database in the Object Explorer

1.2.1   Objects in the Student_course **Database**

A SQL Server database is a collection of many objects, such as tables, views, and synonyms that are defined to support activities performed with data.

In Figure 1.7, expand the **Student_course** database node by clicking on the + sign beside the **Student_course** node. You will see Figure 1.8, which shows the default objects that are in the Student_course database.

Figure 1.8   Viewing the objects in the Student_course database

1.2.2 Default Tables in the Student_course database

A database is a collection of related tables. So far we have created the Student_course database, but we have not created any tables.

To view the default tables in the Student_course database, expand the **Tables** node, as shown in Figure 1.9. The only thing there right now is a folder called **System Tables**. This folder will be populated by SQL Server as we create and use our new database.

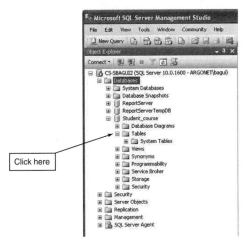

Figure 1.9   Default tables in the Student_course database

At this point you may click on the – sign beside the **Tables** node, and then on the – sign beside the **Student_course** node to close those up; your screen will now look like Figure 1.7.

1.2.3 Default System Databases

SQL Server 2008 comes with some default system databases—`master`, `model`, `msdb`, and `tempdb`. To view these default database nodes, expand the **Database** node and then the **System Databases** node, as shown in Figure 1.10.

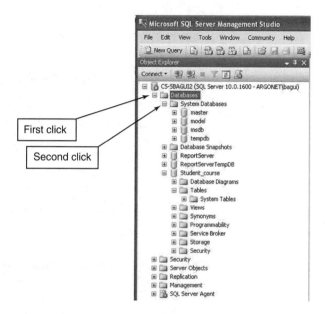

Figure 1.10   Default system databases

`master` is a database comprised of system tables that keeps track of server installation as a whole and all other databases that are subsequently created. SQL Server 2008 defaults to the `master` database.

`model` is a template database. Every time a new database is created, SQL Server makes a copy of the `model` database to form the basis of the new database. If you want all your new databases to inherit certain properties, you could include these properties in your `model` database.

`msdb` is a database that performs scheduled activities such as backups and replication tasks.

`tempdb` is a temporary database or workspace recreated every time SQL Server is restarted. `tempdb` is used to hold temporary tables created by users and intermediate results created internally by SQL Server during query processing and sorting.

1.3 The Query Editor

The most important thing in SQL Server 2008, or any other database for that matter, is querying the database—using the database to find information about the data stored therein. Queries in SQL Server 2008 are typed in the query editor. In this section, we will show you how to open the query editor. The query editor can be opened in two ways: by right-clicking with your mouse or by clicking the **New Query** button. We will illustrate both ways.

1.3.1 Opening the Query Editor by Right-Clicking

Select the Student_course database and right-click. Then select **New Query** as shown in Figure 1.11.

Figure 1.11   Opening the query editor

You will see an image similar to Figure 1.12, which shows the query editor. The query editor can be used to create queries and other SQL scripts and to execute them against SQL Server databases. A script is a prewritten series of queries as opposed to a single, ad hoc query. Scripts are stored in text files and usually are created using an editor such as Notepad.

The first query will be called *SQLQuery1.sql* by default. Later we will show you how to change the name of the query when saving it.

If the query editor is opened in this way, the Student_course database

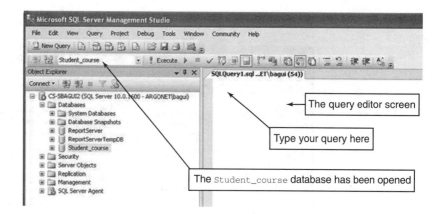

Figure 1.12 The query editor

is automatically activated. If we want to work in our Student_course database, we have to make sure it is active. If it is not active, we have to activate it. We show you how to do this in the following sections.

1.3.2 Opening the Query Editor Using the New Query Button

You can also open the query editor by selecting the **New Query** button from the toolbar (leftmost icon), as shown in Figure 1.13.

Figure 1.13 The New Query button

If you used the New Query button in Figure 1.13 without selecting the Student_course database, you will see the screen shown in Figure 1.14.

Here, note that `master` is the active database rather than `Student_course`.

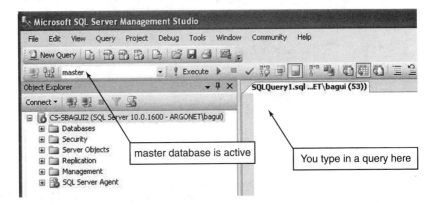

Figure 1.14   The query screen

But we want to use the `Student_course` database that we just created, so we have to activate it. Click on the drop-down icon of the combo box beside `master` and select `Student_course`, as shown in Figure 1.15. This activates (or opens) the `Student_course` database.

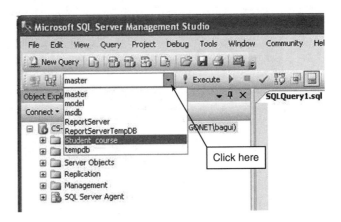

Figure 1.15   Selecting the `Student_course` database

1.3.3   Opening (or Activating) the Database Using USE

You can also activate or open the `Student_course` database by typing the following in the query editor, as shown in Figure 1.16:

USE Student_course

Then click on the **Execute** button in the menu bar above the query editor screen.

You will get the following message in the results pane, as shown in Figure 1.16:

```
Command(s) completed successfully
```

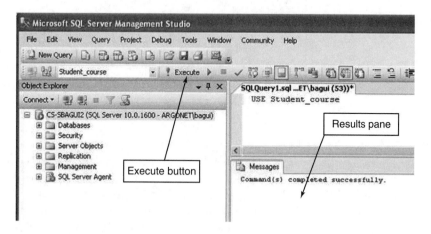

Figure 1.16   Using USE

1.4   Creating Tables Using the Load Script

After we activate the Student_course database, we will create tables in the database and insert data into the tables. To do this, we will run (execute) the load script, *SQLServer2008_load.sql*, which you already downloaded and saved to your working directory.

Go to the directory where you saved the load script, and double-click the script to open it. Then select the entire script and copy it. This script will have to be pasted into SQL Server 2008's query editor.

Open the SQL Server 2008's query editor as shown in Section 1.3.1. Make sure the Student_course database is active. Then paste the load script into the query editor, as shown in Figure 1.17.

Figure 1.17 Pasting the load script into the query editor

Once the script has been pasted into the query editor, execute this script by clicking the **Execute** button. This script only takes a few seconds to execute. You should see the results shown in Figure 1.18.

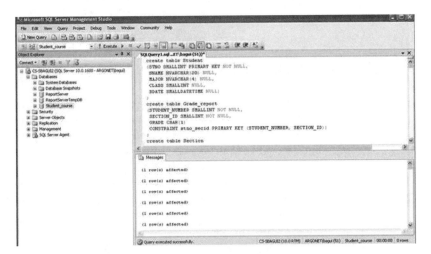

Figure 1.18 Executed load script

This script creates the following tables in the Student_course database and inserts data into them: Course, Department_to_major, Dependent, Grade_report, Languages, Plants, Prereq, Room, Section, Student, and teststu. The tables in the Student_course database are presented in Appendix 1, and the load script is presented in Appendix 2.

To view the tables that were created by the load script, expand the **Student_course** node by clicking on the + sign beside **Student_course**, and then expand the **Tables** node by clicking on the + sign beside **Tables**. (If you don't see the tables you just created, you may need to close Management Studio and restart it.) You should see Figure 1.19. Every table shows up as a node under **Student_course**.

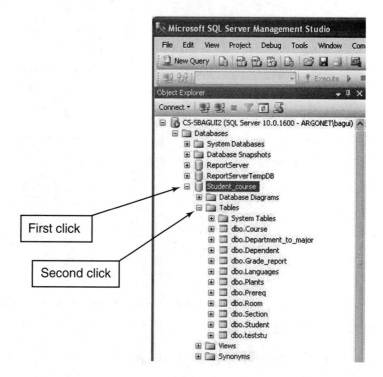

Figure 1.19 Viewing the tables in the Student_course database

1.5 Viewing Table Designs

Every table in SQL Server 2008 has a table design. The table design gives us information about a table such as the column (or field) names, the data types of the columns, and whether the columns allow null (missing) values.

To view the design of the Student table, for example, expand the **Student** node by clicking on the + sign beside it, and then expand the **Columns** node by clicking on the + sign beside it, as shown in Figure 1.20. You will be able to view the columns in the Student table. The columns in the Student table are stno, sname, major, class, and bdate.

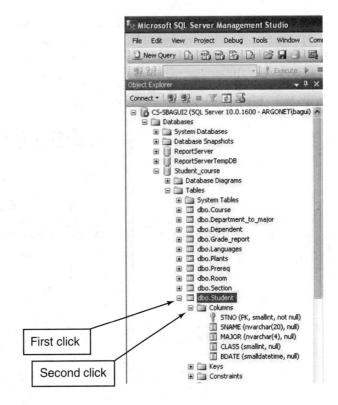

Figure 1.20   Viewing the table design of the Student table

1.6   Modifying Table Designs

If you wish to modify any of the column specifications, for example, if you want to insert or delete columns, rename a column, change the data type of a column, or allow or disallow null fields, you would need to modify the table design. The table design can be modified in two ways by modifying the column design or by modifying the table design. We illustrate both ways to change a table design in the following sections.

1.6.1   Modifying Column Designs

To modify the column design, right-click on the column that you wish to modify. For example, if you wish to modify the design of the **sname** column in the **Student** table, right-click on **SNAME**, as shown in Figure 1.21, and select one of the following options—**New Column, Modify, Rename, Delete, Refresh,** or **Properties**.

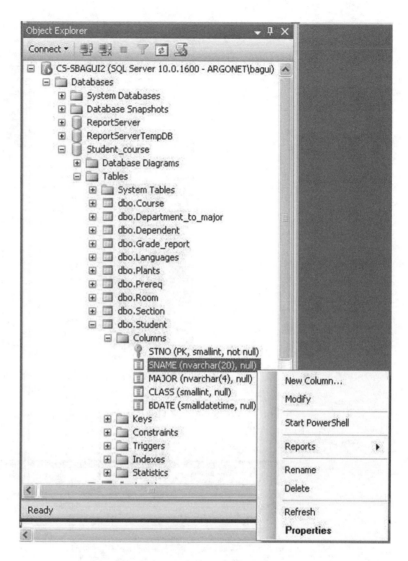

Figure 1.21 Modifying the column design

1.6.2 Modifying the Table Design Directly

Another way to view or modify the table design is to right-click on the table. For example, select **Student** (as shown in Figure 1.22), and then select **Design**.

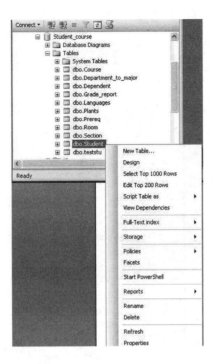

Figure 1.22   Modifying/viewing the table design

The table design of the **Student** table is now displayed, as shown in Figure 1.23.

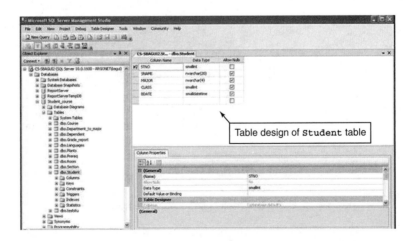

Figure 1.23   Viewing the table design of the **Student** table using the **Design** option

Here, you can delete or insert columns, change the data types, and allow or disallow null fields. Once you have finished making your changes (or just viewing the table design, if that is what you intended to do), you can close this window. You will be asked if you wish to save the changes; select **Yes** or **No**, depending on whether or not you made changes to the table design and you want to save the changes.

1.7   Viewing Table Data

To view the data in a table, right-click on the table, as shown in Figure 1.22, and select **Select Top 1000 Rows**. For example, to view the data of the Student table, right-click on the Student table, and select **Select Top 1000 Rows**. You will see a screen similar to Figure 1.24. Note that the query used by the system shows up on the top portion of the screen (the query editor screen), and the results are presented in the **results pane** (on the bottom portion of the screen).

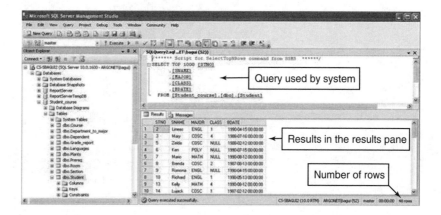

Figure 1.24   Viewing the data in the Student table

This will show all 48 rows of the Student table. The number of rows presented in the output is displayed at the bottom-right corner of the figure.

1.8   Deleting a Table

To delete a table, right-click on the table that you wish to delete (as shown in Figure 1.22), and then select **Delete**. Deleting a table will delete the table, the table design, and the data in the table. Once you delete a table, there is no way to get the table or its data back. Be very careful to ensure that you indeed intend to permanently dispose of data before selecting **Delete**.

Note: Please do NOT delete any tables right now. Just note this section for later, since you may have to delete tables at some point.

1.9 Deleting a Database

To delete a database, right-click on the database that you would like to delete, and select **Delete**, as shown in Figure 1.25.

Note: Please do NOT delete the database right now.

Figure 1.25 Deleting a database

1.10 Entering a SQL Query or Statement

A SQL query or statement is used to give instructions to the computer. A query is a request for data stored in SQL Server. The computer analyzes each instruction and interprets it. If the instruction is "understandable" to the database engine, the program produces a result. If the computer cannot figure out what the instruction means, it will display an error message.

In SQL Server 2008, the SQL query is entered in the query editor screen as shown in Figure 1.12. But before you type your query, make sure the database that you wish to work with is active or open. To type in or work on the queries in this book, the Student_course database should be active or open.

Right-click on **Student_course** and select **New Query** as shown in Figure 1.11. Enter the following SQL query in the query editor screen:

```
USE Student_course
SELECT *
FROM Student
```

"USE Student_course" is used to activate the Student_course database, as shown in Figure 1.12. "SELECT" is the SQL keyword that means "select data" or "retrieve the following data from the database." The "*" is interpreted to mean "show all columns in the result." "FROM" is the keyword that is used before a table name, and "Student" is the name of a table. This is a simple SQL query that tells the system to display all the rows and columns (all the data) in the Student table.

1.11 Parsing a Query

Before you execute your query, you may want to parse it to be sure it is written correctly. The **Parse Query** button is shown in Figure 1.26.

1.12 Executing a Query

To execute a query, click the **Execute** button above the query editor screen.

If the query is correct, the **Execute** button will execute (run) the query and the results will show on the **Results pane** (bottom partition) of the screen, as shown in Figure 1.26. If the query is incorrect, an error message will be presented on the **Results pane** of the screen as shown in Figure 1.26.

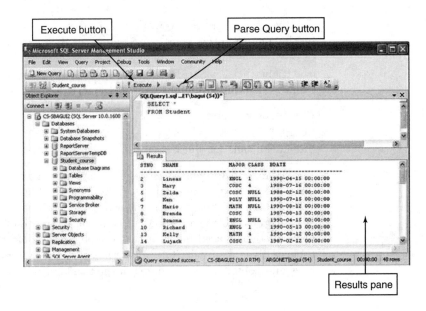

Figure 1.26   Displaying output

1.12.1   Color Coding

The automatic color coding of SQL code in the query editor will help you enter your SQL query correctly as well as prevent and resolve errors. If you are using the default color codes, for example, and you type in a keyword that is not then displayed in blue, the keyword is probably misspelled. If your code is displayed in red, you might have omitted a closing quotation mark for a character string.

1.13   Saving a Query

To save a query while the query is on the query editor screen, select **File** from the main menu, and then select **Save SQLQuery1.sql As....** A dialog box will open up and you will be able to type a name for your query and navigate to a directory where you can save it.

1.14   Displaying the Results

Results in SQL Server 2008 are displayed in the **Results pane**. The Results pane is shown in Figure 1.26. SQL queries can be executed to view results in grid form or text form, or the results can be saved to a file. We discuss each of the options to display or view the results in the following sections.

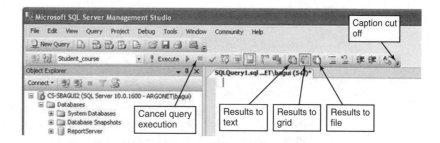

Figure 1.27   Displaying the results icons

1.14.1   Viewing Results in Grid Form

The grid form displays the results in spreadsheet-like grids.

To execute a query and view query results in grid form, first click on the **Results to grid** icon (this icon is shown in Figure 1.27) and then click the **Execute** button. Note that the **Results to grid** option is the default option.

You may also press <F5> on the keyboard to execute queries.

Your results will be in grid form, as shown in Figure 1.28.

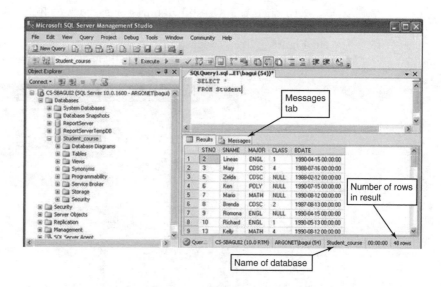

Figure 1.28   Viewing results in grid form

In Figure 1.28, the name of the database and the number of rows in the result set are displayed at the bottom of the screen.

1.14.2 Viewing Results in Text Form

To execute a query and view query results in text form, click the **Results to text** icon (this icon is shown in Figure 1.27) and then click the **Execute** button.

You will now see the results in text form, as shown in Figure 1.26. Viewing the output in text form may make it easier for you to copy and paste the output into a word processor so that you can use it in a report or print it. Figure 1.26 also displays the name of the database and the number of rows in the result set at the bottom of the screen.

1.14.3 Saving Results to File

To save your query results to a file, select the **Results to file** icon (this icon is shown in Figure 1.27), and then click the **Execute** button.

The **Save Results** window will come up and you will be able to select the appropriate directory, enter the appropriate filename, and save the results to file for later use. The RESULTS TO FILE option saves the results as a Crystal Reports file. It is beyond the scope of this book to discuss Crystal Reports, but the report file can be opened with Notepad by right-clicking it and using the **Open With** option if you navigate to the appropriate directory outside of SQL Server.

To open this Crystal Report (or saved file) from within SQL Server, select **File** from the main menu, and then **Open**, and select **File** (as shown in Figure 1.29). Navigate to the directory where you saved your file and select your file; your results will be displayed on the screen.

Figure 1.29 Opening Crystal Reports

1.15 Stopping Execution of a Long Query

If you want to stop or interrupt the execution of a long-running query, you can click on the **Cancel Query Execution** button (shown in Figure 1.27) or press Alt-Break. This option can be used for queries on very large tables but may not be needed with the database used here.

1.16 Viewing Error Messages

To view error messages, click on the **Messages** tab (shown in Figure 1.28). This displays any messages, including error messages, of the SQL query output.

1.17 Printing the Query and Results

Once the SQL query is on the query editor screen, you can print the query by selecting **File** from the main menu and then selecting **Print**.

To print the results displayed in the Results pane, place your cursor in the Results pane by clicking anywhere in the pane (see Figure 1.26 for the Results pane), and then select **File** from the main menu and then **Print**. You can also right-click anywhere in the Results pane and select **Print**.

When the results are saved to file, they can, of course, be retrieved and printed from the file.

1.18 Copying the Query and Results

Once the SQL query is on the query editor screen, you can select the entire query by highlighting it and then right-clicking. Select **Copy**, and paste it wherever you wish.

To copy a portion of the results, highlight the portion that you would like to copy, right-click, and then select **Copy**. The **Results to grid** option has an option of **Copy with Headers**, which copies the results along with the headers.

1.19 Customizing Microsoft® SQL Server® 2008

You can customize some options in SQL Server 2008 by selecting **Tools** from the main menu and then **Options**. Once you select Tools and Options, you will see the following tabs: **Environment**, **Text Editor**, **Query Execution**, **Query Results**, **SQL Server Query Explorer**, **Designers**, and **Source Control**.

1.19.1 The Environment Tab

The **Environment** tab contains the **General, Fonts and Colors, Keyboard**, and **Help** options.

Among other options, the General option allows you to change the default start-up window of SQL Server 2008.

The Fonts and Colors option allows you to change, among other things, an item's foreground and background colors.

The Keyboard option allows you to change keyboarding options like Shortcuts.

1.19.2 The Text Editor Tab

The **Text Editor** tab allows you to change the default editor and set language and text options.

1.19.3 The Query Execution Tab

The **Query Execution** tab allows you to change the default ROWCOUNT options, TEXTSIZE options, execution time-out length, and other settings.

1.19.4 The Query Results Tab

The **Query Results** tab allows you to change the default type of results, the default location for results to be saved, and other settings.

1.19.5 The SQL Server Query Explorer Tab

The **SQL Server Query Explorer** tab allows you to change table and viewing options and scripting options.

1.19.6 The Designer Tab

The **Designer** tab allows you to change the default table and database designer settings.

1.19.7 The Source Control Tab

The **Source Control** tab specifies the source control plug-in to use with Microsoft SQL Server Management Studio and allows changes to plug-in-specific options.

SUMMARY

In this chapter, we have shown you how to start Microsoft® SQL Server® 2008 and SQL Server 2008's Management Studio. We have also shown you how to create the Student_course database that we will be using throughout the rest of this book. In addition, we have demonstrated how to work with tables, and how to type, parse, execute, and save a simple query. In the process, we have also familiarized you with the main screens and workings of SQL Server 2008's Management Studio. Toward the end of the chapter, we showed you how to change some of SQL Server 2008's default settings to suit your needs.

Review Questions

1. If you want to see what columns a table is made of and what the sizes of the fields are, what option do you have to look for?
2. What is a query?
3. A SQL query is typed in the _____.
4. What is the purpose of the model database?
5. What is the purpose of the master database?
6. What is the purpose of the tempdb database?
7. What is the purpose of the USE command?
8. If you delete a table in the database, will the data in the table also be deleted?
9. What is the Parse Query button used for? How does this help you?
10. Tables are created in a _____ in SQL Server 2008.

Chapter 1 Exercises

The tables available in the Student_course database are shown in Appendix 1. You may want to look at Appendix 1 before starting this section.

1. The Student_course database contains the following tables: Student, Department_to_major, Grade_report, Section, Dependent, Course, Prereq, Room, Languages, Plants, and teststu.

   a. View the table design of each of these tables. To save and print your table design, we suggest that you copy and paste your table design into a word processor where you can save it for later use or print it out.
   b. View the data of each of these tables. Save your results to file and also print them out.

2. Write a SQL query to view all the columns and rows in the **Student** table (*Hint*: To retrieve all columns, use "SELECT *" in your query; the "*" means "all columns").

    a. View the results in grid form and print the results.
    b. View the results in text form and print the results.
    c. Save the results to file.
    d. Save the query.

Beginning SQL Commands in Microsoft® SQL Server®

Topics covered in this chapter

In Chapter 1, we introduced you to some of the basics of Microsoft® SQL Server® 2008 and SQL Server 2008's Management Studio. We provided instructions on creating a database, the Student_course database, which we will be using in this chapter and throughout the rest of the book. We also showed you how and where to enter and execute a query.

In this chapter, we discuss how to write (build) simple SQL query statements in SQL Server 2008 using the SELECT statement. We examine how to retrieve data from a table by the use of SELECT statements, how to SELECT columns (fields) and rows from tables, how to use the ORDER BY and WHERE clauses, and how to use the AND, OR, and BETWEEN operators. The concepts of COUNT and null values are also introduced. Then, to make writing queries clearer and simpler, we discuss how to use table and column aliases, table qualifiers, and synonyms, and finally we present a convention for writing SQL statements.

2.1 Displaying Data with the SELECT Statement

One of the first things that you will usually want to do with a database containing a set of tables is to see what information the tables contain. To display the information from a table using a query, you use a SELECT statement on the table. SELECT is *usually* the first word in a SQL statement or query. The SELECT statement returns information from a table (or tables) as a set of records, or a *result set.* The result set is a tabular arrangement of data, comprised of rows and columns. The SELECT statement shows the output on the computer screen (as shown in Figures 1.26 and 1.28 in Chapter 1). It does not save the results. The simplest and most commonly used form of the SELECT syntax is:

SELECT columns
FROM Table

Here, "Table" is the name of the table (from a particular database) from which the data will be displayed, and "columns" are the columns (or fields or attributes) that you chose to display from the named table. If you do not know the names of the columns in the table or you want to display all the columns in the table, you would use an asterisk (*) in place of "columns"; this will list all the columns in the table.

SQL commands in SQL Server 2008 do not have to be terminated by a semicolon, unlike other SQL languages.

Before we use any SELECT statement, we have to make sure that the correct database is open. As we saw in Chapter 1, there are several ways to do this. Here we will open the database we want to use, student_course, by typing the following in the query editor screen (the query editor screen is shown in Figure 1.12):

USE Student_course

Then click the **Execute** button (the Execute button is shown in Figure 1.16). The Student_course database should now be active (as shown in Figure 1.12).

Once the Student_course database is active, type the following in the query editor screen to display all the data from a table called Dependent:

SELECT *
FROM Dependent

The * means "all columns" of the Dependent table.

Click the **Execute** button to execute this query. Your results will display in the Results pane (once again, the Results pane is illustrated in Figures 1.26 and 1.28).

2.1.1 SELECT without the FROM

Most SQL languages require a FROM in a query. But some SELECT statements in SQL Server may be executed without a named table. SQL Server allows us to write some special queries without a FROM clause. For example, using the GETDATE function, we can type:

```
SELECT GETDATE()
```

This query will return the date and time as defined by the host computer, as shown in the following output:

```
-----------------------
2009-03-05 08:16:05.873

(1 row(s) affected)
```

Note that these columns do not have any headings.

In SQL Server 2008, a SELECT statement can also be used to make an assignment. Note the following examples.

Example 2.1

This statement assigns 100 to col1, and 200 to col2.

```
SELECT col1=100, col2=200
```

will give:

```
col1          col2
-----------   -----------
100           200

(1 row(s) affected)
```

col1 and col2 are column aliases. Column aliases are discussed in detail later in this chapter.

Example 2.2

```
SELECT 'A', 'B'
```

will give:

```
----   ----
A      B

(1 row(s) affected)
```

Note that since no equal sign was used in the result set part of the query, the output has no headings.

Example 2.3

SELECT 4+3, 4-3, 4*3, 4/3

will give:

```
-----------  -----------  -----------  -----------
7            1            12           1
```

(1 row(s) affected)

To include meaningful column headings here, we can type:

SELECT Additions=4+3, Subtractions=4-3, Multiplications=4*3, Divisions=4/3

that will give:

```
Additions   Subtractions Multiplications Divisions
----------- ------------ --------------- -----------
7           1            12              1
```

1 row(s) affected)

"/" gives the whole number quotient of a division.

2.2 Displaying or Selecting Columns from a Table

You do not have to display or return all the columns from a table when using a SELECT statement. You may choose to display only certain relevant columns from a table, provided you know the names of the columns. In this section, we show you how to display or return one column from a table, more than one column from a table, and all columns from a table. Then we introduce the ORDER BY clause and show you how to order the output in ascending or descending order by adding the ASC or DESC keywords to the ORDER BY clause.

2.2.1 Displaying or SELECTing One Column from a Table

To display or return particular fields or columns from a table, you need to know the column names. The column names are displayed in the table design for that table. Figure 1.20 shows you how to view table designs.

You may find it odd that a person working with a database does not know the column names. However, one has great latitude with naming columns when creating a table. For example, in a table called Customer that contains a name and address, the table creator could have called the customer's name CustName, CustomerName, or Name. In order to retrieve the data from that column, you would have to use the exact name and not any variation of it.

To view the table design, select the table for which you want to see the design by clicking on the + beside the table and then clicking on the + beside **Columns** (as shown in Figure 1.20). So now, click the + beside the Dependent table and then click on the + beside **Columns**, and you will see the table design for the Dependent table.

Figure 2.1 shows the design of the Dependent table. The table design provides the exact column names, the data types of the column names, the field sizes, and information on whether or not the fields can hold nulls. The data type allows you to enter only a particular kind of data in the columns. The field sizes allow you to enter only up to a certain number of characters in a field. And, null or not null tells you whether the field will allow nulls.

The Dependent table has the following columns: pno (short for parent_number) of data type SMALLINT (small integers), dname (short for dependent name) of data type NVARCHAR (a varying number of characters), relationship (for relationship to parent or student) of data type NVARCHAR, sex of data type CHAR (character), and age of data type SMALLINT. The only field in the Dependent table that cannot be null is pno.

Data types are discussed in detail in the next chapter.

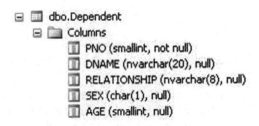

Figure 2.1 Design of the Dependent table

Once you know what columns a table contains, you may choose to display specific columns. Following is the general syntax to display or SELECT the data from one field or column of a table:

SELECT column_name
FROM table

Refer to Appendix 1 for a complete list of tables and columns in the Student_course database.

For example, to display or SELECT data for a column called dname from the Dependent table, type the following query in the query editor (once again, the query editor screen is shown in Figure 1.12):

SELECT dname
FROM Dependent

This query returns a result set containing 39 records or rows (of which the first 10 rows are shown):

```
dname
--------------------
Matt
Mary
Beena
Amit
Shantu
Raju
Rani
Susan
Sam
Donald II
 .
 .
 .

(39 row(s) affected)
```

In SQL Server 2008, if you want the row count displayed at the bottom of your output, you have to display your output in text form. In grid form, the row count is displayed in the **Messages** tab rather than at the bottom of the output.

2.2.2 Displaying or SELECTing More Than One Column from a Table

To display or SELECT (or return) data for more than one column of the table, the column names have to be separated by commas. For example, to display data from the dname and relationship columns in the Dependent table, use the following query:

```
SELECT dname, relationship
FROM Dependent
```

This query also produces 39 rows of output (of which we show the first 12 rows here):

```
dname                    relationship
--------------------     ------------
Matt                     Son
Mary                     Daughter
Beena                    Spouse
Amit                     Son
Shantu                   Daughter
Raju                     Son
Rani
Susan                    Daughter
Sam                      Son
Donald II                Son
Chris                    Son
Susan                    Daughter
  .
  .
  .


(39 row(s) affected)
```

In this example, we see a row where dname (dependent name) is Rani, but no relationship has been assigned or entered. This is a very typical problem in any database—data is missing or unknown (NULL). Preferably, all columns should have a value when data is entered into a table. In this case, an empty string was probably entered because the value for "relationship" was not known at the time of data entry. Hence, SQL Server 2008 assigns a NULL value for that field.

The concept of NULLs will be introduced later in this chapter.

2.2.3   Displaying or SELECTing All Columns of a Table

There are times when you will want to display or select all the columns of a table. To do so, as illustrated previously, you use the * in place of the column names. For example, the following produces an output of 39 rows and all the columns in the Dependent table:

```
SELECT *
FROM Dependent
```

We show the first 11 rows of output here:

```
PNO     DNAME                   RELATIONSHIP SEX   AGE
------  --------------------    ------------ ----  ------
2       Matt                    Son          M     2
2       Mary                    Daughter     F     1
2       Beena                   Spouse       F     19
10      Amit                    Son          M     3
10      Shantu                  Daughter     F     2
14      Raju                    Son          M     1
14      Rani                                 F     3
17      Susan                   Daughter     F     2
17      Sam                     Son          M     1
20      Donald II               Son          M     NULL
20      Chris                   Son          M     4
.
.
.

(39 row(s) affected)
```

2.2.4   ORDER BY

A table maintains the data in the order that the system stores it in, which is unpredictable. Remember that a relational database contains sets of rows of data and sets are not ordered. If you wish to display the contents of a table in a predictable manner, you can use the ORDER BY clause in the SELECT statement. For example, to order the Dependent table by the age field, you would type the following:

```
SELECT dname, age
FROM Dependent
ORDER BY age
```

This produces 39 rows of output ordered by age (of which the first 26 rows are shown here):

```
dname                age
-------------------- ------
Donald II            NULL
Mita                 NULL
Losmith              NULL
Mahesh               1
Sam                  1
Jon                  1
Prakash              1
Mithu                1
Rakhi                1
Mona                 1
Sebastian            1
Susan                1
Monica               1
James                1
Mary                 1
Raju                 1
Shantu               2
Susan                2
Matt                 2
Hillary              2
Jake                 2
Om                   2
Rekha                2
Nita                 2
Mamta                2
Madhu                3
.

.

.

(39 row(s) affected)
```

The ORDER BY clause does not actually change the order of the data in the table as it is stored. It only displays or returns the data (output) in a particular order.

When using ORDER BY in a SELECT statement, you do not have to specify the column that you are ordering by in the SELECT statement. For example, you may display only the dependent name and age while ordering by sex, as follows:

```
SELECT dname, age
FROM Dependent
ORDER BY sex
```

This would produce 39 rows of output, of which we are showing the first 5 rows. In this output, the females are shown first since it is ordered alphabetically and F comes before M, but this is not apparent because sex is not shown in the output.

```
dname                age
-------------------- ------
Mary                 1
Beena                19
Shantu               2
Rani                 3
Susan                2
 .
 .
 .

(39 row(s) affected)
```

Although the preceding output is not wrong, it may appear to be randomly ordered to someone who does not know what was used in the ORDER BY clause. Therefore, it is generally better to also display the column that you are ordering by, as follows:

```
SELECT dname, age, sex
FROM Dependent
ORDER BY sex
```

This would once again produce 39 rows, as shown in the following output:

```
dname                age    sex
-------------------- ------ ----
Mary                 1      F
Beena                19     F
Shantu               2      F
Rani                 3      F
Susan                2      F
Susan                1      F
Monica               1      F
```

Hillary	2	F
Phoebe	3	F
Mita	NULL	F
Nita	2	F
Barbara	18	F
Rekha	2	F
Rakhi	1	F
Mona	1	F
Susan	19	F
Susie	21	F
Xi du	20	F
Barbara	20	F
Madhu	3	F
Mamta	2	F
Sally	20	F
Matt	2	M
Mahesh	1	M
Sebastian	1	M
Jake	2	M
Losmith	NULL	M
James	3	M
Jon	1	M
Om	2	M
Prakash	1	M
Mithu	1	M
Tom	25	M
James	1	M
Sam	1	M
Donald II	NULL	M
Chris	4	M
Raju	1	M
Amit	3	M

```
(39 row(s) affected)
```

2.2.4.1 ORDER BY and NULLs

When data has not been entered for a particular column of a particular row, this cell gets a NULL value. "NULL" means that data is missing or not available; the cell has no assigned value.

If the field that you specify in the ORDER BY clause contains NULLs, the fields that have null values are placed at the top of the output. This is because of the way SQL Server stores null values internally. Take a look at the output of the following query:

```
SELECT dname, age
FROM Dependent
ORDER BY age
```

This produces 39 rows of output (of which we show the first 30 rows):

```
dname                age
-------------------- ------
Donald II            NULL
Mita                 NULL
Losmith              NULL
Mahesh               1
Sam                  1
Jon                  1
Prakash              1
Mithu                1
Rakhi                1
Mona                 1
Sebastian            1
Susan                1
Monica               1
James                1
Mary                 1
Raju                 1
Shantu               2
Susan                2
Matt                 2
Hillary              2
Jake                 2
Om                   2
Rekha                2
Nita                 2
Mamta                2
Madhu                3
Phoebe               3
James                3
Amit                 3
Rani                 3
  .
  .
  .

(39 row(s) affected)
```

If nothing were entered in a column (e.g., an empty string was entered), the column behaves just like a NULL field when using the ORDER BY clause. For example, type in the following query:

```
SELECT dname, relationship
FROM Dependent
ORDER BY relationship
```

You will get 39 rows of output (of which we show the first 8 rows):

```
dname                 relationship
--------------------  ------------
Rani
Susan                 Daughter
Mary                  Daughter
Susan                 Daughter
Monica                Daughter
Hillary               Daughter
Phoebe                Daughter
Shantu                Daughter
 .
 .
 .

(39 row(s) affected)
```

In this table, nothing (an empty string) was entered in the `relationship` column for the `dependent` Rani.

2.2.5 Ascending and Descending Order

In SQL Server, the default order of the ORDER BY clause is ascending, and thus the keyword ASC is unnecessary. To display or order output in descending order, however, the keyword DESC must be appended to the ORDER BY clause.

Note that the following two queries will give you the same output:

```
SELECT dname, age
FROM Dependent
ORDER BY age
```

and

```
SELECT dname, age
FROM Dependent
ORDER BY age ASC
```

The first query returns a result set ordered in ascending order by age by default. The second query has the keyword ASC appended to the ORDER BY clause, so it also orders in ascending order by age (the output for these queries was shown previously).

In order to display or order output in descending order, the keyword DESC must be appended to the ORDER BY clause, as follows:

```
SELECT dname, age
FROM Dependent
ORDER BY age DESC
```

This produces 39 rows of output in descending order of age:

dname	age
Tom	25
Susie	21
Xi du	20
Barbara	20
Sally	20
Susan	19
Beena	19
Barbara	18
Chris	4
Phoebe	3
James	3
Amit	3
Rani	3
Madhu	3
Mamta	2
Susan	2
Shantu	2
Matt	2
Rekha	2
Om	2
Hillary	2
Nita	2
Jake	2
Sebastian	1
Prakash	1
Mithu	1
Rakhi	1
Mona	1
Mary	1

```
Susan                   1
Monica                  1
Jon                     1
James                   1
Raju                    1
Sam                     1
Mahesh                  1
Donald II               NULL
Mita                    NULL
Losmith                 NULL
```

```
(39 row(s) affected)
```

Note that the nulls are at the bottom of the output here since the output was displayed in descending order.

2.2.6 Ordering Within an Order

There will be times when you will want to order within an order. SQL Server syntax allows you to do this. For example, if you want to order all the dependents in the **Dependent** table by sex, and within sex you want to order by age in descending order, you would enter the following query:

```
SELECT dname, sex, age
FROM Dependent
ORDER BY sex, age DESC
```

This would produce 39 rows of output (of which we show the first 25 rows here):

```
dname                   sex   age
-------------------     ----  ------
Susie                   F     21
Xi du                   F     20
Barbara                 F     20
Sally                   F     20
Susan                   F     19
Beena                   F     19
Barbara                 F     18
Phoebe                  F     3
Rani                    F     3
Madhu                   F     3
Mamta                   F     2
Susan                   F     2
Shantu                  F     2
```

```
Hillary              F    2
Rekha                F    2
Nita                 F    2
Rakhi                F    1
Mona                 F    1
Susan                F    1
Monica               F    1
Mary                 F    1
Mita                 F    NULL
Tom                  M    25
Chris                M    4
Amit                 M    3
  .
  .
  .
```

(39 row(s) affected)

You could also order by descending order of sex and descending order of age, as follows:

```
SELECT dname, sex, age
FROM Dependent
ORDER BY sex DESC, age DESC
```

This would return 39 rows of output (of which we show the first 22 rows):

dname	sex	age
Tom	M	25
Chris	M	4
James	M	3
Amit	M	3
Matt	M	2
Om	M	2
Jake	M	2
Prakash	M	1
Mithu	M	1
Raju	M	1
Sam	M	1
Jon	M	1
James	M	1
Mahesh	M	1
Sebastian	M	1
Donald II	M	NULL

```
Losmith              M     NULL
Susie                F     21
Xi du                F     20
Barbara              F     20
Sally                F     20
Susan                F     19

   .

   .

   .


(39 row(s) affected)
```

2.3   Displaying or SELECTing Rows from a Table

In a relational database, a table is called a "relation" and is denoted by the name of the relation followed by the columns (or attributes), as follows:

```
Dependent(pno, dname, relationship, sex, age)
```

An instance of a relation has rows with values in them. Relations are often called "sets of rows." We will use the term "row" to refer to a line of output. Although database literature also uses the term "record" instead of row, we will most often use "row," since that term is more commonly used in commercial relational databases (and SQL Server 2008 is a relational database).

In the previous section, we showed you how to select or display particular columns from a table, but we did not show you how to select or display specific rows. Usually you will want to select or display only particular rows from a table. For example, you may want to list all the dependents that are older than five, or list all the dependents that are female. In this case you want only the rows where the dependents are older than five, or only the rows where the dependents are female. That is, you want to display only the rows that meet a certain condition or criterion.

By using a WHERE clause in a SELECT statement, you can selectively choose rows that you wish to display based on a criterion. For additional filtering, the WHERE clause can be used with logical operators like AND and OR, and the BETWEEN operator and its negation, NOT BETWEEN.

2.3.1   Filtering with WHERE

The WHERE clause is a row filter that is used to restrict the output of rows in a result set. When the WHERE clause is used, the SQL Server database engine selects the rows from the table that meet the conditions listed in the WHERE clause. So, as we have previously illustrated, if no WHERE clause is used in a query, the query will return all rows from the table.

Following is the general syntax of a SELECT statement with a WHERE clause:

```
SELECT column-names
FROM Table
WHERE criteria
```

For example, consider the following query:

```
SELECT *
FROM Dependent
WHERE sex = 'F'
```

This produces the following 22 rows of output:

PNO	DNAME	RELATIONSHIP	SEX	AGE
2	Mary	Daughter	F	1
2	Beena	Spouse	F	19
10	Shantu	Daughter	F	2
14	Rani		F	3
17	Susan	Daughter	F	2
34	Susan	Daughter	F	1
34	Monica	Daughter	F	1
62	Hillary	Daughter	F	2
62	Phoebe	Daughter	F	3
128	Mita	Daughter	F	NULL
128	Nita	Daughter	F	2
128	Barbara	Wife	F	18
132	Rekha	Daughter	F	2
142	Rakhi	Daughter	F	1
143	Mona	Daughter	F	1
144	Susan	Wife	F	19
145	Susie	Wife	F	21
146	Xi du	Wife	F	20
147	Barbara	Wife	F	20
153	Madhu	Daughter	F	3
153	Mamta	Daughter	F	2
158	Sally	Wife	F	20

```
(22 row(s) affected)
```

The output for this query lists all the columns of the **Dependent** table but only the rows where the sex attribute has been assigned a value of **'F'**.

The WHERE clause can be used with the following comparison operators:

>   greater than
<   less than
<>   not equal
=   equal
>=   greater than or equal to
<=   less than or equal to

WHERE may also be used in a query with ORDER BY. The following query displays the **dname** and **age** from the **Dependent** table where the age of the dependent is less than or equal to 5, ordered by age:

```
SELECT dname, age
FROM Dependent
WHERE age <= 5
ORDER BY age
```

This produces the following 28 rows of output:

```
dname                  age
--------------------   ------
Mary                   1
Raju                   1
Sam                    1
Susan                  1
Monica                 1
James                  1
Prakash                1
Mithu                  1
Rakhi                  1
Mona                   1
Sebastian              1
Jon                    1
Mahesh                 1
Om                     2
Susan                  2
Mamta                  2
Jake                   2
Nita                   2
Rekha                  2
```

```
Hillary            2
Matt               2
Shantu             2
Amit               3
Rani               3
Phoebe             3
James              3
Madhu              3
Chris              4
```

(28 row(s) affected)

So far we have shown you how to include only one condition in your WHERE clause. If you want to include multiple conditions in your WHERE clause, you can use logical operators like AND and OR, and other operators like BETWEEN and its negation, NOT BETWEEN. The following sections discuss and illustrate the use of the AND, OR, and BETWEEN operators, and NOT BETWEEN in the WHERE clause.

As you peruse the examples, note that the order of the clauses is always SELECT, followed by FROM (if used), followed by WHERE (if used), followed by ORDER BY (again, if used).

2.3.2 The AND Operator

An AND operator is used in a WHERE clause if more than one condition is required. Using AND further restricts the output of rows in the result set. For example, consider the following query:

```
SELECT *
FROM Dependent
WHERE age <= 5
AND sex = 'F'
```

This produces the following output:

PNO	DNAME	RELATIONSHIP	SEX	AGE
2	Mary	Daughter	F	1
10	Shantu	Daughter	F	2
14	Rani		F	3
17	Susan	Daughter	F	2
34	Susan	Daughter	F	1
34	Monica	Daughter	F	1
62	Hillary	Daughter	F	2

62	Phoebe	Daughter	F	3
128	Nita	Daughter	F	2
132	Rekha	Daughter	F	2
142	Rakhi	Daughter	F	1
143	Mona	Daughter	F	1
153	Madhu	Daughter	F	3
153	Mamta	Daughter	F	2

```
(14 row(s) affected)
```

The output for this query lists all the columns of the **Dependent** table, but only the rows where the value of the age attribute is less than or equal to 5 *and* the sex is female. The AND means that *both* criteria—"**age** <= 5" and "**sex** = '**F**'"—have to be met for the row to be included in the result set. '**F**' is in single quotes in this query because sex was defined as character data (CHAR) in the table. Text or character data must be in single quotes in SQL Server 2008; double quotes are not acceptable. Numeric data (e.g., age <= 5) should not be in quotes.

An extensive discussion of data types is presented in Chapter 3.

2.3.3 The OR Operator

OR is another way of combining conditions in a WHERE clause. Unlike the AND operator, the OR operator allows the database engine to select the row to be included in the result set if *either* of the conditions in the WHERE clause is met. So, although you could use the OR operator with your WHERE clause if you wanted to include more than one condition, either of the conditions in the WHERE clause can be met for a row to be included in the result set.

Consider the following query:

```
SELECT *
FROM Dependent
WHERE age >20
OR sex = 'F'
```

This produces 23 rows of output:

PNO	DNAME	RELATIONSHIP	SEX	AGE
2	Mary	Daughter	F	1
2	Beena	Spouse	F	19
10	Shantu	Daughter	F	2
14	Rani		F	3

17	Susan	Daughter	F	2
34	Susan	Daughter	F	1
34	Monica	Daughter	F	1
62	Tom	Husband	M	25
62	Hillary	Daughter	F	2
62	Phoebe	Daughter	F	3
128	Mita	Daughter	F	NULL
128	Nita	Daughter	F	2
128	Barbara	Wife	F	18
132	Rekha	Daughter	F	2
142	Rakhi	Daughter	F	1
143	Mona	Daughter	F	1
144	Susan	Wife	F	19
145	Susie	Wife	F	21
146	Xi du	Wife	F	20
147	Barbara	Wife	F	20
153	Madhu	Daughter	F	3
153	Mamta	Daughter	F	2
158	Sally	Wife	F	20

(23 row(s) affected)

This output lists all dependents that are either greater than 20 years of age *or* are female. The OR means that either of the criteria—"**age** > 20" or "sex = 'F'"—has to be met for the row to be included in the output.

2.3.4 The BETWEEN Operator

The BETWEEN operator is yet another way of combining filtering conditions in a WHERE clause. In SQL Server 2008, the BETWEEN operator allows you to determine whether a value falls within a given range of values (inclusive). The general syntax of the BETWEEN operator is:

```
SELECT ...
FROM
WHERE
BETWEEN value1 AND value2
```

For example, if we want to find all the dependents from the ages of 3 to 5, we would enter the following:

```
SELECT dname, age
FROM Dependent
WHERE age
BETWEEN 3 AND 5
```

This produces the following output:

```
dname                age
-------------------- ------
Amit                 3
Rani                 3
Chris                4
Phoebe               3
James                3
Madhu                3

(6 row(s) affected)
```

In SQL Server, "value1" in the BETWEEN clause has to be less than "value2." In some SQL languages (for example, in Access SQL), "value1" does not have to be less than "value2."

Because the operator is inclusive, the end points of the comparison are included in the output; that is, the BETWEEN clause takes the values from "value1" to "value2."

As we will often point out, SQL statements may be written in several ways. For example, the preceding query may also be written as follows:

```
SELECT dname, age
FROM Dependent
WHERE age >=3
AND age <=5
```

This will produce the same output as the previous query. So, BETWEEN can be considered shorthand for greater-than-or-equal-to AND less-than-or-equal-to some value.

2.3.5 Negating the BETWEEN Operator

The BETWEEN operator can be negated by preceding it with the keyword NOT. NOT BETWEEN allows you to determine whether a value does not occur within a given range of values. The general syntax of NOT BETWEEN is:

```
SELECT ...
FROM
WHERE
NOT BETWEEN value1 AND value2
```

For example, if we want to find all the dependents that are not between the ages of 3 and 15, we would enter the following:

SELECT dname, age
FROM Dependent
WHERE age
NOT BETWEEN 3 AND 15

This would give us the following output:

dname	age
Matt	2
Mary	1
Beena	19
Shantu	2
Raju	1
Susan	2
Sam	1
Susan	1
Monica	1
Tom	25
James	1
Hillary	2
Jon	1
Om	2
Prakash	1
Mithu	1
Nita	2
Barbara	18
Rekha	2
Rakhi	1
Mona	1
Susan	19
Susie	21
Xi du	20
Barbara	20
Sebastian	1
Jake	2
Mamta	2
Mahesh	1
Sally	20

(30 row(s) affected)

Here the end points of the comparison are *not* included in the result set.

The preceding NOT BETWEEN query could also be written as follows:

```
SELECT dname, age
FROM Dependent
WHERE age <3
OR age >15
```

NOT BETWEEN could be considered shorthand for less-than OR greater-than some value.

2.4   The COUNT Function

The COUNT function is used to return the number of rows that the output will produce without actually displaying the rows themselves. This function often comes in handy when you have large tables or you expect a large output. In such situations, it is desirable to determine the number of rows of output that you will be getting before actually displaying the output. In this section, we introduce the COUNT function and we take another look at the concept of null values.

The following query produces output that includes all the rows of the **Dependent** table plus all the values for all columns in those rows:

```
SELECT *
FROM Dependent
```

If you want to know only the *number* of rows in the output (rather than view the actual rows themselves), you would use the following:

```
SELECT COUNT(*)
FROM Dependent
```

This produces the following output:

```
-----------
39

(1 row(s) affected)
```

This output says that there are 39 rows in the **Dependent** table. Note that the actual rows themselves are not displayed.

It is often useful to count the number of column values that have a value. For example, to find out how many non-null rows are in a particular column, enter the following:

```
SELECT COUNT(age)
FROM Dependent
```

You will get:

```
-----------
36
```

```
Warning: Null value is eliminated by an aggregate or other SET
operation.
```

```
(1 row(s) affected)
```

"COUNT(age)" counts only the rows in which age is not null, meaning it counts only the rows that have a defined value. Therefore, the preceding output is 36 rows rather than 39 rows because the **age** column in the **Dependent** table includes 3 null values. If you want COUNT to count rows and include rows that have fields with null values, you would use "COUNT(*)." In the next section, we discuss null values in more detail.

2.4.1   IS NULL

Null values are used to designate missing data in columns. The IS NULL condition is the only condition that directly tests for nulls. Null values are unmatched by all other conditions in WHERE clauses. Rows with null values cannot be retrieved by using "= NULL" in a WHERE clause, since NULL signifies a missing value. No value is considered to be equal to, greater than, or less than NULL. Even a space character is not considered to be a NULL, and a null is not considered to be a space. The internal representation of nulls is such that there is no distinction between nulls in numeric, text, or date columns.

The following query provides names and ages of dependents (from the **Dependent** table) that have null values for their age columns:

```
SELECT dname, age
FROM Dependent
WHERE age IS NULL
```

This produces the following three rows of output:

```
dname                age
-------------------- ------
Donald II            NULL
Mita                 NULL
Losmith              NULL
```

(3 row(s) affected)

2.4.2 IS NOT NULL

To retrieve all rows where age is not null, IS NOT NULL can be used. The following query will return all the rows in the **Dependent** table with non-null ages—the remaining 36 rows of the table:

SELECT dname, age
FROM Dependent
WHERE age IS NOT NULL

This produces 36 rows of output:

```
dname                age
-------------------- ------
Matt                 2
Mary                 1
Beena                19
Amit                 3
Shantu               2
Raju                 1
Rani                 3
Susan                2
Sam                  1
Chris                4
Susan                1
Monica               1
Tom                  25
James                1
Hillary              2
Phoebe               3
James                3
Jon                  1
Om                   2
Prakash              1
Mithu                1
```

```
Nita                   2
Barbara                18
Rekha                  2
Rakhi                  1
Mona                   1
Susan                  19
Susie                  21
Xi du                  20
Barbara                20
Sebastian              1
Jake                   2
Madhu                  3
Mamta                  2
Mahesh                 1
Sally                  20
```

```
(36 row(s) affected)
```

2.5   The ROWCOUNT Function

In an earlier section, we discussed how we can limit the number of rows returned by a SELECT statement with the use of a WHERE clause and logical operators. In this section, we introduce the ROWCOUNT function, which is another way of limiting the number of rows returned by a SELECT statement.

The WHERE clause assumes that you have knowledge of the actual data values present in a data set. But what if you want to see only a sample of a result set, and you have no idea which range of values are present in the table? In this case, the ROWCOUNT function can be quite handy.

For example, to see the first 10 rows of the **Dependent** table, enter:

```
SET ROWCOUNT 10
SELECT *
FROM Dependent
```

This will give you the following 10 rows of output:

PNO	DNAME	RELATIONSHIP	SEX	AGE
2	Matt	Son	M	2
2	Mary	Daughter	F	1
2	Beena	Spouse	F	19
10	Amit	Son	M	3

10	Shantu	Daughter	F	2
14	Raju	Son	M	1
14	Rani		F	3
17	Susan	Daughter	F	2
17	Sam	Son	M	1
20	Donald II	Son	M	NULL

(10 row(s) affected)

After using ROWCOUNT, you should reset the ROWCOUNT property with:

SET ROWCOUNT 0

If you do not reset the ROWCOUNT property, you will keep getting the number of rows specified in ROWCOUNT for the remainder of the session (that is, until you log off).

If you set ROWCOUNT and then execute other queries without resetting ROWCOUNT, you will restrict your output. For example, if you set ROWCOUNT to 10 and then executed the query **SELECT * FROM Student** without resetting, you would see only 10 rows. (Try it!)

Other important functions are discussed in Chapter 5, but ROWCOUNT is used so frequently that we introduced it here.

2.6   Using Aliases

Column aliases and table aliases are temporary names assigned within a query to columns and tables, respectively. They are created "on the fly" in a query, and do not exist after the query is run. We will discuss both column aliases and table aliases in this section.

2.6.1   Column Aliases

Column aliases are used to improve the readability of a query and its output. In SQL Server 2008, a column alias can be declared either before or after the column designation in the SELECT statement.

We will first display a query *without* a column alias:

SELECT dname, age, sex
FROM Dependent
WHERE age > 5

This produces the following output:

```
dname                  age    sex
-------------------    ------ ----
Beena                  19     F
Tom                    25     M
Barbara                18     F
Susan                  19     F
Susie                  21     F
Xi du                  20     F
Barbara                20     F
Sally                  20     F
```

(8 row(s) affected)

You will notice that (by default) SQL Server uses the column names from the table you are using for the column headings. These column names may not be very explicit or descriptive, however. For example, what is **dname**? We would probably assume it's a name of some sort, but what does the "d" in front of "**name**" stand for? Using more descriptive headings in the output would considerably increase readability. To use more descriptive column headings, you can include column aliases just before or after the column name by using AS in the SELECT statement, as shown in the following query (in the first few examples, we will place the descriptive column headings after the column names):

SELECT dname AS Dependent_name, age AS Dependent_age, sex AS Dependent_sex
FROM Dependent
WHERE age > 5

This produces the following output:

```
Dependent_name         Dependent_age Dependent_sex
-------------------    ------------- -------------
Beena                  19            F
Tom                    25            M
Barbara                18            F
Susan                  19            F
Susie                  21            F
Xi du                  20            F
Barbara                20            F
Sally                  20            F
```

(8 row(s) affected)

Clearly, the preceding output has more descriptive headings and the output makes more sense.

To embed a blank space in the column alias, you must put the column alias in single or double quotes, as shown in the following example:

```
SELECT dname AS "Dependent Name", age AS "Dependent Age", sex AS
"Dependent Sex"
FROM Dependent
WHERE age > 5
```

This produces the following output:

```
Dependent Name         Dependent Age Dependent Sex
--------------------   ------------- -------------
Beena                   19            F
Tom                     25            M
Barbara                 18            F
Susan                   19            F
Susie                   21            F
Xi du                   20            F
Barbara                 20            F
Sally                   20            F

(8 row(s) affected)
```

If you use single quotes in the preceding query, you can omit the AS. That is, the following query will give you the same output as the previous query:

```
SELECT dname 'Dependent Name', age 'Dependent Age', sex 'Dependent
Sex'
FROM Dependent
WHERE age > 5
```

Column aliases can also be placed in brackets ([ ]) as shown in the following query:

```
SELECT dname AS [Dependent Name], age AS [Dependent Age], sex AS
[Dependent Sex]
FROM Dependent
WHERE age > 5
```

Finally, column aliases can be placed in brackets ([ ]) before "= column name":

SELECT [Dependent Name] = dname, [Dependent Age] = age, [Dependent Sex] = sex
FROM Dependent
WHERE age > 5

These last two queries will produce the same output and headings as the query preceding them.

If we wish to eliminate the brackets in the previous query, we can use a one-word alias before "= column name":

SELECT Name = dname, Age = age, Sex = sex
FROM Dependent WHERE age > 5

This will produce the following output:

```
Name                     Age    Sex
--------------------     ------ ----
Beena                    19     F
Tom                      25     M
Barbara                  18     F
Susan                    19     F
Susie                    21     F
Xi du                    20     F
Barbara                  20     F
Sally                    20     F

(8 row(s) affected)
```

2.6.2 Table Aliases

A table alias, usually used in multitable queries (we will introduce and discuss multitable queries in Chapter 4), allows us to use a shorter name for a table when we reference the table in the query. A table alias is temporary and does not exist after the query is run. We make extensive use of multitable queries in future chapters. Following is an example of a query written with a one-letter table alias:

SELECT d.dname
FROM Dependent d
WHERE d.age > 5

This produces the following output:

```
dname
--------------------
Beena
Tom
Barbara
Susan
Susie
Xi du
Barbara
Sally

(8 row(s) affected)
```

In the preceding query, the table alias is the letter d *after* the table name, `Dependent`. A table alias can also be defined by a short, meaningful word or expression after the table name, rather than a one-letter table alias, but the one-letter table alias is commonly used by SQL programmers. Once a table alias has been defined in a query, it can be used in place of the table name. So, d could be used in place of `Dependent` if the table name needed to be used again in this particular query; the table alias is not reusable in multiple queries because the definition is local to only that query. For example, if you enter "SELECT * from d" in another query, you will get an error message. There is no such table as d, since d was only locally defined as the table alias for that one particular query and is only valid in that particular query.

2.6.3 Table Aliases Used as Table Qualifiers

In the previous example, the construction "d.dname" contains a table qualifier (the "d." part). Table qualifiers are used when we have a situation where the same column name has been used in more than one table. Table qualifiers before the column names determine which table the column is from. For example, if `TableA` has a column called `Field1` and `TableB` also has a column called `Field1`, there is no way the query engine will know which Field1 the query is referring to if we do not use a table qualifier in a multitable query. To correctly handle this situation, we would have to use a table qualifier in the form `Table1.FieldA`, where `Table1` is the table qualifier (this is also an alias in a way).

Once again, multitable queries will be discussed from Chapter 4 onward.

Following is an example of a query with a table qualifier used for the age column:

```
SELECT *
FROM Dependent
WHERE Dependent.age > 5
```

This produces the following output:

```
PNO     DNAME                    RELATIONSHIP SEX  AGE
------  --------------------     ------------ ---- ------
2       Beena                    Spouse       F    19
62      Tom                      Husband      M    25
128     Barbara                  Wife         F    18
144     Susan                    Wife         F    19
145     Susie                    Wife         F    21
146     Xi du                    Wife         F    20
147     Barbara                  Wife         F    20
158     Sally                    Wife         F    20

(8 row(s) affected)
```

It is very common in SQL to alias a table and then use the table alias as a table qualifier, as illustrated here:

```
SELECT *
FROM Dependent d
WHERE d.age > 5
```

The output of this query is the same as the output of the previous query.

In this query, d (the table alias) is also the table qualifier. Not only is a construction like this very common, but it also helps to prevent typing errors when writing commands.

The advantages of using table qualifiers and table aliases may not be so apparent in the examples presented in this chapter since we are only working with single tables here. As we start working with multiple tables (from Chapter 4 onward), their advantages will become more obvious.

2.7 Synonyms

In the last section, we discussed one way of referring to a table—through the use of table aliases. Table aliases are not permanent in the sense that they do not exist after the query has been executed. Here we will show you another way of referring to a table—through the use of synonyms. Synonyms are more permanent in the sense that they are available for use until they are deleted. In this section, we show you how to create, use, and delete synonyms.

SQL Server 2008 allows you to create synonyms for your tables. Synonyms are usually shorter names or more meaningful names that can be used in place of a table name itself. If a change is made in the original table or its data, this change will be reflected when the synonym is used. If a change is made in the data of the table using a synonym, this change will also be reflected in the original table. However, you cannot alter the table's design using a synonym. ALTER TABLE commands (covered in Chapter 3) can only be used on the actual tables themselves.

The general syntax to create a synonym is:

CREATE SYNONYM synonym_name
FOR Table_name

For example, to create a synonym called **s1** for the **Student** table, enter:

CREATE SYNONYM s1
FOR Student

To view the synonym that you just created, from the Object Explorer, expand the **Student_course** database and then expand **Synonyms** as shown in Figure 2.2, and you will see the synonym **s1**.

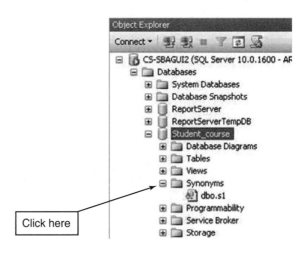

Figure 2.2 The Synonym

You can now use:

```
SELECT *
FROM s1
```

You will get the same output as if you entered:

```
SELECT *
FROM Student
```

A synonym exists until you delete it. The general syntax to delete a synonym is:

```
DROP SYNONYM synonym_name
```

So, if you want to delete the synonym, s1, enter:

```
DROP SYNONYM s1
```

You may also delete the synonym by right-clicking on the synonym and selecting **Delete**.

If you forget which synonym has been created for which table, right-click on the synonym and select **Properties**. Under the **General** tab, the **Object name** shows the table for which the synonym has been created.

2.8   Adding Comments to SQL Statements

Comments are nonexecutable words or phrases included in SQL queries to make the queries easier to understand (particularly by other people). Comments are ignored by the SQL engine, but they are very useful to programmers in determining what the statement does, when it was written, who wrote it, and so on. There are two ways of including comments in SQL Server 2008. The first way is by the use of dashes:

```
SELECT *            – displays all attributes
FROM Dependent d    – of the Dependent table
WHERE d.age > 5     – where the age of the dependent is greater than 5.
```

The second way of including comments in SQL Server 2008 is by the use of /* ... */. The following is an example of a commented statement that uses this format:

```
SELECT dname, age /* displays the dependent name and age */
FROM Dependent d  /* from the Dependent table */
WHERE d.age > 5   /* where the age of the dependent is greater than 5 */
```

SQL Server 2008 allows you to include comments above the first line in a query and below the last line in a query.

We wish to encourage the use of comments in writing SQL queries, particularly for complex queries and when queries will be debugged or enhanced by others.

SQL Server 2008 also has icons to turn lines into comment lines. There are times in query development where a line of the query seems to be incorrect or needs to be debugged. For example, if you enter the query as shown in Figure 2.3, and then you wish to make the last line a comment line, highlight the last line and click the **Comment Lines** button; the last line will become a comment line. This is a quick and easy way to see what the query result would be if the WHERE clause were omitted ("commented out"). If you wish to remove the comment, click the **Uncomment Lines** button, and the comment line will turn into a regular line.

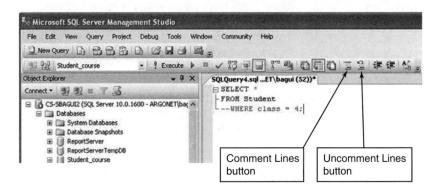

Figure 2.3   Icons for commenting/uncommenting lines

2.9 Some Conventions for Writing SQL Statements

Although SQL statements often contain multiple commands and multiple lines, there are no fixed rules for writing SQL statements; SQL is a "free-form" language. We suggest that you use the following conventions to increase the readability of your queries, especially as your statements or queries become more complex:

■ Use uppercase letters for keywords like SELECT, FROM, and WHERE. Use lowercase letters for user-supplied words. (SQL Server 2008 is not case sensitive for commands.)

■ Place the keywords SELECT, FROM, and WHERE on separate lines, like this:

```
SELECT *
FROM Dependent
WHERE age > 5
```

2.10 A Few Notes about Microsoft® SQL Server® 2008 Syntax

Here are a few things that you need to know about syntax in SQL Server 2008:

■ SQL Server 2008 allows blank lines in the SQL window.
■ Queries in SQL Server 2008 do not have to end in a semicolon as is required in other versions of SQL.
■ SQL Server 2008 allows you to include comments anywhere in a SQL script or query. Many other SQL languages will not let you include a comment as the first line of a script or query. While these other SQL languages will look for a SQL statement beginning with a command like SELECT on the first line of a script or query, SQL Server 2008 will allow you to include a comment on the first line of a script or query. SQL Server 2008 also allows comments after the semicolon (which may have been used to end a query). Many SQL languages will not allow anything to be typed after the semicolon.
■ SQL Server 2008 lets you enter multiple queries in the query editor screen at one time, and you may execute only the ones that you wish to execute. For example, if you enter the following three queries in the query editor screen:

```
SELECT *
FROM Dependent

SELECT *
FROM Student

SELECT *
FROM Course
```

And you wish to first execute the middle query, "SELECT * FROM Student," highlight this query and click the **Execute** button. If you then wish to execute the first query, "SELECT * FROM Dependent," highlight this query and click on the **Execute** button. You can, of course, do this as many times as you wish, and in any combination you wish.

SUMMARY

In this chapter, we have shown how to use the basic SELECT statement and how to extract columns and rows from tables using SELECT. We introduced the COUNT and ROWCOUNT functions; examined the AND, OR, and BETWEEN operators in WHERE clauses; and discussed table and column aliases and synonyms. We also touched on the concept of nulls and have shown you how to include comments in SQL scripts. Toward the end of the chapter, we presented some conventions for writing SQL statements and a few notes about SQL Server syntax. You will need this basic knowledge and understanding to work on the forthcoming chapters.

Review Questions

1. What is usually the first word in a SQL query?
2. Does a SQL Server 2008 SELECT statement require a FROM clause in a query?
3. Can a SELECT statement in SQL Server 2008 be used to make an assignment? Explain with examples.
4. What is the ORDER BY clause used for?
5. Does ORDER BY actually change the order of the data in the tables or does it just change the output?
6. What is the default order of an ORDER BY clause?
7. What kind of comparison operators can be used in a WHERE clause?
8. What are four major operators that can be used to combine conditions in a WHERE clause? Explain the operators with examples.
9. What are the logical operators that can be used in the WHERE clause?
10. In a WHERE clause, do you need to enclose a text column in quotes? Do you need to enclose a numeric column in quotes?
11. Is a NULL value equal to anything? Can a space in a column be considered a NULL value? Why or why not?
12. Will "COUNT(column)" include columns with NULL values in its count?
13. What are column aliases? Why would you want to use column aliases? How can you embed blank spaces in column aliases?
14. What are table aliases?
15. What are table qualifiers? When should table qualifiers be used?
16. Are semicolons required at the end of SQL statements in SQL Server 2008?
17. Do comments need to go in a special place in SQL Server 2008?
18. When would you use the ROWCOUNT function versus using the WHERE clause?
19. Is SQL case sensitive? Is SQL Server 2008 case sensitive?

20. What is a synonym? Why would you want to create a synonym?

21. Can a synonym of a table be used instead of a table name in a SELECT statement?

22. Can a synonym of a table be used when you are trying to alter the design of a table?

23. Can you enter more than one query in the query editor screen at one time?

Chapter 2 Exercises

Unless specified otherwise, use the `Student_course` database to answer the following questions.

In writing out the following queries, use table and column aliases wherever you feel that they would improve the readability of your output. Follow the conventions we presented for writing SQL statements. Also, for future reference, you may want to get into the practice of saving your queries by question number. For example, save the query you write for question 2-2a as *query2-2a*. Print the queries and your results.

Refer to Appendix 1 for a complete listing of all tables (and their columns) available in the `Student_course` database.

1. The `Student_course` database used in this book has the following tables: `Student`, `Dependent`, `Course`, `Section`, `Prereq` (for prerequisite), `Grade_report`, `Department_to_major`, `Languages`, `Room`, `Plants`, and `teststu`.

a. Display the data from each of these tables by using the simple form of the SELECT * statement.

b. Display the first five rows from each of these tables.

2. a. Display the student name and student number of all students who are juniors (*hint:* `class` = 3).

b. Display the student names and numbers from part (a) in descending order by name.

3. a. Display the course name and course number of all courses that are three credit hours.

b. Display all the course names and course numbers in ascending order by course name.

4. Display the building number, room number, and room capacity of all rooms in descending order by room capacity. Use appropriate column aliases to make your output more readable.

5. Display the course number, instructor, and building number of all courses that were offered in the fall semester of 2008. Use appropriate column aliases to make your output more readable.

6. List the student number of all students who have grades of C or D.

7. List the offering_dept of all courses that are more than three credit hours.

8. Display the student name of all students who have a major of "COSC."

9. Find the capacity of room 120 in Bldg 36.

10. Display a list of all student names ordered by major.

11. Display a list of all student names ordered by major, and by class within major. Use appropriate table and column aliases.

12. Count the number of departments in the Department_to_major table.

13. Count the number of buildings in the Room table.

14. What output will the following query produce?

```
SELECT COUNT(class)
FROM Student
WHERE class IS NULL
```

Why do you get this output?

15. Use the BETWEEN operator to list all the sophomores, juniors, and seniors from the Student table.

16. Use the NOT BETWEEN operator to list all the sophomores and juniors from the Student table.

17. Create synonyms for each of the tables available in the Student_course database. View your synonyms in the Object Explorer.

chapter

3

Creating, Populating, Altering, and Deleting Tables

Topics covered in this chapter

In the Microsoft® SQL Server® 2008 database, data is stored in tables (also known as *relations* in relational database theory). In Chapter 2, we discussed how to write queries to retrieve data from *existing* tables by using a SELECT statement. In this chapter, we will discuss how to create tables and insert data into them, and how to alter, update, and delete tables and their data using SQL.

We start the chapter with a discussion of data types, since you need to know the different data types before you can use the CREATE TABLE command to create tables. In the CREATE TABLE command, we have to give names to columns and also provide data types and sizes for the data to be included in the columns. Therefore, before we get into a discussion of how to create tables and insert data into them, we will first discuss the data types available in SQL Server 2008.

3.1 Data Types in Microsoft® SQL Server® 2008

Every column in a table has a data type. The data type of a column is used to determine what kind of information or values can be stored in that column (a domain of values), and what kind of operations can be performed on those values. Defining a column, therefore, is a matter of mapping the domain values you need to store to the corresponding data type. In selecting a data type, you also want to avoid wasting storage space while allowing enough space for a sufficient range of possible values over the life of your application. SQL Server 2008 supports more than 30 different data types and has introduced seven new ones. We will present the most commonly used data types by breaking the data types into four major categories: numeric, character, date and time, and miscellaneous.

Domain values are the set of all possible values that a column can have. For example, the domain of values for a GPA column would likely be 0.00 to 4.00.

Several of the primary data types also have valid synonyms that can be used instead of the regular data types. The synonyms are external names that are intended to make one SQL product compatible with another.

The more specific you are when selecting a data type for a column, the more accurately the information in your database will be represented. The following sections briefly describe each data type and its valid synonyms.

In this discussion of data types, the choices may seem a little overwhelming. Although admittedly subjective, we have characterized the data types as common (C), those used only for specific applications (U), and those used rarely or for very specific applications (R). For beginning SQL programmers, you will likely use only the "C" data types.

3.1.1   Numeric Data Types

Numeric data types should be used for storing numeric data—data on which you want to perform numeric comparisons or arithmetic operations. Numeric data types can further be broken into two groups: integers and decimals.

3.1.1.1   Integer Data Types

Integer data types have no digits after the decimal point, and range in size from 1 to 8 bytes of internal storage. Integer data types in SQL Server 2008 include:

- BIGINT (R), which uses 8 bytes of storage and can be used to store numbers from -2^{63} to $2^{63} -1$. You should avoid using the BIGINT data type unless you really need its additional storage capacity.
- INT (C), which uses 4 bytes of storage and can be used to store numbers from -2^{31} to $2^{31} -1$. The synonym for INT is INTEGER.
- SMALLINT (C), which uses 2 bytes of storage and can be used to store numbers from -2^{15} to $2^{15} -1$.
- TINYINT (U), which uses 1 byte of storage and can be used to store numbers from 0 to 255.
- MONEY (U), which uses 8 bytes of storage.
- SMALLMONEY (U), which uses 4 bytes of storage.

MONEY and SMALLMONEY are included among the integer types because they are internally stored the same way as integers and their internal representation is converted when they are used.

3.1.1.2   Decimal Data Types

Decimal data types allow a larger range of values as well as a higher degree of accuracy than integer data types. For decimal data types, you can specify a precision and a scale. Precision is the total number of digits stored, and scale is the maximum number of digits to the right of the decimal point. The storage space of decimal data varies according to the precision. Decimals with a precision of 1 to 9 would take up 5 bytes of storage space; decimals with a precision of 10 to 19 would take up 9 bytes of storage space, and so on.

Decimal data types include:

- REAL (U), which uses 4 bytes for storage and has a precision of 7 digits. The synonym for REAL is FLOAT$[(n)]$, where $n = 1$ to 7.

- FLOAT (R), which uses 8 bytes for storage and has a precision of 15 digits. The synonym for FLOAT is DOUBLE PRECISION and FLOAT$[(n)]$ where $n = 8$ to 15.
- DECIMAL (C), whose storage size varies based on the specified precision and uses 2 to 17 bytes for storage. The synonyms for DECIMAL are DEC and NUMERIC.

Rounding errors can occur when using the REAL (or FLOAT) data types. NUMERIC or DECIMAL may be used to avoid the rounding problems associated with REALs.

When you are trying to select the numeric data type to use, your decision should be based on the maximum range of possible values that you want to store, and the precision and scale that you need. But, at the same time, you have to realize that data types that can store a greater range of values take up more space.

The NUMERIC data type most closely resembles Oracle's NUMBER data type.

3.1.2 Character Data Types

Character data types are used to store any combination of letters, numbers, and symbols. Single quotes must be used when entering character data. SQL Server 2008 has the following character data types: CHAR (C), VARCHAR (C), TEXT (U), NTEXT (U), NCHAR (U), and NVARCHAR (U).

3.1.2.1 The CHAR Data Type

The CHAR(n) is a commonly used fixed-length single-byte character string that can be used to store up to 8000 bytes of data. CHAR data is used when the column size is known and unvarying. For example, a U.S. Social Security number could be of CHAR(9) data type. Since CHARs use a fixed storage length, CHARs are accessed faster than VARCHARs (variable-length character strings). You can and should specify the maximum byte length of a CHAR(n) data type with a value for n; otherwise, the default size will be used, which may be set to a size much higher than what you need. The synonym for CHAR is CHARACTER.

3.1.2.2 The VARCHAR Data Type

The VARCHAR(n) is a commonly used variable-length single-byte character string that can also be used to store up to 8000 bytes of data. Here, too, you can and should specify the maximum byte length of VARCHARs; otherwise, as with the CHAR data type, the default size will be used and may be set much higher than what you need. "Variable length" means that if less data than the specified n bytes is used, the storage size will be the actual length of the data entered. The synonym for VARCHAR is CHAR VARYING. VARCHAR is the most commonly used character (string) type. An example of the use of VARCHAR(n) would be a column containing names that could be defined as VARCHAR(20) to store names up to 20 characters long.

VARCHAR2 is the Oracle equivalent of VARCHAR.

3.1.2.3 The TEXT Data Type

The TEXT data type is also a variable-length single-byte character string and can be used to store up to 2 GB of text data. TEXT is much less common than VARCHAR and is a large object data type. TEXT is used to store large strings of data like a paragraph or a lengthy explanation. TEXT has extra overhead that may slow performance and should be used only in rare circumstances.

LONG is the Oracle equivalent of TEXT.

3.1.2.4 The NCHAR Data Type

The NCHAR is a fixed-length Unicode character string used in specific circumstances. You can also specify the maximum byte length of NCHAR with n. The synonym for NCHAR is NATIONAL CHAR. This data type may be used if symbols or non-English characters (e.g., Chinese) are stored.

3.1.2.5 The NVARCHAR Data Type

The NVARCHAR is a variable-length Unicode character string. You can specify the maximum byte length of NVARCHAR with n. The synonym for NVARCHAR is NATIONAL CHARACTER VARYING.

3.1.2.6 The NTEXT Data Type

An NTEXT is a Unicode character string that is rarely used. NTEXT is only used to support legacy applications and has likely been replaced by NVARCHAR or VARCHAR.

3.1.2.7 Unicode Character Strings

Unicode character strings (e.g., NVARCHAR) need 2 bytes for each stored character. Most English and European alphabets can be stored as single-byte characters. Single-byte character strings can store up to 8000 characters, while Unicode character strings can store up to 4000 characters.

3.1.2.8   General Rules on Selecting Character Data Types

Here we present some general rules for determining which character data type to use:

- Use the variable-length data types (VARCHAR) over fixed-length data types (CHAR) when you expect a lot of null values or a lot of variation in the size of data.
- If a column's data does not vary widely in number of characters, consider using CHAR instead of VARCHAR.
- NVARCHAR or NCHAR data types should not be used unless you need to store 16-bit character (Unicode) data. NVARCHARs and NCHARs take up twice as much space as VARCHAR or CHAR data types, reducing I/O performance.

3.1.3   Date and Time Data Types

Earlier SQL Server versions, e.g., SQL Server 2005, had two data types for storing date and time information: DATETIME and SMALLDATETIME. SQL Server 2008, with its introduction of four additional date and time data types, gives us the ability to work with date and time information separately. These new data types are: DATE, TIME, DATETIME2, and DATETIMEOFFSET. These new data types also simplify working with date and time data by providing for increased data range, precision of seconds, fractional seconds, and time zone support.[1]

3.1.3.1   The DATE Data Type

The DATE data type, which will store dates through December 31, 9999, has a precision of 10 digits. This data type does not have a time component.

3.1.3.2   The TIME Data Type

The TIME data type stores hours, minutes, seconds, and fractional seconds through 23:59:59.9999999, hence you can specify up to the fractional second. This data type does not include the date component.

3.1.3.3   The DATETIMEOFFSET Data Type

The DATETIMEOFFSET data type allows for time-zone awareness by including + or − hh:mm.

3.1.3.4   The DATETIME2 Data Type

The DATETIME2 data type is an improved version of the DATETIME data type. While the original version of DATETIME only supported three digits of precision, this newer version, DATETIME2, allows you to specify the precision and supports a larger date range.

3.1.4   Miscellaneous Data Types

Among other data types available in SQL Server 2008 are BINARY, IMAGE, BIT, TABLE, SQL_VARIANT, UNIQUEIDENTIFIER, XML, and hierarchyid (this last data type is one of SQL Server 2008's newest enhancements).

3.1.4.1   The BINARY Data Type

The BINARY data types are BINARY and VARBINARY. Both are used for very specific applications.

BINARY data types are used to store strings of bits; values are entered and displayed using their hexadecimal (hex) representation. The maximum length of the BINARY data type is 8000 bytes. You can specify the maximum byte length of BINARY(n) data with n, (e.g., BINARY(500)).

The VARBINARY data type can store up to 8000 bytes of variable-length binary data. Once again, you can specify the maximum byte length with n. The VARBINARY data type should be used (instead of the BINARY data type) when you expect to have NULL values or a variation in data size.

RAW is the Oracle equivalent of VARBINARY.

3.1.4.2   The IMAGE Data Type

The IMAGE data type is a large object binary data type that stores more than 8000 bytes. The IMAGE data type is used to store both binary values and pictures.

LONG RAW is the Oracle equivalent of IMAGE.

3.1.4.3   The BIT Data Type

The BIT data type, which is rarely used, is actually an integer data type that can only store a 0 or a 1 and can consume only a single bit of storage space. However, if there is only a 1-bit column in a table, it will take up a whole byte. The BIT data type is usually used for true/false or yes/no types of data. BIT columns cannot be NULL and cannot have indexes on them.

3.1.4.4   The Monetary Data Types

Monetary data types are generally used to store monetary values. SQL Server 2008 has two monetary data types:

- MONEY, which uses 8 bytes of storage
- SMALLMONEY, which uses 4 bytes of storage

3.1.4.5   The TABLE Data Type

The TABLE data type can be used to store the result of a function and can be used as the data type of local variables. Columns in tables, however, cannot be of type TABLE. Table variables are sometimes preferable to temporary tables because table variables are erased automatically at the end of a function or stored procedure.

Temporary tables are covered in Chapter 6. Discussing stored procedures is beyond the scope of this book.

3.1.4.6   The SQL_VARIANT Data Type

Values stored in a SQL_VARIANT column can be of any data type except TEXT or IMAGE. The usage of the SQL_VARIANT data type should be avoided for several reasons: (1) a SQL_VARIANT column cannot be part of a primary or foreign key; (2) a SQL_VARIANT column cannot be part of a computed column; (3) a SQL_VARIANT column can be used in indexes or as other unique keys only if they are shorter than 900 bytes; and (4) a SQL_VARIANT column must convert the data to another data type when moving data to objects with other data types. Since good database practice dictates that columns have consistent data types, the use of this variant type is rarely justified.

Foreign keys are discussed in Chapter 11.

3.1.4.7   The UNIQUEIDENTIFIER Data Type

The UNIQUEIDENTIFIER data type, also referred to as a globally unique identifier (GUID) or a universal unique identifier (UUID), is a 128-bit generated value that guarantees uniqueness worldwide, even among unconnected computers. This is an advanced data type used in multiuser, multilocation settings.

3.1.4.8   The XML Data Type

XML is a globally standardized markup language similar in style to HTML that is used to exchange data over the Internet. The XML data type, introduced with SQL Server 2005, is used to handle XML data. XML can model complex data structures, and XML columns can be typed or untyped. Like other data types, the XML data type must meet specific formatting criteria. It must conform to well-formatted XML criteria (which is untyped) and you can optionally add additional conformance criteria by specifying a schema collection (typed). SQL Server will also allow you to store XML documents associated with multiple schema definitions. The XML data type will allow you to store complete XML documents or fragments of XML documents. XML documents are limited to 2 GB of data.

3.1.4.9 The Hierarchyid Data Type

Typically, tables in relational databases do not have any imposed structure. However, there are some circumstances in business that may require a hierarchical structuring of data (e.g., organization charts or critical path diagrams). This new SQL Server data type, hierarchyid, allows you to construct relationships among data elements within a table, specifically to represent a position in a hierarchy. This advanced feature will likely be used only in rare circumstances where data representation cannot be accomplished more traditionally.

3.1.5 General Rules on Selecting Data Types

Here we present some general rules that you can follow to determine which data type to use to define a column:

- Use the smallest possible column sizes. The smaller the column size, the less the amount of data that SQL Server has to store and process, and the faster SQL Server will be able to read and write the data. In addition, the narrower the column, the faster a sort will be performed on that column.
- Use the smallest possible data type that will hold your data for a column. For example, if you are going to be storing numbers from 1 to 99 in a column, you would be better off selecting the TINYINT data type instead of the INT data type.
- For numeric data, it is better to use a numeric data type such as INTEGER rather than using VARCHAR or CHAR, since numeric data types generally require less space to hold numeric values then character data types. Also, if numeric data is stored as characters, it will have to be converted to numbers to be used in calculations. Smaller columns can improve performance when the columns are searched, joined with other columns, or sorted.

Joins are discussed in Chapter 4.

FLOATs or REALs should not be used to define primary keys. Integer data types are most commonly used for primary keys.

Avoid selecting the fixed-length columns—CHAR or NCHAR—if your column will have a lot of NULLs. The NULL in a CHAR or NCHAR field will take up the entire fixed length of 255 characters. This is a large waste of space and reduces SQL Server's overall performance.

If you are going to be using a column for frequent sorts, consider an integer-based column rather than a character-based column. SQL Server sorts integer data faster than character data.[2]

3.2 Creating a Table

In SQL Server, a relational database system, data is loaded into tables that are created in a database. In Chapter 1, we showed you how to create a database. In this section, we will concentrate on creating tables within an existing database.

In SQL, the CREATE TABLE command is used to create a table. In SQL Server, the CREATE TABLE command has to be entered in the query editor screen (shown in Figure 1.12).

Instructions on opening the query editor screen are presented in Chapter 1.

The general syntax of the CREATE TABLE statement is:

```
CREATE TABLE Tablename
(column_name type, column_name, type, .....)
```

To demonstrate how this CREATE TABLE command works, we provide two examples.

Example 3.1 For the first example, we will create a table called `Employee` that has four columns (attributes). First, enter the following in the query editor screen (make sure that you have selected the `Student_course` database before typing this; if you do not remember how to select the `Student_course` database, refer to Figure 1.15):

```
CREATE TABLE Employee (names VARCHAR(20),
                       address VARCHAR(20),
                       employee_number INT,
                       salary SMALLMONEY)
```

Execute the query.

You will get:

```
Command(s) completed successfully.
```

This CREATE TABLE query created a table called `Employee` with four columns (in the `Student_course` database): names, address, `employee_number`, and `salary`. The data type of `names` is VARCHAR (variable-length character), with a maximum length of 20 characters. The data type of `address` is VARCHAR, with a maximum length of 20 characters. The data type of `employee_number` is INT, and the data type of `salary` is SMALLMONEY.

To view the `Employee` table in the `Student_course` database, expand the `Student_course` node (under the Object Explorer) and the **Tables** node, and you should be able to see the `Employee` table, as shown in Figure 3.1:

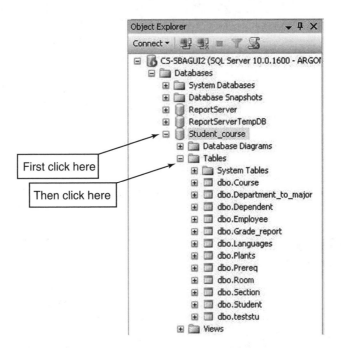

Figure 3.1   Viewing the `Employee` table

To see the table design of the table you just created, right-click on the table, `Employee`, and select **Design**. Figure 3.2 shows the table design of the `Employee` table.

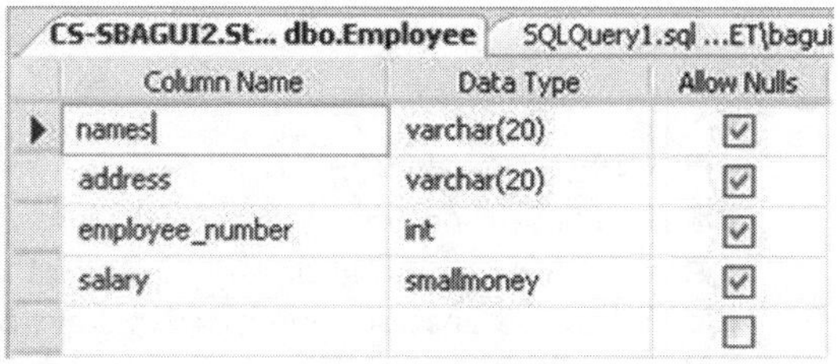

Figure 3.2   Table Design of the Employee table

Example 3.2   For the second example to demonstrate the use of the CREATE TABLE command, we will create a table called Names. Enter the following query:

```
CREATE TABLE Names
(fullname VARCHAR(20))
```

This table has only one column, fullname. Its data type is VARCHAR, and the maximum length of a name in this table is 20 characters.

3.3   Inserting Values into a Table

There are several ways to insert values into a table using SQL in SQL Server. We will illustrate the two most commonly used ways: using INSERT INTO .. VALUES and using INSERT INTO .. SELECT.

3.3.1   Using INSERT INTO .. VALUES

One way to insert values into *one* row of a table is to use the INSERT INTO command with the VALUES option. The INSERT INTO .. VALUES option needs the column list and all the columns in the correct order.

The general syntax for the INSERT INTO .. VALUES option is:

```
INSERT INTO TableName
VALUES ('character_attribute_value', numeric_attribute_value, ... )
```

We will first illustrate inserting data with the INSERT INTO .. VALUES option using the Names table we created in the preceding section. So, type the following in the query editor:

```
INSERT INTO Names
VALUES ('Joe Smith')
```

where:

- INSERT is the SQL command to insert data into a table.
- INTO is a necessary keyword.
- `names` is the name of an existing table.
- VALUES is another necessary keyword.
- `'Joe Smith'` is a string of letters corresponding to the VARCHAR data type (refer to the `Names` table example in the preceding section).

Then click the **Execute** button.

You will get a message that tells you how many rows were inserted by the query:

```
(1 row(s) affected)
```

Now, if you type the following SQL query:

```
SELECT *
FROM Names
```

you will get:

```
fullname
--------------------
Joe Smith

(1 row(s) affected)
```

The INSERT INTO .. VALUES option appends rows to a table (that is, rows are added to the end of the table). So, if you use the INSERT INTO .. VALUES option again as follows:

```
INSERT INTO Names
VALUES ('Sudip Kumar')
```

and then type:

```
SELECT *
FROM Names
```

you get this result:

```
fullname
--------------------
Joe Smith
Sudip Kumar

(2 row(s) affected)
```

If you created a table with n attributes (columns), you usually will have n values in the INSERT INTO .. VALUES statement in the order of the design of the columns. For example, to insert information into the `Employee` table that you created earlier, the INSERT INTO .. VALUES statement to insert a row would have to match column for column and would look like this:

INSERT INTO Employee
VALUES ('Joe Smith', '123 4th St.', 101, 2500)

Note that character data is entered with single quotes around it. Numeric data does not use quotes (as shown by the 101 and 2500).

Now if you type:

SELECT *
FROM Employee

you get the following:

```
names                address              employee_number salary
-------------------- -------------------- --------------- ------------
Joe Smith            123 4th St.          101             2500.00

(1 row(s) affected)
```

An INSERT that looks like the following is incorrect because it does not include all four columns of the `Employee` table:

INSERT INTO Employee
VALUES ('Joe Smith', '123 4th St.')

You may insert a row that does not include all the columns by naming the columns you want to insert into, like this:

INSERT INTO Employee (names, address)
VALUES ('Joe Smith', '123 4th St.')

In this case, the row will contain nulls or default values for the values left out, which you will see if you type:

```
SELECT *
FROM Employee
```

This will give:

```
names                 address               employee_number salary
-------------------- --------------------- --------------- ------------
Joe Smith            123 4th St.           101             2500.00
Joe Smith            123 4th St.           NULL            NULL

(2 row(s) affected)
```

An INSERT that looks like the following is incorrect because it does not have the values in the same order as the design of the table:

```
INSERT INTO Employee
VALUES (2500, 'Joe Smith', 101, '123 4th St.')
```

If for some reason the data had to be entered in this order, the preceding statement could be corrected by specifying the column names as follows:

```
INSERT INTO Employee (salary, names, employee_number, address)
VALUES (2500, 'Joe Smith', 101, '123 4th St.')
```

At this point, entering:

```
SELECT *
FROM Employee
```

would give us the following output:

```
names                 address               employee_number salary
-------------------- --------------------- --------------- ------------
Joe Smith            123 4th St.           101             2500.00
Joe Smith            123 4th St.           NULL            NULL
Joe Smith            123 4th St.           101             2500.00

(3 row(s) affected)
```

You may actually include the keyword NULL if the address and salary are unknown:

INSERT INTO Employee
VALUES ('Joe Smith', NULL, 101, NULL)

Now having added four rows to our table, enter:

SELECT *
FROM Employee

This will give the following output:

```
names                address              employee_number salary
-------------------- -------------------- ---------------- ------------
Joe Smith            123 4th St.          101              2500.00
Joe Smith            123 4th St.          NULL             NULL
Joe Smith            123 4th St.          101              2500.00
Joe Smith            NULL                 101              NULL

(4 row(s) affected)
```

To delete all the rows in the `Employee` table as well as in the `Names` table, type:

DELETE FROM Employee

Then:

DELETE FROM Names

We will revisit the DELETE command later in the chapter.

We will now set up our `Employee` table with more meaningful data to use the rest of this chapter. Delete all the test rows you entered earlier with a DELETE statement and then use the INSERT INTO .. VALUES option to insert valid data into the `Employee` table so it looks like this:

```
names                address              employee_number salary
-------------------- -------------------- ---------------- ------------
Joe Smith            123 4th St.          101              2500.00
Pradeep Saha         27 Shillingford      103              3300.00
Sumit Kumar          95 Oxford Rd         105              1200.00
Joya Das             23 Pesterfield Cr    114              2290.00
Terry Livingstone    465 Easter Ave       95               3309.00

(5 row(s) affected)
```

More than one INSERT INTO .. VALUES command can be entered on one screen in SQL Server.

3.3.2   Using **INSERT INTO .. SELECT**

With the INSERT INTO .. VALUES option, you insert only one row at a time into a table. With the INSERT INTO .. SELECT option, you may (and usually do) insert *many* rows into a table at one time.

The general syntax for the INSERT INTO .. SELECT option is:

```
INSERT INTO target_table(column1, column2, column3, ... )
"SELECT clause"
```

We will first illustrate inserting with the INSERT INTO .. SELECT statement by populating the **Names** table (that you created earlier in this chapter and then removed all rows with "DELETE FROM Names.") To copy all the names from the **Employee** table into the **Names** table, enter the following:

```
INSERT INTO Names(fullname)
SELECT names
FROM Employee
```

Now enter:

```
SELECT *
FROM Names
```

This will produce the following five rows of output:

```
fullname
-------------------
Joe Smith
Pradeep Saha
Sumit Kumar
Joya Das
Terry Livingstone

(5 row(s) affected)
```

At this point, delete all the data from the **Names** table once again with:

```
DELETE FROM Names
```

We do not have to copy all the names from the **Employee** table to the **Names** table. For example, we could restrict the INSERT INTO .. SELECT like this:

```
INSERT INTO Names(fullname)
SELECT names
FROM Employee
WHERE salary > 2600
```

This would give us only the following two rows in `Names`:

```
fullname
--------------------
Pradeep Saha
Terry Livingstone


(2 row(s) affected)
```

As with the INSERT INTO .. VALUES option, if you create a table with n columns, you usually have n values in the INSERT INTO .. SELECT option in the order of the table design, or you have to name the columns you are inserting. For example, suppose we have a table called `Emp1` with three columns:

```
Emp1 (addr, sal, empno)
```

The columns `addr`, `sal`, and `empno`, stand for address, salary, and employee number, respectively.

Now suppose that we want to load the existing empty table called `Emp1` from the `Employee` table with the appropriate columns.

As with the INSERT INTO .. VALUES option, the INSERT INTO .. SELECT option has to match column for column.

An INSERT INTO .. SELECT statement would look like this:

```
INSERT INTO Emp1(addr, sal, empno)
SELECT address, salary, employee_number
FROM Employee
```

The `Emp1` table would now have the following five rows:

```
addr                 sal           empno
--------------------  ------------  -----------
123 4th St.          2500.00       101
27 Shillingford      3300.00       103
95 Oxford Rd         1200.00       105
23 Pesterfield Cr    2290.00       114
465 Easter Ave       3309.00       95


(5 row(s) affected)
```

If we created another table, Emp2, with columns (or attributes) identical to Emp1, we could use the following INSERT to load data from table Emp1 to Emp2:

```
INSERT INTO Emp2
SELECT *
FROM Emp1
```

The Emp2 table would now have the same data as the Emp1 table. This is one way of creating a copy or a backup of a table.

Note that the Emp2 table has to exist (be created with the same columns and types) before loading it with the INSERT INTO .. SELECT option.

One caution should be observed here. The INSERT INTO .. SELECT could succeed if the data types of the SELECT match the data types of the columns in the table to which we are inserting, but might result in incorrect data. For example, execute the following statement (remember that both sal and empno are numeric types):

```
INSERT INTO Emp1 (addr, sal, empno)
SELECT address, employee_number, salary
FROM Employee
```

This INSERT will succeed because the data types match. The following output is the result of executing the preceding INSERT statement:

```
addr                    sal           empno
--------------------    ------------  -----------
123 4th St.             101.00        2500
27 Shillingford         103.00        3300
95 Oxford Rd            105.00        1200
23 Pesterfield Cr       114.00        2290
465 Easter Ave          95.00         3309

(5 row(s) affected)
```

The wrong information has been inserted in Emp1's columns. The employee_number from Employee has been inserted into the sal column in Emp1, and the salary from Employee has been inserted into the empno column of Emp1. Therefore, it is most prudent to be careful and line up or match up the columns (attributes) in the INSERT INTO and SELECT statements when using an INSERT INTO .. SELECT.

As you might have already guessed from the INSERT INTO .. VALUES section, you do not have to insert the entire row with an INSERT INTO ..

SELECT. You may load fewer columns. For example, once again delete all rows from `Emp1`, and then execute a statement like this:

```
INSERT INTO Emp1 (addr, sal)
SELECT address, salary
FROM Employee
```

This INSERT would leave the other column, `empno` (of the `Emp1` table), with a value of NULL as shown here:

```
SELECT *
FROM Emp1
```

This produces the following output:

```
addr                    sal           empno
--------------------    ------------  -----------
123 4th St.             2500.00       NULL
27 Shillingford         3300.00       NULL
95 Oxford Rd            1200.00       NULL
23 Pesterfield Cr       2290.00       NULL
465 Easter Ave          3309.00       NULL

(5 row(s) affected)
```

In conclusion, you must be careful with the INSERT INTO .. SELECT option, because, unlike the INSERT INTO .. VALUES option (which inserts one row at a time), you almost always insert multiple rows, and if types match, the insert will take place whether or not it makes sense.

3.4 The UPDATE Command

Another common command used for setting or changing data values in a table is UPDATE. Although quite useful, the UPDATE command must be handled with care because you often update more than one row, as with INSERT INTO .. SELECT. To examine how the UPDATE command works, we will use the tables we created in the previous section.

The general format for the UPDATE command is:

```
UPDATE TableName
SET fieldname . . .
```

For example, if you want to set *all* salaries in the table `Emp2` to zero, you may do so with one UPDATE command:

```
UPDATE Emp2
SET sal = 0
```

Now, if you type:

```
SELECT *
FROM Emp2
```

you will get:

```
addr                    sal           empno
--------------------    ------------  -----------
123 4th St.             0.00          101
27 Shillingford         0.00          103
95 Oxford Rd            0.00          105
23 Pesterfield Cr       0.00          114
465 Easter Ave          0.00           95

(5 row(s) affected)
```

This UPDATE command sets all salaries in all rows of the `Emp2` table to zero, regardless of previous values. As with any statement that affects all rows, this may be viewed as a dangerous command and caution should be observed.

    It is often useful to include a WHERE clause in the UPDATE command so that values are set selectively. For example, if we assume that employee numbers are unique, we can update a specific employee from the `Employee` table with the following statement:

```
UPDATE Employee
SET salary = 0
WHERE employee_number=101
```

This produces the following output:

```
names                 address               employee_number salary
--------------------  --------------------  --------------- ------------
Joe Smith             123 4th St.           101             0.00
Pradeep Saha          27 Shillingford       103             3300.00
Sumit Kumar           95 Oxford Rd          105             1200.00
Joya Das              23 Pesterfield Cr     114             2290.00
Terry Livingstone     465 Easter Ave        95              3390.00

(5 row(s) affected)
```

Only the row for employee number 101 is updated since we are using equality in the WHERE and a primary key. Observe that we do not use quotes around 101, since employee_number is defined as an INT column (a numeric column). Quotes would have to be used around any character or string columns.

3.5   The ALTER TABLE Command

In the last few sections, we looked at how to add, change, and update rows in a table with the INSERT and UPDATE commands. In this section, we will discuss how you can add, modify, and delete *columns* in a table's design by using SQL's ALTER TABLE command. ALTER TABLE commands are known as data definition language (DDL) commands since they change the design or definition of a table. This section is perhaps less interesting to SQL Server users because of the ease of use of Microsoft SQL Server's Management Studio; however, for completeness in learning SQL, this section is included and shows how altering tables is carried out in noninteractive interfaces.

3.5.1   Adding a Column to a Table

You may add columns to a table using SQL. The general syntax for adding a column to a table is:

```
ALTER TABLE Tablename
ADD column-name type
```

For example, to add a column called bonus (a SMALLMONEY column) to the Employee table, you enter the following:

```
ALTER TABLE Employee
ADD bonus SMALLMONEY
```

This query alters the table design of the Employee table, as shown in Figure 3.3 (to get Figure 3.3, click on the + beside the Employee table and then click on the + beside **Columns** in the Object Explorer on the left side of your screen).

When columns are added to existing tables, they will initially contain NULL values. Data may be added to the new column using an UPDATE command.

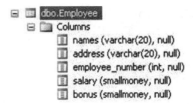

Figure 3.3   Column added to the Employee table

3.5.2   Changing a Column's Data Type in a Table

In SQL Server 2008, you can change the data type of a column with existing data in it provided the new data type will accommodate the existing data. The general syntax for changing a column's data type in a table is:

ALTER TABLE Tablename
ALTER COLUMN column-name new_type

For example, to change the data type of the **bonus** column from SMALL-MONEY to FLOAT, you would type the following:

ALTER TABLE Employee
ALTER COLUMN bonus FLOAT

This would produce the table design of the Employee table shown in Figure 3.4.

	Column Name	Data Type	Allow Nulls
▶	names	varchar(20)	☑
	address	varchar(20)	☑
	employee_number	int	☑
	salary	smallmoney	☑
	bonus	float	☑

Figure 3.4   Altered column's data type for bonus column in the Employee table

You may have to refresh the Employee table before you can see this change made to the table design. To refresh the Employee table, right-click on the table and select **Refresh**. Then, select the Employee table, right-click, and select **Design**.

3.5.3 Changing a Column's Size in a Table

You may want to change the size of a column in a table. You typically will make a column larger, and SQL Server will not have a problem with that because larger columns will accommodate existing data. But if you wanted to make a column smaller (which is unusual), sometimes SQL Server will let you do it and other times it will not.

When will SQL Server 2008 allow you to reduce the size of your column without any problems? When you do not have any data in that column yet (it is all NULL) and when all the data in that column is still less than the size to which you are changing the column.

If you try to reduce the column size to a size where you would be truncating some of the data, SQL Server will give you an error message and will not let you do it.

For example, if you type in the following ALTER TABLE statement, trying to change the **names** column of the **Employee** table to a size of 5 (where you would be losing some data):

```
ALTER TABLE Employee
ALTER COLUMN names VARCHAR(5)
```

you will get the following error message:

```
Msg 8152, Level 16, State 14, Line 1
String or binary data would be truncated.
The statement has been terminated.
```

Upon viewing the table design of the **Employee** table, you will find that the column size of the **names** column was not altered.

If, however, you type:

```
ALTER TABLE Employee
ALTER COLUMN names VARCHAR(19)
```

you will get the message:

```
Command(s) completed successfully.
```

Now if you look at the table design of the **Employee** table, you will see that the **names** column has been changed to a size of 19 characters, as shown in Figure 3.5.

Column Name	Data Type	Allow Nulls
names	varchar(19)	☑
address	varchar(20)	☑
employee_number	int	☑
salary	smallmoney	☑
bonus	float	☑

Figure 3.5 Altering a column's length in the `Employee` table

Remember that you may have to refresh the `Employee` table before you can view this change.

SQL Server 2008 allowed this reduction in column size since all the data in the names column was less than 19 characters in length.

Before you proceed to the following section, please change the size of the `names` column back to 20.

3.5.4 Deleting a Column from a Table

The following is the general syntax for deleting a column from a table:

```
ALTER TABLE Tablename
DROP column column-name
```

For example, to delete the column called `bonus` from the `Employee` table, type the following:

```
ALTER TABLE Employee
DROP column bonus
```

This produces the design of the `Employee` table shown in Figure 3.6, which matches the original design for the table shown in Figure 3.2.

Column Name	Data Type	Allow Nulls
names	varchar(20)	☑
address	varchar(20)	☑
employee_number	int	☑
salary	smallmoney	☑

Figure 3.6 Design of the `Employee` table after dropping a column

Note that this DROP column command will delete a column even if there is data in it, so you have to be very careful when using it. This is another command that affects multiple rows, and thus caution must be observed.

We will discuss a few other uses of the ALTER TABLE command in subsequent chapters. For example, you can use it to define or change a default column value, enable or disable an integrity constraint, manage internal space, etc.

3.6   The DELETE Command

Earlier in the chapter, we saw that the DELETE command can be used to remove all rows of a table. In this section we revisit DELETE. Keep in mind as you read this that the DELETE command can affect multiple rows as we have seen and hence caution must be observed when using it. Following is the general syntax of the DELETE command used to delete rows from a table:

DELETE FROM Table
WHERE (condition)

The (condition) determines which rows of the table will be deleted. As we saw earlier, if no WHERE condition is used, all the rows of the table will be deleted.

Multiple rows can be affected by the DELETE command, so be careful when using it.

The following is an example of using the DELETE command on our original Employee table:

DELETE FROM Employee
WHERE salary < 1500

Now if you type:

SELECT *
FROM EMPLOYEE

you will get the following four rows of output:

names	address	employee_number	salary
Joe Smith	123 4th St.	101	2500.00
Pradeep Saha	27 Shillingford	103	3300.00
Joya Das	23 Pesterfield Cr	114	2290.00
Terry Livingstone	465 Easter Ave	95	3390.00

(4 row(s) affected)

3.7 Deleting a Table

The general syntax to delete or remove an entire table and its contents is:

DROP TABLE Tablename

For example, to delete the table called Names from your database, you would type the following:

DROP TABLE Names

There are times when it is appropriate to delete all the data in a table, and there are times when the entire table should be eliminated. When a table is dropped, it no longer exists; its design is removed from the database. But when data is deleted from a table with a DELETE statement (maybe with a WHERE condition), the table may be repopulated because only the data from the table was removed; the design is intact.

SUMMARY

In this chapter, we introduced the basic data types available in SQL Server 2008 and covered basic table manipulations. We illustrated how to create tables, insert data into tables, update data in tables, add and delete columns in tables, alter column types and sizes, and delete entire tables.

Review Questions

1. The INSERT INTO .. VALUES option will insert rows into the _____ of a table.
2. While you are inserting values into a table with the INSERT INTO .. VALUES option, does the order of the columns in the INSERT statement have to be the same as the order of the columns in the table?
3. While you are inserting values into a table with the INSERT INTO .. SELECT option, does the order of the columns in the INSERT statement have to be the same as the order of the columns in the table?
4. When would you use an INSERT INTO .. SELECT option versus an INSERT INTO .. VALUES option? Give an example of each.
5. What does the UPDATE command do?
6. Can you change the data type of a column in a table after the table has been created? If so, which command would you use?
7. Will SQL Server 2008 allow you to reduce the size of a column?
8. What integer data types are available in SQL Server 2008?
9. What is the default value of an integer data type in SQL Server 2008?

10. What decimal data types are available in SQL Server 2008?
11. What is the difference between a CHAR and a VARCHAR data type?
12. Does Server SQL treat CHAR as a variable-length or fixed-length column? Do other SQL implementations treat it the same way?
13. If you are going to have many nulls in a column, what would be the best data type to use?
14. When columns are added to existing tables, what do they initially contain?
15. What command would you use to add a column to a table in SQL Server?
16. In SQL Server, which data type is used to store large object data types?
17. If you do not need to store decimal places, what would be a good numeric data type to use?
18. If you need to store decimal places but are not worried about rounding errors, what would be a good data type to use?
19. Should a column be defined as a FLOAT if it is going to be used as a primary key?
20. What are the new date data types available in SQL Server 2008?

Chapter 3 Exercises

Unless specified otherwise, use the `Student_course` **database to answer the following questions. Also, use appropriate column headings when displaying your output.**

1. Create a table called `Cust` with a customer number as a fixed-length character string of 3, an address with a variable-length character string of up to 20, and a numeric balance.
   a. Insert values into the table with the INSERT INTO .. VALUES option. Use the form of INSERT INTO .. VALUES that requires you to have a value for each column; therefore, if you have a customer number, address, and balance, you must insert three values with INSERT INTO .. VALUES.
   b. Create at least five rows with customer numbers 101 to 105 and balances from 200 to 2000.
   c. Display the table's data with a simple SELECT.
   d. Show the balances for customers with customer numbers 103 and 104.
   e. Add a customer number 90 to your `Cust` table.
   f. Show a listing of the customers in balance order (high to low), using ORDER BY in your SELECT. (The result should be five rows or however many you created.)

2. From the **Student** table (from our **Student_course** database), display the student names, classes, and majors for freshmen or sophomores (class <= 2) in descending order of class.

3. From your **Cust** table, show a listing of only the customer balances in ascending order where balance > 400. (You can choose some other constant or relation if you want, such as balance <= 600.) The results will depend on your data.

4. Create two more tables with the same data types as **Cust** but without the customer addresses. Call one table **Cust1** and the other **Cust2**. Use column names **cnum** for customer number and **bal** for balance. Load the tables with the data from the **Cust** table, but with one less row. Use an INSERT INTO .. SELECT with appropriate columns and an appropriate WHERE clause.

   a. Display the design of the new tables and their data.

5. Alter the **Cust1** table by adding a **date_opened** column with an appropriate date data type. View the table design of **Cust1**.

   a. Add some more data into the **Cust1** table by using INSERT INTO .. VALUES.

   After each of the following, display the table.

   b. Set the **date_opened** value in all rows to '01-JAN-10'.

   c. Set all balances to zero.

   d. Set the **date_opened** value of one of your rows to '21-OCT-10'.

   e. Change the type of the balance column in the **Cust1** table to FLOAT. Display the table design. Set the balance for one row to 888.88 and display the table data.

   f. Try changing the data type of balance to INTEGER. Does this work in SQL Server?

   g. Delete the **date_opened** column of the **Cust1** table.

   h. When you are finished with the exercise (but be sure you are finished), delete the tables **Cust**, **Cust1**, and **Cust2**.

References

1. http://www.technet.microsoft.com/en-us/magazine/2008.04.datatypes .aspx

2. http://www.sql-server-performance.com/datatypes.asp

chapter

4

Joins

Topics covered in this chapter

This chapter discusses joins, which are a common way to combine tables in SQL. In Chapter 2, you learned how to write simple query statements in SQL using *one* table. In real databases, however, data is usually spread over many tables. This chapter shows you how to combine tables in a database so that you can retrieve data from more than one table. The join operation is used to combine related rows from two tables (relations) into a result set. The join is a binary operation. More than two tables can be combined pairwise using multiple join operations.

We begin the chapter by discussing the "regular" join in Microsoft® SQL Server® 2008. The regular join is accomplished using the JOIN command. Then, we show how the same join could also be achieved with an INNER JOIN or a WHERE clause. The concepts of the Cartesian product, equi-joins, non-equi-joins, and self-joins are also introduced. We also show how multiple table joins can be performed with nested JOINs or a WHERE clause. Finally, the concept of OUTER JOINs, with specific illustrations of the LEFT and RIGHT OUTER joins and the FULL OUTER JOIN, is also discussed.

4.1 The JOIN

In SQL Server 2008, the join is accomplished using the ANSI JOIN SQL syntax, which uses the JOIN keyword and an ON clause. The ANSI JOIN syntax requires the use of an ON clause to specify how the tables are related. One ON clause is used for each pair of tables being joined. The general form of the ANSI JOIN SQL syntax is:

```
SELECT columns
FROM Table1 JOIN Table2
ON Table1.column1=Table2.column1
```

The following example demonstrates the basic idea of a join. Suppose we have the following two tables, Table 4.1 and Table 4.2:

The common column between the two tables is ColumnA. So the join would be performed on ColumnA. A SQL JOIN would result in a table where

ColumnA	ColumnB	ColumnC
X1	Y1	Z1
X2	Y2	Z2
X3	Y3	Z3

Table 4.1

ColumnA	ColumnD	ColumnE
X1	D1	E1
X2	D2	E2
X3	D3	E3

Table 4.2

"ColumnA of Table1 = columnA of Table2." This would produce a new table, Table 4.3, which is the result of the join:

ColumnA	ColumnB	ColumnC	ColumnA	ColumnD	ColumnE
X1	Y1	Z1	X1	D1	E1
X2	Y2	Z2	X2	D2	E2
X3	Y3	Z3	X3	D3	E3

Table 4.3

There are several types of joins in SQL. The preceding model refers to an "inner join" where the two tables being joined must share at least one common column. The columns of the two tables being joined by the JOIN command are matched using an ON clause. SQL Server will actually translate the preceding JOIN statement to an unambiguous INNER JOIN form, as we shall see. When inner-joining two tables, the JOIN returns rows from both tables only if there is a corresponding value in both tables as described by the ON clause column. In other words, the JOIN disregards any rows in which the specific join condition in the ON clause is not met.

To illustrate the JOIN using our database (the Student_course database), we present two examples.

Example 4.1 To find the student names and dependent names of all the students who have dependents, we need to join the Student table with the Dependent table because the data that we want to display is spread across these two tables. Before we can formulate the JOIN query, we have to examine both tables and find out what relationship exists between the two tables. Usually this relationship is one in which one table has a column as a primary key and the other table has a column as a foreign key. A *primary key* is a unique identifier for a row in a table. A *foreign key* is so called because the key it references is "foreign" to the table where it exists. An example will clarify this point.

Let us first look at the table designs of the Student and Dependent tables, shown in Figures 4.1 and 4.2, respectively.

CS-SBAGUI2.St... - dbo.Student		
Column Name	Data Type	Allow Nulls
STNO	smallint	☐
SNAME	nvarchar(20)	☑
MAJOR	nvarchar(4)	☑
CLASS	smallint	☑
BDATE	smalldatetime	☑

Figure 4.1   Design of the Student table

CS-SBAGUI2.St... dbo.Dependent		
Column Name	Data Type	Allow Nulls
PNO	smallint	☐
DNAME	nvarchar(20)	☑
RELATIONSHIP	nvarchar(8)	☑
SEX	char(1)	☑
AGE	smallint	☑

Figure 4.2   Design of the Dependent table

In examining these two tables, we note that student number (stno in the Student table) is the primary key of the Student table. stno is the unique identifier for each student. The Dependent table, which was not created with a primary key of its own, contains a reference to the Student table in that for each dependent, a parent number (pno) is recorded. pno in the Dependent table is a foreign key—it represents a primary key from the table it is referencing. pno in the Dependent table is not unique since a student can have more than one dependent; that is, one stno can be linked to more than one pno.

From the table designs, we can see that the Student table (which has columns stno, sname, major, class and bdate) can be joined with the Dependent table (which has columns pno, dname, relationship, sex, and age) by the column stno from the Student table and the pno column from the Dependent table. Following the ANSI JOIN syntax, we can join the two tables as follows:

```
SELECT s.stno, s.sname, d.relationship, d.age
FROM Student s JOIN Dependent d
ON s.stno=d.pno
```

In this query, Student refers to the table and s is the table alias of the Student table. Likewise, Dependent refers to the Dependent table and d is the table alias of that table. The table alias simplifies and clarifies writing queries and expressions. Typically, SQL programmers use single-letter table aliases. We very strongly recommend using table aliases in all multitable queries. This query requests the student number (stno) and student name (sname) from the Student table, and the relationship and age from the Dependent table when the student number in the Student table (stno) matches a parent number (pno) in the Dependent table.

Table aliases were discussed in detail in Chapter 2.

When the preceding query is entered and executed, you will get the following output showing the dependents of the students:

stno	sname	relationship	age
2	Lineas	Son	2
2	Lineas	Daughter	1
2	Lineas	Spouse	19
10	Richard	Son	3
10	Richard	Daughter	2
14	Lujack	Son	1
14	Lujack		3
17	Elainie	Daughter	2
17	Elainie	Son	1
20	Donald	Son	NULL
20	Donald	Son	4
34	Lynette	Daughter	1
34	Lynette	Daughter	1
62	Monica	Husband	25
62	Monica	Son	1
62	Monica	Daughter	2
62	Monica	Daughter	3
123	Holly	Son	3
123	Holly	Son	1
126	Jessica	Son	2
126	Jessica	Son	1
128	Brad	Son	1
128	Brad	Daughter	NULL
128	Brad	Daughter	2
128	Brad	Wife	18
132	George	Daughter	2
142	Jerry	Daughter	1
143	Cramer	Daughter	1
144	Fraiser	Wife	19

145	Harrison	Wife	21
146	Francis	Wife	20
147	Smithly	Wife	20
147	Smithly	Son	1
147	Smithly	Son	2
147	Smithly	Son	NULL
153	Genevieve	Daughter	3
153	Genevieve	Daughter	2
153	Genevieve	Son	1
158	Thornton	Wife	20

(39 row(s) affected)

Example 4.2   To find the course names and the prerequisites of all the courses that have prerequisites, we need to join the Prereq table with the Course table. Course names are in the Course table, and the Prereq table contains the course number of each prerequisite. The descriptions of the Prereq and Course tables are shown in Figures 4.3 and 4.4, respectively.

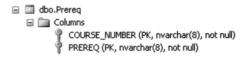

Figure 4.3   Design of the Prereq table

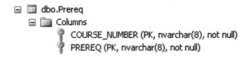

Figure 4.4   Design of the Course table

From these table designs, we note that the Course table has course_number as its primary key—the unique identifier for each course. The Prereq table also contains a course_number column but the course number in the Prereq table is not unique—there are often several prerequisites for any given course. The course number in the Prereq table is a foreign key referencing the primary key of the Course table. The Prereq table (which has columns course_number and prereq) can be joined with the Course table (which has columns course_name, course_number, credit_hours, and offering_dept) by the relationship column in both tables, course_number, as follows:

```
SELECT *
FROM COURSE c JOIN Prereq p
ON c.course_number=p.course_number
```

The preceding query could be written without the table alias (using a table qualifier) as follows:

```
SELECT * FROM Course JOIN Prereq
ON Course.course_number=Prereq.course_number
```

However, the use of the table alias is so common that the table alias form should be used. Also, aliases let you select columns that have the same names in different tables. This query will display those rows (12 rows) that have `course_number` in the `Course` table equal to `course_number` in the `Prereq` table, as follows:

```
COURSE_NAME          COURSE_NUMBER CREDIT_HOURS OFFERING_DEPT COURSE_NUMBER PREREQ
-------------------- ------------- ------------ ------------- ------------- --------
MANAGERIAL FINANCE   ACCT3333      3            ACCT          ACCT3333      ACCT2220
ORGANIC CHEMISTRY    CHEM3001      3            CHEM          CHEM3001      CHEM2001
DATA STRUCTURES      COSC3320      4            COSC          COSC3320      COSC1310
DATABASE             COSC3380      3            COSC          COSC3380      COSC3320
DATABASE             COSC3380      3            COSC          COSC3380      MATH2410
ADA - INTRODUCTION   COSC5234      4            COSC          COSC5234      COSC3320
ENGLISH COMP II      ENGL1011      3            ENGL          ENGL1011      ENGL1010
FUND. TECH. WRITING  ENGL3401      3            ENGL          ENGL3401      ENGL1011
WRITING FOR NON MAJO ENGL3520      2            ENGL          ENGL3520      ENGL1011
MATH ANALYSIS        MATH5501      3            MATH          MATH5501      MATH2333
AMERICAN GOVERNMENT  POLY2103      2            POLY          POLY2103      POLY1201
POLITICS OF CUBA     POLY5501      4            POLY          POLY5501      POLY4103

(12 row(s) affected)
```

Rows from the `Course` table without a matching row in the `Prereq` table are eliminated from the JOIN result; hence, courses that do not have prerequisites are not in the result set.

A primary key is a column or a minimal set of columns whose values uniquely identify a row in a table. A primary key cannot have a NULL value. Creation of primary keys is discussed in Chapter 11.

The inner join uses equality in the ON clause (the join condition). When an equal sign is used as a join condition, the join is called an "equi-join." The use of equi-joins is so common that many people use the phrase "join" synonymously with "equi-join"; when the term "join" is used without qualification, "equi-join" is inferred.

When dealing with table combinations, specifically joins, it is a good idea to estimate the number of rows one might expect in the result set. To find out how many rows will actually occur in the result set, the COUNT function is used. For example:

```
SELECT COUNT(*)
FROM Course c JOIN Prereq p
ON c.course_number = p.course_number
```

will tell us that there are 12 rows in the result set.

Suppose that the two tables to be equi-joined have X number of rows and Y number of rows, respectively. How many rows does one expect in the join? $MAX(X, Y)$ provides a good guideline. In our case, we have 12 rows in the Prereq table and 32 rows in the Course table. $MAX(12, 32) = 32$, but we actually got 12 rows. Note that $MAX(X, Y)$ is just a guideline. If you executed the COUNT as in the preceding query and got some number greater than 32 in this case, something would be wrong with the query. The actual and expected number of rows need not match exactly (and likely won't).

4.1.1   The INNER JOIN

In SQL Server, the keyword combination INNER JOIN behaves just like the JOIN discussed in the previous section. The general syntax for INNER JOIN is:

```
SELECT columns
FROM table1 INNER JOIN table2
ON table1.column1=table2.column1
```

Using INNER JOIN, the JOIN query presented in the previous section also could be written as:

```
SELECT *
FROM Course INNER JOIN Prereq
ON Course.course_number=Prereq.course_number
```

This query would produce the same result as given in the previous section.

As with the JOIN, the INNER JOIN cannot be used without the ON clause.

4.1.2   Using a WHERE Clause Instead of a JOIN

Another way of joining tables in SQL Server is to use a WHERE clause instead of using JOIN or INNER JOIN. To perform a join with a WHERE clause, the tables to be joined are listed in the FROM clause of a SELECT statement and the join condition between the tables to be joined is specified in the WHERE clause.

The JOIN from the preceding section could be written with a WHERE clause as follows:

```
SELECT *
FROM Course c, Prereq p
WHERE c.course_number = p.course_number
```

This command will display the same 12 rows as was previously shown (when JOIN was used). As a side note, this form of a join with the WHERE clause is extremely common in legacy databases. Almost all JOINs written more than 10 or so years ago will be in this form.

4.1.3 Associative Property of the JOIN

The algebraic associative property holds for an equi-join between two tables. That is, when two tables are being joined, it does not matter whether `TableA` is joined with `TableB`, or `TableB` is joined with `TableA`. For example, the following two queries would essentially give the same output:

```
SELECT *
FROM Course c JOIN Prereq p
ON c.course_number = p.course_number
```

and

```
SELECT *
FROM Prereq p JOIN Course c
ON p.course_number=c.course_number
```

The only difference in the two result sets would be the order of the columns. But the result set column order can be controlled by listing the columns in the order that you want them after the SELECT statement instead of using the "SELECT *" syntax.

4.1.4 Column Types in Joins

Joins have to be performed on "compatible" columns; that is, a character column may be joined to another character column, a numeric column may be joined to another numeric column, and so forth. So, for example, a CHAR column can be joined to a VARCHAR or NVARCHAR column (all being character columns). An INT column can be joined to a REAL column (both being numeric columns). Having made the point that compatible columns are required, and keeping in mind that SQL is not logical, it is up to the programmer to match semantics. If you ask SQL to join a `job_title` column with a `last_name` column, it will try to do so even though it makes no sense!

Some column types, such as IMAGE, cannot be joined since these columns will generally not contain "like" columns. Joins cannot be written on binary data types.

To create efficient joins, try to always join on the narrowest columns possible. The narrower the column, the less storage space will be used by SQL Server, and the faster SQL Server will be able to read and write the data.

4.2   The Cartesian Product

The Cartesian product is mathematically a binary operation in which two objects or sets (or tables) are combined in an "everything in combination with everything" fashion. In a SQL statement, a Cartesian product is where every row of the first table in the FROM clause is joined with every row of the second table in the FROM clause. A Cartesian product is produced when the WHERE form of the JOIN is used without the WHERE. An example of a Cartesian product (join) would be:

```
SELECT *
FROM Course c, Prereq p
```

The preceding command combines all the data in both the tables and makes a new result set. All rows in the `Course` table are combined with all rows in the `Prereq` table (a Cartesian product). This produces 384 rows of output, of which we show the first 10 rows:

```
COURSE_NAME         COURSE_NUMBER CREDIT_HOURS OFFERING_DEPT COURSE_NUMBER PREREQ
------------------- ------------- ------------ ------------- ------------- --------
ACCOUNTING I        ACCT2020      3            ACCT          ACCT3333      ACCT2220
ACCOUNTING II       ACCT2220      3            ACCT          ACCT3333      ACCT2220
MANAGERIAL FINANCE  ACCT3333      3            ACCT          ACCT3333      ACCT2220
ACCOUNTING INFO SYST ACCT3464     3            ACCT          ACCT3333      ACCT2220
INTRO TO CHEMISTRY  CHEM2001      3            CHEM          ACCT3333      ACCT2220
ORGANIC CHEMISTRY   CHEM3001      3            CHEM          ACCT3333      ACCT2220
INTRO TO COMPUTER SC COSC1310     4            COSC          ACCT3333      ACCT2220
TURBO PASCAL        COSC2025      3            COSC          ACCT3333      ACCT2220
ADVANCED COBOL      COSC2303      3            COSC          ACCT3333      ACCT2220
DATA STRUCTURES     COSC3320      4            COSC          ACCT3333      ACCT2220
.
.
.

(384 row(s) affected)
```

As we pointed out earlier, it is a good idea to get a count of the number of rows one might expect before actually combining tables. This can be done by:

SELECT COUNT(*) AS [COUNT OF CARTESIAN]
FROM Course c, Prereq p

This produces the following output:

```
COUNT OF CARTESIAN
------------------
384
```

From these results, we can see that the results of a Cartesian "join" will be a relation, say Q, which will have $n * m$ rows (where n is the number of rows from the first relation, and m is the number of rows from the second relation). In the preceding example, the result set has 384 rows (32 times 12), with all possible combinations of rows from the Course table and the Prereq table. If we compare these results with the results of the earlier query (with the WHERE clause), we can see that both results have the same structure, but the earlier one has been filtered by row with the WHERE clause to include only those rows where there is equality between Course.course_number and Prereq.course_number. Put another way, the earlier results make more sense because they present only those rows that correspond to one another. In this example, the Cartesian product produces extra, meaningless rows.

The Cartesian product can be called a join with no join (WHERE) condition. Usually, the Cartesian product result represents an error. Oftentimes, the Cartesian product is the result of a user having forgotten to use an appropriate WHERE clause in the SELECT statement when formulating a join using the WHERE format. The "forgetting to use a WHERE condition" usually occurs when many tables are involved in a query and some condition is accidentally left out. Note that if the JOIN or INNER JOIN syntax (ANSI JOIN syntax) is used, one cannot avoid the ON clause (omitting the ON clause produces a syntax error). Hence, producing a Cartesian product inadvertently in SQL Server 2008 using JOIN/INNER JOIN is much harder to do.

4.2.1 Uses of the Cartesian Product

Though the Cartesian product is generally regarded as not so useful in SQL per se, if harnessed properly, it can be used to produce exceptionally useful result sets, such as the following:

■ The Cartesian product can be used to generate sample or test data.

■ The simplest Cartesian product of two sets is a two-dimensional table or a cross-tabulation whose cells may be used to enter frequencies or to designate possibilities.

■ The Cartesian product is needed if you want a collection of all ordered *n*-rows (rows with *n* columns) that can be formed so that they contain one element of the first set, one element of the second set, ..., and one element of the *n*th set. For example, if set (or table) X is the 13-element set { A, K, Q, J, 10, 9, 8, 7, 6, 5, 4, 3, 2 } and set (or table) Y is the 4-element set { spades, hearts, diamonds, clubs }, then the Cartesian product of those two sets is the 52-element set { (A, spades), (K, spades), ... , (2, spades), (A, hearts), ... , (3, clubs), (2, clubs) }.

4.2.2   Generating a Cartesian Product with a CROSS JOIN

In SQL Server, a CROSS JOIN can be used to return a Cartesian product of two tables. The form of the CROSS JOIN is:

```
SELECT *
FROM Table1 CROSS JOIN Table2
```

Using our database, `Student_course`, the following CROSS JOIN would produce the same result (Cartesian product) as the query without the WHERE clause used earlier:

```
SELECT *
FROM Course CROSS JOIN Prereq p
```

4.3   Equi-Joins and Non-Equi-Joins

Joins with comparison (nonequal) operators, i.e., =, >, >=, <, <=, and <>, in the WHERE or ON clauses are called theta-joins, where theta represents the relational operator. Joins with an = operator are called equi-joins and joins with an operator other than an = sign are sometimes also called non-equi-joins.

4.3.1   Equi-Joins

The most common join involves join conditions with equality comparisons (equi-join). The following is an example:

```
SELECT *
FROM Course c JOIN Prereq p
ON c.course_number=p.course_number
```

Another way to look at a join of any kind is that it is the Cartesian product with an added condition. The output for this query was shown earlier in this chapter. You will note that the result of the join is simply the

Cartesian product with the rows where the course numbers are equal. As per the output, you will see that this query displays all rows that have `course_number` in the `Course` table equal to `course_number` in the `Prereq` table. All the join columns have been included in this result set. This means that `course_number` has been shown twice—once from the `Course` table, and once from the `Prereq` table—and this duplicate column is, of course, redundant.

4.3.2 Non-Equi-Joins

Joins that do not test for equality are called *non-equi-joins* (or *theta-joins*). Non-equi-joins are somewhat rare. The following section on self-joins provides an example of a theta-join without an equality operator (=); this is a non-equi-join.

4.4 Self-Joins

On some occasions, you will need to join a table with itself. Joining a table with itself is known as a self-join.

In a regular join, a row of a table (`TableA`) is joined with a row of another table (`TableB`) if the column value used for the join in `TableA` matches the column value used for the join in `TableB`. One row of a table is processed at a time. But if the information that you need is contained in several different rows of the same table, for example, if you need to compare `row1, column1` with `row2, column1`, you will need to join the table with itself.

Suppose we want to find all the students who are more senior than other students. We have to join the `Student` table with itself. Logically, we need to take a row from the `Student` table and look through the rest of the `Student` table to see which rows fit the criterion ("more senior"). To accomplish this, we will use two versions of the `Student` table. Here is our query:

```
SELECT 'SENIORITY' = x.sname + ' is in a higher class than ' + y.sname
FROM Student AS x, Student AS y
WHERE y.class = 3
AND x.class > y.class
```

First we alias the `Student` table as x, and then we alias another instance of the `Student` table as y. Then we join where `x.class` is greater than `y.class` and we add the WHERE qualifier "y.class = 3," so this effectively gives us only the seniors (we restricted the result to just seniors to keep the result set smaller and to show that the WHERE may contain criteria other than the join.) The use of the > sign is an example of a non-equi-join.

+ is a string concatenation operator in SQL Server. String concatenation is discussed in detail in Chapter 5.

This query produces 70 rows of output (of which we show a sample):

```
SENIORITY
------------------------------------------------------------------
Mary is in a higher class than Susan
Kelly is in a higher class than Susan
Donald is in a higher class than Susan
Chris is in a higher class than Susan
Jake is in a higher class than Susan
Holly is in a higher class than Susan
Jerry is in a higher class than Susan
Harrison is in a higher class than Susan
Francis is in a higher class than Susan
Benny is in a higher class than Susan
Mary is in a higher class than Monica
Kelly is in a higher class than Monica
Donald is in a higher class than Monica
       .
       .
       .

Mary is in a higher class than Phoebe
Kelly is in a higher class than Phoebe
Donald is in a higher class than Phoebe
       .
       .
       .

Mary is in a higher class than Rachel
Kelly is in a higher class than Rachel
       .
       .
       .

Mary is in a higher class than Cramer
Kelly is in a higher class than Cramer
       .
       .
       .

(70 row(s) affected)
```

In this join, all the rows where x.class is greater than y.class (which is restricted to "y.class = 3") are joined to the rows that have "y.class =

3." So, Mary, the first row that has "x.class = 4," is joined to the first row where `class = 3` ("y.class = 3"), which is Susan. Then, the next row in the `Student` table with `x.class = 4` is Kelly, so Kelly is joined to Susan ("y.class = 3"), etc.

To more fully understand how the self-join is working, view the data in the `Student` table.

The alternative INNER JOIN syntax for this non-equi-join is:

SELECT 'SENIORITY' = x.sname + 'is more senior than ' + y.sname
FROM Student AS x INNER JOIN Student AS y
ON x.class > y.class – the join condition
WHERE y.class = 3 – another criterion

4.5 Using ORDER BY with a Join

As with other SELECT statements, the ORDER BY clause can be used in joins to order the result set. For example, to order the result set of one of the queries presented earlier in this chapter by the `course_number` column, we would type the following:

SELECT c.course_name, c.course_number, c.credit_hours, c.offering_dept,
        p.prereq
FROM Course c JOIN Prereq p
ON c.course_number=p.course_number
ORDER BY c.course_number

This interesting alternative will also work:

SELECT c.course_name, c.course_number, c.credit_hours, c.offering_dept,
        p.prereq
FROM Course c JOIN Prereq p
ON c.course_number=p.course_number
ORDER BY 2

"ORDER BY 2" means to order by the second column of the result set.

This produces the same 12 rows as the preceding query, but ordered alphabetically in the order of course_number:

course_name	course_number	credit_hours	offering_dept	prereq
MANAGERIAL FINANCE	ACCT3333	3	ACCT	ACCT2220
ORGANIC CHEMISTRY	CHEM3001	3	CHEM	CHEM2001
DATA STRUCTURES	COSC3320	4	COSC	COSC1310
DATABASE	COSC3380	3	COSC	COSC3320
DATABASE	COSC3380	3	COSC	MATH2410

```
ADA - INTRODUCTION    COSC5234    4          COSC       COSC3320
ENGLISH COMP II       ENGL1011    3          ENGL       ENGL1010
FUND. TECH. WRITING   ENGL3401    3          ENGL       ENGL1011
WRITING FOR NON MAJO  ENGL3520    2          ENGL       ENGL1011
MATH ANALYSIS         MATH5501    3          MATH       MATH2333
AMERICAN GOVERNMENT   POLY2103    2          POLY       POLY1201
POLITICS OF CUBA      POLY5501    4          POLY       POLY4103

(12 row(s) affected)
```

4.6   Joining More than Two Tables

You will frequently need to perform a join in which you have to get data from more than two tables. A join is a pairwise (binary) operation. In SQL Server, you can join more than two tables in either of two ways: by using a nested JOIN or by using a WHERE clause. Joins are always done pairwise.

4.6.1   Joining Multiple Tables Using a Nested JOIN

The simplest form of the nested JOIN is as follows:

```
SELECT columns
FROM table1 JOIN
(table2 JOIN table3
ON table3.column3=table2.column2)
ON table1.column1=table2.column2
```

Here `table2` and `table3` are joined to form a virtual table that is then joined to `table1` to create the result set. The join in parentheses is completed first.

As an example of a nested join, suppose we want to see the courses (course names and numbers) that have prerequisites and the departments (department names) offering those courses. To do so, we will have to join three tables—`Course`, `Prereq`, and `Department_to_major`. This is because the data that we want to display is spread among these three tables. We could choose to first join the `Course` table with the `Prereq` table, and then join that result to the `Department_to_major` table. The `Department_to_major` table contains the names of the departments. To determine which columns of the `Department_to_major` table can be used in the join, we have to look at the description of the `Department_to_major` table, which is shown in Figure 4.5.

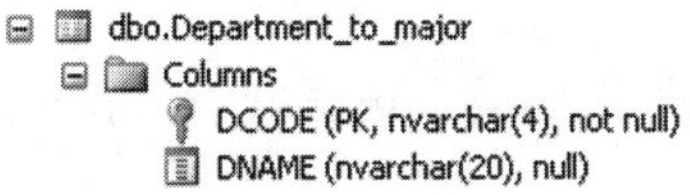

dbo.Department_to_major
  Columns
    DCODE (PK, nvarchar(4), not null)
    DNAME (nvarchar(20), null)

Figure 4.5   Description of the `Department_to_major` table

The query to join the `Course` table to the `Prereq` table to the `Department_to_major` table with the `Course/Prereq` join done first is:

```
SELECT c.course_name, c.course_number, d2m.dname
FROM department_to_major d2m JOIN
(course c JOIN prereq p
ON c.course_number=p.course_number)
ON c.offering_dept=d2m.dcode
```

In the previously nested JOIN, the part within the parentheses, "course c JOIN prereq p ON c.course_number=p.course_number," is performed first to produce an intermediate, virtual result set. The internal result is then used to join to the third table, `Department_to_major`.

The result of the join is the following 12 rows:

```
course_name           course_number dname
-------------------   ------------- --------------------
MANAGERIAL FINANCE    ACCT3333      Accounting
ORGANIC CHEMISTRY     CHEM3001      Chemistry
DATA STRUCTURES       COSC3320      Computer Science
DATABASE              COSC3380      Computer Science
DATABASE              COSC3380      Computer Science
ADA - INTRODUCTION    COSC5234      Computer Science
ENGLISH COMP II       ENGL1011      English
FUND. TECH. WRITING   ENGL3401      English
WRITING FOR NON MAJO  ENGL3520      English
MATH ANALYSIS         MATH5501      Mathematics
AMERICAN GOVERNMENT   POLY2103      Political Science
POLITICS OF CUBA      POLY5501      Political Science

(12 row(s) affected)
```

Which join is performed first has performance implications. We could choose to do the `Course/Department_to_major` table join first, in which case the query could be written as follows:

```
SELECT c.course_name, c.course_number, d.dname
FROM (course c JOIN department_to_major d
ON c.offering_dept = d.dcode)
```

```
JOIN prereq p
ON p.course_number = c.course_number
```

For larger tables and multitable joins ("multi" meaning three or more here), experimentation with different join queries is encouraged and typically done for "production queries" (queries used over and over again). It is difficult to predict which version of the query would be most efficient.

4.6.2 Joining Multiple Tables Using the WHERE Clause

Multiple tables can also be joined using a WHERE clause. For example, the nested JOIN query in the preceding section could be written as follows:

```
SELECT c.course_name, c.course_number, d.dname
FROM Course c, Prereq p, Department_to_major d
WHERE c.course_number=p.course_number
AND c.offering_dept = d.dcode
```

Again, a JOIN is a pairwise operation. This "triple join" is actually either ((the `Course` table JOIN the `Prereq` table) JOIN the `Department_to_major` table) or (the `Course` table JOIN (the `Prereq` table JOIN the `Department_to_major`)), depending on the database engine. This WHERE clause version of the three-table join would have exactly the same result as shown in the preceding section using the nested JOIN, but performance may be enhanced by tinkering with the order of joining. In SQL Server, the order of joins is most easily controlled using the JOIN syntax. One further note here: Remember that we mentioned "forgetting a WHERE condition" in the section on Cartesian products? Imagine a query like this with perhaps 10 or 15 tables and not using the INNER JOIN form. Accidentally leaving out a join condition is not at all hard to do when developing a large query; hence, using COUNT is particularly encouraged.

4.7 The OUTER JOIN

In an equi-inner join, rows without matching values are eliminated from the join result. For example, with the following join, we did not see information on any course that did not have a prerequisite:

```
SELECT *
FROM Course c, Prereq p
WHERE c.course_number = p.course_number
```

In some cases, it may be desirable to include rows from one table even though it does not have matching rows in the other table. This is done with the use of an outer join. Outer joins are used when we want to keep all the rows from one table, say `Course`, or all the rows from the other, regardless of whether they have matching rows in the other relation. In SQL Server, an outer join in which we want to keep all the rows from the first (left) table is called a *left outer join*, and an outer join in which we want to keep all the rows from the second table (or right relation) is called a *right outer join*. The term "full outer join" is used to designate the union of the left and right outer joins. We illustrate these three outer joins in the following sections.

4.7.1 The LEFT OUTER JOIN

Left outer joins include all the rows from the first (left) of the two tables, even if there are no matching values for the rows in the second (right) table. Left outer joins are performed in SQL Server using a LEFT OUTER JOIN statement.

LEFT JOIN is the same as LEFT OUTER JOIN. The inclusion of the word OUTER is optional in SQL Server SQL, but we will use LEFT OUTER JOIN instead of LEFT JOIN for clarity.

The following is the simplest form of a LEFT OUTER JOIN statement:

```
SELECT columns
FROM table1 LEFT OUTER JOIN table2
ON table1.column1=table2.column1
```

For example, if we want to list all the rows in the `Course` table (the left, or first table), even if these courses do not have prerequisites, we can use the following LEFT OUTER JOIN statement:

```
SELECT *
FROM Course c LEFT OUTER JOIN Prereq p
ON c.course_number = p.course_number
```

The LEFT OUTER JOIN is processed as follows: All rows from the `Course` table that have `course_number` equal to the `course_number` in the `Prereq` table are joined. When a row (with a course_number) from the `Course` table (first table) has no match in the `Prereq` table (second table), the rows from the `Course` table are added to the result set with a partial subrow of NULL values joined to the right side. This means that the courses that do not have prerequisites will get a set of NULL values for prerequisites. So, the output of a LEFT OUTER JOIN statement includes all rows from the left (first) table, `Course`, along with matching and nonmatching rows from the `Prereq` table.

There is a legacy operator for LEFT JOINS: *=. The use of the *= operator for the LEFT OUTER JOIN is considered old syntax, and hence its use is not at all encouraged. It is prone to ambiguities, especially when joining three or more tables and it is unusual among SQL versions.

The preceding query will produce 33 rows of output (of which we show the first 13 rows):

```
COURSE_NAME          COURSE_NUMBER CREDIT_HOURS OFFERING_DEPT COURSE_NUMBER PREREQ
-------------------- ------------- ------------ ------------- ------------- --------
ACCOUNTING I         ACCT2020      3            ACCT          NULL          NULL
ACCOUNTING II        ACCT2220      3            ACCT          NULL          NULL
MANAGERIAL FINANCE   ACCT3333      3            ACCT          ACCT3333      ACCT2220
ACCOUNTING INFO SYST ACCT3464      3            ACCT          NULL          NULL
INTRO TO CHEMISTRY   CHEM2001      3            CHEM          NULL          NULL
ORGANIC CHEMISTRY    CHEM3001      3            CHEM          CHEM3001      CHEM2001
INTRO TO COMPUTER SC COSC1310      4            COSC          NULL          NULL
TURBO PASCAL         COSC2025      3            COSC          NULL          NULL
ADVANCED COBOL       COSC2303      3            COSC          NULL          NULL
DATA STRUCTURES      COSC3320      4            COSC          COSC3320      COSC1310
DATABASE             COSC3380      3            COSC          COSC3380      COSC3320
DATABASE             COSC3380      3            COSC          COSC3380      MATH2410
OPERATIONS RESEARCH  COSC3701      3            COSC          NULL          NULL
.
.
.

(33 row(s) affected)
```

Note that the NULLs added to the courses (due to the LEFT OUTER JOIN) like `ACCOUNTING I`, `ACCOUNTING II`, `ACCOUNTING INFO SYST`, and so on, are the courses in the `Course` table that do not have prerequisites.

4.7.2   The RIGHT OUTER JOIN

Right outer joins include all the rows from the second (right) of the two tables, even if there are no matching values for the rows in the first (left) table. Right outer joins are performed in SQL Server using a RIGHT OUTER JOIN statement.

RIGHT JOIN is the same as RIGHT OUTER JOIN. The inclusion of the word OUTER is optional in SQL Server SQL, but we will use RIGHT OUTER JOIN instead of RIGHT JOIN for clarity's sake.

The following is the simplest form of a RIGHT OUTER JOIN statement:

```
SELECT columns
FROM table1 RIGHT OUTER JOIN table2
ON table1.fieldcolumn1=table2.column1
```

As an example, we will redo the previous query from the right side. If we want to list all the rows in the `Course` table (the right, or second table), even if these courses do not have prerequisites, we can use the following RIGHT OUTER JOIN statement:

```
SELECT *
FROM Prereq p RIGHT OUTER JOIN Course c
ON p.course_number = c.course_number
```

The RIGHT OUTER JOIN is processed like this: All rows from the `Prereq` table that have `course_number` equal to the `course_number` in the `Course` table are joined. When a row with a `course_number` from the `Course` table (second table) has no match in the `Prereq` table (first table), the rows from the `Course` table are added to the result set with NULL values joined to the left side. This means that courses that do not have prerequisities will get a set of NULL values included on the left side of the row. The output of a RIGHT OUTER JOIN statement includes all rows from the right (second) table, which in this case is the `Course` table, producing output similar to that obtained in the previous section.

The output consists of 33 rows (of which the first 13 rows are shown):

```
COURSE_NUMBER PREREQ   COURSE_NAME          COURSE_NUMBER CREDIT_HOURS OFFERING_DEPT
------------- -------- -------------------- ------------- ------------ -------------
NULL          NULL     ACCOUNTING I         ACCT2020      3            ACCT
NULL          NULL     ACCOUNTING II        ACCT2220      3            ACCT
ACCT3333      ACCT2220 MANAGERIAL FINANCE   ACCT3333      3            ACCT
NULL          NULL     ACCOUNTING INFO SYST ACCT3464      3            ACCT
NULL          NULL     INTRO TO CHEMISTRY   CHEM2001      3            CHEM
CHEM3001      CHEM2001 ORGANIC CHEMISTRY    CHEM3001      3            CHEM
NULL          NULL     INTRO TO COMPUTER SC COSC1310      4            COSC
NULL          NULL     TURBO PASCAL         COSC2025      3            COSC
NULL          NULL     ADVANCED COBOL       COSC2303      3            COSC
COSC3320      COSC1310 DATA STRUCTURES      COSC3320      4            COSC
COSC3380      COSC3320 DATABASE             COSC3380      3            COSC
COSC3380      MATH2410 DATABASE             COSC3380      3            COSC
NULL          NULL     OPERATIONS RESEARCH  COSC3701      3            COSC
.
.
.

(33 row(s) affected)
```

Once again, note the NULLs added to the unmatched rows from the second table due to the use of the RIGHT OUTER JOIN.

4.7.3 The FULL OUTER JOIN

The FULL OUTER JOIN includes the rows that are equi-joined from both tables, plus the remaining unmatched rows from the first and second tables. NULLs are added to the unmatched rows on both sides.

The following is the simplest form of a FULL OUTER JOIN statement:

```
SELECT columns
FROM table1 FULL OUTER JOIN table2
ON table1.column1=table2.column1
```

If we want to list all the rows for which a connection exists between the Prereq table and the Course table (the result of a regular JOIN), and then in addition, we want all rows from the Prereq table for which there is no corresponding row in the Course table (LEFT OUTER JOIN) and all rows in the Course table for which there is no corresponding row in the Prereq table (RIGHT OUTER JOIN), we would use the following FULL OUTER JOIN statement:

```
SELECT *
FROM Prereq p FULL OUTER JOIN Course c
ON p.course_number = c.course_number
```

We will get the following 33 rows:

COURSE_NUMBER	PREREQ	COURSE_NAME	COURSE_NUMBER	CREDIT_HOURS	OFFERING_DEPT
NULL	NULL	ACCOUNTING I	ACCT2020	3	ACCT
NULL	NULL	ACCOUNTING II	ACCT2220	3	ACCT
ACCT3333	ACCT2220	MANAGERIAL FINANCE	ACCT3333	3	ACCT
NULL	NULL	ACCOUNTING INFO SYST	ACCT3464	3	ACCT
NULL	NULL	INTRO TO CHEMISTRY	CHEM2001	3	CHEM
CHEM3001	CHEM2001	ORGANIC CHEMISTRY	CHEM3001	3	CHEM
NULL	NULL	INTRO TO COMPUTER SC	COSC1310	4	COSC
NULL	NULL	TURBO PASCAL	COSC2025	3	COSC
NULL	NULL	ADVANCED COBOL	COSC2303	3	COSC
COSC3320	COSC1310	DATA STRUCTURES	COSC3320	4	COSC
COSC3380	COSC3320	DATABASE	COSC3380	3	COSC
COSC3380	MATH2410	DATABASE	COSC3380	3	COSC
NULL	NULL	OPERATIONS RESEARCH	COSC3701	3	COSC
NULL	NULL	ADVANCED ASSEMBLER	COSC4301	3	COSC
NULL	NULL	SYSTEM PROJECT	COSC4309	3	COSC
COSC5234	COSC3320	ADA - INTRODUCTION	COSC5234	4	COSC
NULL	NULL	NETWORKS	COSC5920	3	COSC
NULL	NULL	ENGLISH COMP I	ENGL1010	3	ENGL
ENGL1011	ENGL1010	ENGLISH COMP II	ENGL1011	3	ENGL
ENGL3401	ENGL1011	FUND. TECH. WRITING	ENGL3401	3	ENGL
NULL	NULL	TECHNICAL WRITING	ENGL3402	2	ENGL
ENGL3520	ENGL1011	WRITING FOR NON MAJO	ENGL3520	2	ENGL
NULL	NULL	CALCULUS 1	MATH1501	4	MATH
NULL	NULL	CALCULUS 2	MATH1502	3	MATH
NULL	NULL	CALCULUS 3	MATH1503	3	MATH
NULL	NULL	ALGEBRA	MATH2333	3	MATH
NULL	NULL	DISCRETE MATHEMATICS	MATH2410	3	MATH
MATH5501	MATH2333	MATH ANALYSIS	MATH5501	3	MATH
NULL	NULL	AMERICAN CONSTITUTIO	POLY1201	1	POLY
NULL	NULL	INTRO TO POLITICAL S	POLY2001	3	POLY
POLY2103	POLY1201	AMERICAN GOVERNMENT	POLY2103	2	POLY
NULL	NULL	SOCIALISM AND COMMUN	POLY4103	4	POLY
POLY5501	POLY4103	POLITICS OF CUBA	POLY5501	4	POLY

```
(33 row(s) affected)
```

At first you might think that the full outer join is the same as the Cartesian product. This is not the case. The Cartesian product combines tables by combining rows regardless of any criteria. The full outer join combines rows by doing both equi-join matches and then showing the non-matches with NULL values.

SUMMARY

This chapter was about combining tables in a relational database. The join is a powerful, common operation to combine tables in a meaningful way. The join is a binary operation, meaning that tables are combined pairwise. We illustrated the regular equi-join (JOIN), the CROSS JOIN, and the Cartesian product. We also discussed how multiple tables can be joined using a nested JOIN as well as the common WHERE clause join. We explained a non-equi-join with a self-join. Finally, we demonstrated the LEFT OUTER JOIN, RIGHT OUTER JOIN, and FULL OUTER JOIN statements.

Review Questions

1. What is a join? Why do you need a join?
2. What is an inner join?
3. Which clause(s) can be used in place of JOIN in SQL Server?
4. What is the Cartesian product?
5. What would be the Cartesian product of a table with 15 rows and another table with 23 rows?
6. List some uses of the Cartesian product.
7. What is an equi-join?
8. What is a non-equi-join? Give an example of a non-equi-join.
9. What is a self-join? Give an example of a self-join.
10. What is a LEFT OUTER JOIN?
11. What is a RIGHT OUTER JOIN?
12. What is a CROSS JOIN?
13. What is a FULL OUTER JOIN?
14. Does SQL Server allow the use of *= to perform outer joins?
15. What is the maximum number of rows that a self-join can produce?
16. For what kinds of joins will the associative property hold?
17. What would be the Cartesian product of two sets {a, b, c} and {c, d, e} ?

Chapter 4 Exercises

Unless specified otherwise, use the Student_course database to answer the following questions. Also, use appropriate column headings when displaying your output.

1. Create two tables, Stu(name, majorcode) and Major(majorcode, majordesc), with the following data. Use VARCHAR for the codes and appropriate data types for the other columns.

```
Stu                       Major
name     majorCode    majorCode   majorDesc
----     ---------    ---------   ---------
Jones    CS           AC          Accounting
Smith    AC           CS          Computer Science
Evans    MA           MA          Math
Adams    CS           HI          History
Sumon
Sudip
```

a. Display the Cartesian product (no WHERE clause) of the two tables. Use SELECT * ... . How many rows did you get? How many rows will you always get when combining two tables with n and m rows in them (Cartesian product)?

b. Display an equi-join of the Stu and Major tables on majorCode. First do this using the INNER JOIN statement, and then display the results using the equi-join with an appropriate WHERE clause. Use appropriate table aliases. How many rows did you get?

c. Display whatever you get if you leave off the column qualifiers (the aliases) on the equi-join in step b. (Note: This will give an error because of ambiguous column names.)

d. Use the COUNT(*) function instead of SELECT * in the query. Use COUNT to show the number of rows in the result set of the equi-join.

e. Display the name, majorCode, and majorDesc of all students regardless of whether they have a declared major (even if the major column is null). (*Hint*: You need to use a LEFT OUTER JOIN statement here if Stu is the first table in your equi-join query.)

f. Display a list of majorDescs available (even if the majorDesc does not have students yet) and the students in each of the majors. (*Hint*: You need to use a RIGHT OUTER JOIN statement here.)

g. Display the Cartesian product of the two tables using CROSS JOIN.

2. Create two tables, T1(name, jobno) and T2(jobno, jobdesc). Let jobno be data type INT, and use appropriate data types for the other columns. Insert three rows into T1 and two rows into T2. Give T1.jobno values 1, 2, 3 for the three rows: < ... ,1>,< ... ,2,>,< ... ,3>, where ... represents any value you choose. Give T2.jobno the values 1, 2: <1, ... >,<2, ... >.

a. How many rows are in the equi-join (on jobno) of T1 and T2?

b. If the values of T2.jobno were <2, ... >, <2, ... > (with different jobdesc values), how many rows would you expect to get and why? Why would the rows have to have different descriptions?

    c. If the values of `T2.jobno` were 4, 5 as in $<4, \ldots >,<5, \ldots >$, how many rows would you expect to get?

    d. If the values of `T1.jobno` were $< \ldots ,1>,< \ldots ,1>,< \ldots ,1>$ (with different names) and the values of `T2.jobno` were $<1, \ldots >$, $<1 \ldots >$ (with different descriptions), how many rows would you expect to get?

    e. If you have two tables, what is the number of rows you may expect from an equi-join operation (and with what conditions)? A Cartesian product?

    f. The number of rows in an equi-join of two tables, whose sizes are m and n rows, is from ___ to ____ depending on these conditions: _____.

3. Use tables `T1` and `T2` in this exercise. Create another table called `T3(jobdesc, minpay)`. Let `minpay` be of data type SMALLMONEY. Populate the table with at least one occurrence of each `jobdesc` from table `T2` plus one more `jobdesc` that is not in `T2`. Write and display the result of a triple equi-join of `T1`, `T2`, and `T3`. Use an appropriate comment on each of the lines of the WHERE clause on which there are equi-join conditions. (Note that you will need two equi-join conditions.)

    a. How many rows did you get in the equi-join?

    b. Use the COUNT(*) function and display the number of rows in the equi-join.

    c. How many rows would you get in this meaningless, triple Cartesian product (use COUNT(*))?

    d. In an equi-join of n tables, you always have _____ equi-join conditions in the WHERE clause.

In the preceding three exercises, you created tables `T1`, `T2`, `T3`, `Stu`, and `Major`. When you have completed the three exercises, delete these tables.

Answer questions 4 through 12 by using the `Student_course` database.

4. Display a list of course names for all of the prerequisite courses.

5. Use a JOIN or INNER JOIN to join the `Section` and `Course` tables.

    a. List the course names, instructors, and the semesters and years they were teaching.

    b. List the instructor, course names, and departments of each of the courses the instructors were teaching.

6. Use a LEFT OUTER JOIN statement to join the `Section` and `Course` tables.

    a. List the course names, instructors, and the semesters and years they were teaching in. Order in descending order by instructors.

    b. List the instructor, course names, and departments of each of the courses the instructors were teaching.

7. Use a RIGHT OUTER JOIN statement to join the `Section` and `Course` tables.
    a. For each instructor, list the name of each course they teach and the semester and year in which they teach that course.
    b. For each course, list the name of the instructor and the name of the department that offers it.
8. a. Are there any differences in the answers for questions 5, 6, and 7? Why? Explain.
    b. Use a FULL OUTER JOIN statement to join the `Section` and `Course` tables. How do the results vary from the results of questions 5, 6, and 7?
9. Discuss the output that the following query would produce:

```
SELECT *
FROM Course AS c, Prereq AS p
WHERE c.course_number<>p.course_number
```

10. Find all the sophomores who are more senior than other students. (*Hint:* Use a self-join.)
11. Find all the courses that have more credit hours than other courses. (*Hint:* Use a self-join.)
12. Display a list of the names of all students who have dependents, and the dependent's name, relationship, and age, ordered by age of dependent.

chapter

5

Functions

Topics covered in this chapter

Summary

Review Questions

Chapter 5 Exercises

Functions are preprogrammed mini-programs that perform a certain task. As with mathematics, functions transform values into another result. Microsoft® SQL Server® 2008 has a wide range of built-in functions to carry out various tasks. In this chapter, we introduce several of SQL Server 2008's useful built-in functions, which can broadly be divided into row-level functions, aggregate functions, and other special functions. Row-level functions operate one row at a time, whereas aggregate functions operate on many rows at once.

In SQL Server, we can broadly group the row-level functions into four types: numeric, string, conversion, and date functions. Numeric functions are used for calculations; they transform a value found in a row of a table. An example of a numeric function is SQUARE, which returns the square of a number. String functions are used to manipulate strings (combine them, break them apart, or get information about a string). An example of a string function is SUBSTRING, which is used to extract characters from a string. Conversion functions are used to convert data from one data type to another. Date functions operate on date data to extract days or years or do date arithmetic.

The second category of functions that we will discuss is aggregate functions. Aggregate functions provide a one-number result after calculations based on multiple rows. Examples of aggregate functions are MIN and AVG, which return the minimum or average value, respectively, of multiple rows in a particular column.

The third category of functions that we will discuss is a special class of "other functions." These other functions produce a smaller subset of rows from multiple rows. Examples of these functions would be the DISTINCT function and the TOP function, both of which produce a smaller subset of rows from the complete set.

Most of the functions discussed in this chapter are placed in a SELECT statement, and so they are parts of result sets. A SELECTed function will not change the underlying data in the database. To change the underlying data in a database, UPDATE (instead of SELECT) would have to be used (see Chapter 3).

We begin the chapter by discussing aggregate functions.

5.1 Aggregate Functions

An aggregate function (aka, group function) is a function that returns a result (one number) after calculations based on multiple rows. We will use the term *aggregate* instead of group, because it avoids confusion later in the book (we discuss other GROUP functions in Chapter 9). Aggregate functions can be used for tasks like counting the number of rows, finding the sum or average of all the values in a given numeric column, and finding the largest or smallest of the entries in a given column. In SQL, aggregate functions include COUNT, SUM, AVG, MAX, and MIN. In this section we examine and illustrate several of these aggregate functions.

5.1.1 The COUNT Function

The COUNT function is used to count *how many* (rows) there are in a result set. Following is the general syntax for the COUNT function:

SELECT COUNT(*)
FROM Table-name(s)

The following query counts the number of rows in the table **Grade_report**:

SELECT COUNT(*) AS [Count]
FROM Grade_report

The following is its output:

```
Count
-----------
209
```

```
(1 row(s) affected)
```

COUNT(*) counts all rows, including rows that have some (or even all) null values in some columns.

In Figure 5.1, we present the table design of the **Grade_report** table to show the columns that are available.

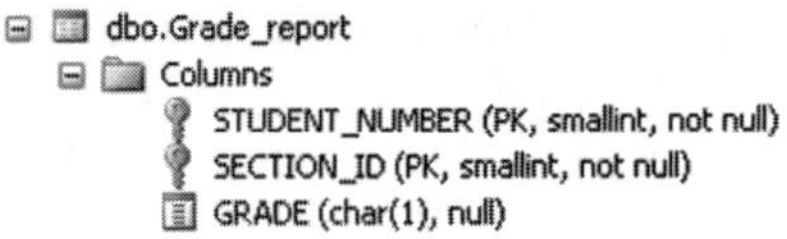

Figure 5.1   Design of the **Grade_report** table

Sometimes we may want to count how many non-null values we have in a specific column. The general syntax for counting the number of valued items in a specific column is:

SELECT COUNT(attribute_name)
FROM Table-name(s)

For example, to count the number of grades in the grade column of the `Grade_report` table, we could enter the following:

SELECT COUNT(grade) AS [Count of Grade]
FROM Grade_report

This produces the following output:

```
Count of Grade
--------------
114
Warning: Null value is eliminated by an aggregate or other SET operation.

(1 row(s) affected)
```

COUNT(column) counts only non-null columns. Although the `Grade_report` table has 209 rows, you get a count of 114 grades rather than 209 grades because there are 95 null grades in the grade column.

The COUNT feature can be used to answer "how many" queries without looking at the row values themselves. COUNT can also be quite useful because it can save you from unexpectedly long result sets. In Chapter 4, which showed how Cartesian products are generated, you learned that SQL does not prevent programmers from asking questions that have very long or even meaningless answers. Thus, when dealing with larger tables, it is good to first ask the question "How many rows can I expect in my answer?" This question may be vital if a printout is involved. For example, consider the question, "How many rows are there in the Cartesian product of the `Student`, `Section`, and `Grade_report` tables in our database?" This can be answered by the query:

SELECT COUNT(*) AS Count
FROM Student, Section, Grade_report

The following output shows the count from this query, which will be equal to the product of the sizes of the three tables (the Cartesian product of the three tables). Obviously, in this example, it would be a good idea to find out the number of rows in this result set before printing it.

```
Count
-----------
321024
```

```
(1 row(s) affected)
```

Contrast the previous COUNT query and its Cartesian product result to this query:

```
SELECT COUNT(*) AS [Count of Grade]
FROM Student, Grade_report, Section
WHERE Student.stno = Grade_report.student_number
AND Grade_report.section_id = Section.section_id
```

The following is the result of this query:

```
Count
-----------
209
```

```
(1 row(s) affected)
```

What is requested here is a count of a three-way equi-join rather than a three-way Cartesian product, the result of which is something you probably would be much more willing to work with. Note also that you expect a count of about 209 from the sizes of the tables involved: **Student** (48 rows), **Grade_report** (209 rows), and **Section** (32 rows). The expected count of a join operation is of the order of magnitude of the larger number of rows in the tables.

SQL syntax will *not* allow you to count two or more columns at the same time. Thus, the following query will not work:

```
SELECT COUNT (grade, section_id)
FROM Grade_report
```

You will get:

```
Msg 174, Level 15, State 1, Line 2
The COUNT function requires 1 argument(s).
```

In summary, the COUNT function can be used in several ways—to count rows, to count non-null attribute values, and to audit rows in the database. The function will tell us how many rows a result set will contain without providing the actual result. This "how many rows" feature will help us to test the reasonableness of results and hence possibly discover incorrect queries.

5.1.2 The SUM Function

The SUM function totals the values in a numeric column. For example, suppose you have a table called **Employee** that looks like this:

```
names                 wage                  hours
--------------------  --------------------  ------
Sumon Bagui           10.00                 40
Sudip Bagui           15.00                 30
Priyashi Saha         18.00                 NULL
Ed Evans              NULL                  10
Genny George          20.00                 40

(5 row(s) affected)
```

In this **Employee** table, **names** is defined as NVARCHAR, **wage** is defined as SMALLMONEY, and **hours** is defined as SMALLINT.

The **Employee** table has not been created for you in the **Student_course** database. You have to create it and insert data into it in order to run the following queries.

Although the numbers in the **wage** column show two decimal places, internally the numbers in the **wage** column are stored as four decimal places since the **wage** column is defined as SMALLMONEY.

To find the sum of hours worked, use the SUM function like this:

```
SELECT SUM(Hours) AS [Total hours]
FROM Employee
```

This query produces the following output:

```
Total hours
-----------
120
Warning: Null value is eliminated by an aggregate or other SET operation.

(1 row(s) affected)
```

Columns that contain NULL values are not included in the SUM (and not in any aggregate numeric function except COUNT(*)).

AS [Total hours] is an illustration of an alternative way of giving a title to the column.

5.1.3 The AVG Function

The AVG function calculates the arithmetic mean (the sum of non-null values divided by the number of non-null values) of a set of values contained in a numeric column in a query. For example, if you want to find the average hours worked from the `Employee` table, use:

```
SELECT AVG(hours) AS [Average hours]
FROM Employee
```

This produces the following output:

```
Average hours
-------------
30
Warning: Null value is eliminated by an aggregate or other SET
operation.

(1 row(s) affected)
```

Again, note that the NULL value is ignored in the calculation of the average, so the total hours (120) are divided by 4 rather than 5.

5.1.4   The MIN and MAX Functions

The MIN function finds the minimum value from a column, and the MAX function finds the maximum value (once again, nulls are ignored). For example, to find the minimum and maximum wage from the `Employee` table, you could type the following:

```
SELECT MIN(wage) AS [Minimum Wage], MAX(wage) AS [Maximum Wage]
FROM Employee
```

This produces the following output:

```
Minimum Wage          Maximum Wage
--------------------- ---------------------
10.00                 20.00
Warning: Null value is eliminated by an aggregate or other SET
operation.

(1 row(s) affected)
```

The MIN and MAX functions also work with character columns. For example, if we type:

```
SELECT "First name in alphabetical order" = MIN(names)
FROM     Employee
```

we will get:

```
First name in alphabetical order
--------------------------------
Ed Evans

(1 row(s) affected)
```

And if we type:

```
SELECT "Last name in alphabetical order" = MAX(names)
FROM Employee
```

we will get:

```
Last name in alphabetical order
--------------------------------
Sumon Bagui

(1 row(s) affected)
```

In the case of strings, MIN and MAX use the collating sequence of the letters in the string. Internally, the column that we are trying to determine the MIN or MAX of is sorted alphabetically. Then, MIN returns the first (top) of the internally sorted alphabetical list, and MAX returns the last sorted value.

5.2   Row-Level Functions

Whereas aggregate functions operate on multiple rows to obtain a result, row-level functions operate on values in single rows, one value in a row at a time. In this section, we look at row-level functions that are used in calculations, e.g., row-level functions that are used to add a number to a column, the ROUND function, the ISNULL function, and others.

5.2.1   Arithmetic Operations on a Column

To illustrate how row-level functions work on a value in a row, we will first demonstrate a value transformation with arithmetic.

Strictly speaking, arithmetic transformations on values are not functions per se, but operations performed in a result set. However, the use of arithmetic operations in result sets behave like functions.

For an arithmetic example using the `Employee` table, if we wanted to display every person's wage plus 5, we could use the following:

```
SELECT wage, (wage + 5) AS [wage + 5]
FROM Employee
```

In this query, first the wage is displayed, then the wage is incremented by five with (wage + 5), and the new wage is displayed.

This produces the following output:

```
wage                    wage + 5
--------------------    --------------------
10.00                   15.00
15.00                   20.00
18.00                   23.00
NULL                    NULL
20.00                   25.00

(5 row(s) affected)
```

Similarly, values can be subtracted (with the − operator), multiplied (with the * operator), and divided (with the / operator) to and from other values.

The (wage + 5) value is a "read-only" or "display-only" result set value. The wage field in the `Employee` table is not actually changing. We are only displaying the computation `wage + 5`. To actually increase the wage in the `Employee` table by 5, we would have to use the UPDATE command.

Any other combination of arithmetic operations may be performed on numeric data in result sets.

5.2.2 The ROUND Function

Functions perform transformations. For example, the square root function transforms a number into its square root. Functions are of the form:

```
Function name(argument list)
```

where "function name" is the name of the function and "argument list" contains the "input" to the function—the data on which the function will perform its transformation.

The ROUND function, a built-in function in SQL Server, rounds numbers to a specified number of decimal places. This function has the basic form:

```
ROUND(target value, precision)
```

where "target value" is the what you want to round, and "precision" is the number of decimal places that you desire.

For example, in the Employee table, if you wanted to divide every person's wage by 3 (one-third of the wage) and round this result, you would enter (wage/3) as the target value. To specify the number of decimal places, you must specify the precision and include it as the second argument to the function. In query form, this would be:

SELECT names, wage, ROUND((wage/3), 2) AS [wage/3]
FROM Employee

This produces the following output:

names	wage	wage/3
Sumon Bagui	10.00	3.33
Sudip Bagui	15.00	5.00
Priyashi Saha	18.00	6.00
Ed Evans	NULL	NULL
Genny George	20.00	6.67

(5 row(s) affected)

In this example, the values of (wage/3) are rounded up to two decimal places because of the "2" as the second argument.

Actually, the ROUND function may have a third, optional argument that further specifies how rounding is to take place. However, this third attribute is rarely used and not illustrated here. Many of the functions available in SQL Server have "extra" arguments that are needed only in certain well-defined circumstances.

Other common numeric functions that are used in a way similar to ROUND include:

- CEILING(numeric value), which returns the next larger integer value when a number contains decimal places.

- FLOOR(numeric value), which returns the next lower integer value when a number contains decimal places.

- SQRT(numeric value), which returns the square root of positive numeric values.

- ABS(numeric value), which returns the absolute value of any numeric value.

- SQUARE(numeric value), which returns a number squared.

5.2.3 The ISNULL Function

The result of the SUM or AVG aggregate functions shown earlier demonstrate that nulls are ignored when aggregate functions are used on multiple rows. In row-level functions, if a null is contained in a calculation on a row, the result is always null. We will illustrate, with a couple of examples, how to handle this NULL-calculation issue.

Example 5.1

In the first example, we will illustrate how to handle the NULL issue and also show how to create variables on the fly. SQL Server 2008 allows you to create variables on the fly (virtual variables) using a DECLARE statement followed by an @, the variable name (*a* and *b*, in our example below), and then the data type of the variable (both declared as FLOAT in our example). Variables are assigned values using the SET statement and can then be added to a SELECT statement.

A variable is a special place used to temporarily hold data.

Enter the following sequence to declare the variables (*a* and *b*), assign values to them, and then add them together:

```
DECLARE @a FLOAT, @b FLOAT
SET @a = 3
SET @b = 2
SELECT @a + @b AS 'A + B = '
```

This gives the result:

```
A + B =
----------------------
5

(1 row(s) affected)
```

SQL Server allows the use of SELECT with no FROM clause for such calculations.

Now, if you set the variable *a* to NULL, as follows:

```
DECLARE @a FLOAT, @b FLOAT
SET @a = NULL
SET @b = 2
SELECT @a + @b AS 'A + B = '
```

you get this:

```
A + B =
----------------------
NULL
```

```
(1 row(s) affected)
```

To handle the null problem, SQL Server 2008 provides a row-level function, ISNULL, which returns a value if a table value is null. The ISNULL function has the following form:

ISNULL(expression1, ValueIfNull)

The ISNULL function says that if the expression (or column value) *is not* null, return the value, but if the value *is* null, return `ValueIfNull`. For example, if you wanted to use a default value of zero for a null in the previous example, you could do this:

```
DECLARE @a FLOAT, @b FLOAT
SET @a = NULL
SET @b = 2
SELECT ISNULL(@a, 0) + ISNULL(@b, 0) AS 'A + B = '
```

This query would give:

```
A + B =
----------------------
2
```

```
(1 row(s) affected)
```

Here, @b is unaffected, but @a is set to zero for the result set as a result of the ISNULL function. @a is not actually changed but is replaced for the purposes of the query.

Example 5.2 For the second example, we will again use the `Employee` table. To multiply the wage by hours and avoid the Null-result problem by making the nulls act like zeros, a query could read:

```
SELECT names, wage, hours, ISNULL(wage, 0)*ISNULL(hours,0) AS
          [wage*hours]
FROM Employee
```

This would produce the following output:

```
names                 wage                   hours  wage*hours
-------------------   --------------------   -----  --------------------
Sumon Bagui           10.00                  40     400.00
Sudip Bagui           15.00                  30     450.00
Priyashi Saha         18.00                  NULL   0.00
Ed Evans              NULL                   10     0.00
Genny George          20.00                  40     800.00

(5 row(s) affected)
```

ISNULL does not have to have a `ValueIfNull` equal to zero. For example, if you want to assume that the wage is 40 if the value for wage is null, then you could use the following expression:

SELECT names, wage, new_wage = ISNULL(wage, 40)
FROM Employee

This would give:

```
names                 wage                   new_wage
-------------------   --------------------   --------------------
Sumon Bagui           10.00                  10.00
Sudip Bagui           15.00                  15.00
Priyashi Saha         18.00                  18.00
Ed Evans              NULL                   40.00
Genny George          20.00                  20.00

(5 row(s) affected)
```

5.2.4 The NULLIF Function

SQL Server 2008 also has a NULLIF function that returns a NULL if expression1 = expression2. If the expressions are not equal, then expression1 is returned. The NULLIF function has the following form:

NULLIF(expression1, expression2)

For example, if we want to see if the wage is 0, we would type:

SELECT names, wage, new_wage = NULLIF(wage, 0)
FROM Employee

This would give:

names	wage	new_wage
Sumon Bagui	10.00	10.00
Sudip Bagui	15.00	15.00
Priyashi Saha	18.00	18.00
Ed Evans	NULL	NULL
Genny George	20.00	20.00

(5 row(s) affected)

From these results we can see that, since none of the wages are equal to 0, the wage(expression1) is returned in every case. Even the NULL wage (Ed Evans's wage) is not equal to 0, but NULL is returned anyway since the value in question is NULL.

If, for some reason, a wage of, say, 15 were unacceptable, you could null out the value of 15 using the NULLIF function like this:

```
SELECT names, wage, new_wage = NULLIF(wage, 15)
FROM Employee
```

This would give:

names	wage	new_wage
Sumon Bagui	10.00	10.00
Sudip Bagui	15.00	NULL
Priyashi Saha	18.00	18.00
Ed Evans	NULL	NULL
Genny George	20.00	20.00

(5 row(s) affected)

Again, as can be noted from the preceding set of results, you have to be very careful about the interpretation of the output obtained from a NULLIF function if there were already nulls present in the columns being tested. Ed Evans's wage was not equal to 15 but had a NULL originally, and thus may be wrongly interpreted when the NULLIF function is being used.

5.2.5 Other Row-Level Functions

Other row-level functions in SQL Server 2008 include ABS, which returns the absolute value of a numeric expression. For example, if we wanted to find the absolute value of –999.99, we could type the following:

```
SELECT ABS(-999.99) AS [Absolute Value]
```

This would produce the following output:

```
Absolute Value
---------------------------------------
999.99

(1 row(s) affected)
```

There are also several row-level trigonometric functions available in SQL Server 2008 including SIN, COS, TAN, LOG, and so forth. Because these functions are less commonly used, we will not discuss them here.

5.3   Other Functions

This section discusses some other useful functions including TOP, TOP with PERCENT, and DISTINCT. These functions help us in selecting rows from a larger set of rows. Often it is prudent to look at a sample of a result set, and the TOP functions allow us to do that. TOP is most often used in conjunction with a sorted result set. DISTINCT is often useful when values are repeated in a column and you want to look at only the values that are present. Some examples will clarify these uses.

5.3.1   The TOP Function

The TOP function returns a specified number of rows. Often it is used to display rows that fall at the top of a range specified by an ORDER BY clause. Suppose you want the names of the "top 2" employees with the lowest wages from the `Employee` table (top 2 refers to the results in the first two rows). You would use:

```
SELECT TOP 2 names, wage
FROM Employee
ORDER BY wage ASC
```

This would produce the following output:

```
names                wage
--------------------  ----------------------
Ed Evans             NULL
Sumon Bagui          10.00

(2 row(s) affected)
```

To get this output, first the wage column was ordered in ascending order, and then the top two wages were selected from that ordered result set. Because ASC (ascending) was used, the columns with the null wages are placed on top.

With the TOP command, if you do not include the ORDER BY clause, the query will return rows based on the order in which the rows appear in the table (usually, but not always the order in which the rows were entered in the table). For example, the following query does not include the ORDER BY clause:

```
SELECT TOP 2 names, wage
FROM Employee
```

And this returns the following output:

```
names                  wage
-------------------    ---------------------
Sumon Bagui            10.00
Sudip Bagui            15.00

(2 row(s) affected)
```

Remember that in a relational database, you can never depend on where rows are in tables. Tables are sets of rows, and at times the database engines may insert rows in unoccupied physical spaces. You should never depend on retrieving rows in some particular order; if you desire an ordering you should always use ORDER BY.

5.3.1.1 Handling the Bottom

Since there is only a TOP command and no similar BOTTOM command, if you want to get the "bottom" two employees (the values in the last two ordered rows) instead of the top two employees from the sorted `Employee` table, the top two employees (the highest paid in this case) would have to be selected from the table ordered in descending order, as follows:

```
SELECT TOP 2 names, wage
FROM Employee
ORDER BY wage DESC
```

This would produce the following output:

```
names                wage
-------------------- ----------------------
Genny George         20.00
Priyashi Saha        18.00

(2 row(s) affected)
```

5.3.1.2 Handling a Tie

This section answers an interesting question—what if there is a tie in the ordering process? For example, what if you are looking for the top two wages, and two employees have the same amount in the **wage** column? To handle ties, SQL Server has a WITH TIES option that can be used with the TOP function.

To demonstrate WITH TIES, make one change in the data in your **Employee** table, so that the value in the **wage** column for Sudip Bagui is 10, as shown below:

```
Names             Wage           Hours
---------------   ------------   ------------
Sumon Bagui       10.00          40
Sudip Bagui       10.00          30
Priyashi Saha     18.00          NULL
Ed Evans          NULL           10
Genny George      20.00          40
```

You can use the following UPDATE statement to make the change in the **Employee** table:

```
UPDATE Employee
SET WAGE = 10
WHERE names LIKE '%Sudip%'
```

The LIKE operator is explained later in the chapter.

You can also make this change in the data of the **Employee** table by right-clicking on the **Employee** table from your Object Explorer, selecting **Edit Top 200 Rows**, and then changing the data.

Now type the following query:

```
SELECT TOP 2 WITH TIES names, wage
FROM Employee
ORDER BY wage ASC
```

Although you requested only the Top two employees, this query produced three rows, as shown by the following output, because there was a tie in the column that you were looking for, and you used with the WITH TIES option:

```
names                 wage
-------------------- ----------------------
Ed Evans              NULL
Sumon Bagui           10.00
Sudip Bagui           10.00
```

(3 row(s) affected)

The WITH TIES option is not allowed without a corresponding ORDER BY clause.

Remember to change the data in your `Employee` table back to its original state if you are doing the exercises as you read the material.

5.3.2   The TOP Function with PERCENT

PERCENT returns a certain percentage of rows that fall at the top of a specified range. For example, the following query returns the top 10% (by count) of the student names from the `Student` table based on the order of names:

```
SELECT TOP 10 PERCENT sname
FROM Student
ORDER BY sname ASC
```

This produces the following output:

```
sname
--------------------
Alan
Benny
Bill
Brad
Brenda
```

(5 row(s) affected)

Again, since there is no BOTTOM PERCENT function, in order to get the bottom 10%, you would have to order the `sname` column in descending order and then select the top 10%, as follows:

```
SELECT TOP 10 PERCENT sname
FROM Student
ORDER BY sname DESC
```

This would produce the following output:

```
sname
--------------------
Zelda
Thornton
Susan
Steve
Stephanie

(5 row(s) affected)
```

Note that the query can be used without the ORDER BY, but since the rows are unordered, the result is simply a sample of the first 10% of the data drawn from the table. Here is the same query without the use of the ORDER BY:

```
SELECT TOP 10 PERCENT sname
FROM Student
```

As output, this query returns the first 10% of the names based on the number of rows. But because the rows are unordered, your output would depend on where in the database these rows resided.

```
sname
--------------------
Lineas
Mary
Zelda
Ken
Mario

(5 row(s) affected)
```

Once again, ties in this section could be handled in the same way as they were handled in the preceding section, with the WITH TIES option as shown here:

```
SELECT TOP 10 PERCENT WITH TIES sname
FROM Student
ORDER BY sname DESC
```

The WITH TIES option cannot be used without a corresponding ORDER BY clause.

5.3.3 The DISTINCT Function

The DISTINCT function omits rows in the result set that contain duplicate data in the selected columns. Suppose you'd like to know what grades are entered in the `Grade_report` table. You don't need to know how many of each or who got what grade—you just want a report of the grades entered. To select all grades from the `Grade_report` table, you would type:

```
SELECT grade
FROM Grade_report
```

This results in 209 rows—all the grades in the `Grade_report` table.

To SELECT all *distinct* grades from the `Grade_report` table, you would type:

```
SELECT DISTINCT grade
FROM Grade_report
```

This result set would look like this:

```
grade
-----
NULL
A
B
C
D
F
```

```
(6 row(s) affected)
```

Observe that the syntax requires you to put the word DISTINCT first in the string of attributes because DISTINCT implies distinct rows in the result set. The preceding statement also produces a row for NULL grades (regarded here as a distinct grade). Note also that the result set is sorted (ordered). The fact that the result set is sorted could cause some response inefficiency in larger table queries.

5.3.3.1 Using DISTINCT with Aggregate Functions

In SQL Server 2008, DISTINCT can also be used as an option with aggregate functions like COUNT, SUM, and AVG. For example, to count the distinct grades from the `Grade_report` table, we can enter:

SELECT "Count of distinct grades" = COUNT(DISTINCT(grade))
FROM Grade_report

This will give:

```
Count of distinct grades
-----------------------
5
Warning: Null value is eliminated by an aggregate or other SET
operation.

(1 row(s) affected)
```

Since an aggregate function, COUNT, is being used here with an argument, NULL values are not included in this result set.

As another example, to sum the distinct wages from the `Employee` table, we can type:

SELECT "Sum of distinct wages" = SUM(DISTINCT(wage))
FROM Employee

This will give:

```
Sum of distinct wages
--------------------
63.00
Warning: Null value is eliminated by an aggregate or other SET
operation.

(1 row(s) affected)
```

5.4 String Functions

SQL Server 2008 has several functions that operate on strings. What is done with strings? They are often parsed for content (taken apart) and stuck together (concatenated). There are a variety of ways of looking for elements in strings, as we shall see. More specific examples of string functions include functions for the extraction of parts of a string, functions to find the length of a string, and functions to find matching characters in strings. String functions are not aggregates; they are row-level functions, as they operate on one value in one row at a time. String functions are read-only functions and will not change the underlying data in the database unless the UPDATE command is used. We start our discussion of string functions with string concatenation.

5.4.1 String Concatenation

String manipulations often require *concatenation*, which means to connect things together. In this section, we look at the string concatenation operator available in SQL Server 2008, the +.

To see an example of concatenation, list the names of the employees in the Employee table with the following statement:

```
SELECT names
FROM Employee
```

This produces the following output:

```
names
--------------------
Sumon Bagui
Sudip Bagui
Priyashi Saha
Ed Evans
Genny George


(5 row(s) affected)
```

Now, suppose you would like to concatenate each of the names with ", Esq." Type the following:

```
SELECT names + ', Esq.' AS [Employee Names]
FROM Employee
```

This produces:

```
Employee Names
--------------------------
Sumon Bagui, Esq.
Sudip Bagui, Esq.
Priyashi Saha, Esq.
Ed Evans, Esq.
Genny George, Esq.


(5 row(s) affected)
```

As another example, suppose you want to add a series of dots (.....) to the left side of the names column. You would type:

```
SELECT ('.....'+ names) AS [Employee Names]
FROM Employee
```

This produces the following output:

```
Employee Names
------------------------
.....Sumon Bagui
.....Sudip Bagui
.....Priyashi Saha
.....Ed Evans
.....Genny George


(5 row(s) affected)
```

Similarly, to add ..... to the right side of the names column, type:

```
SELECT (names + '.....') AS [Employee Names]
FROM Employee
```

This produces:

```
Employee Names
------------------------
Sumon Bagui.....
Sudip Bagui.....
Priyashi Saha.....
Ed Evans.....
Genny George.....


(5 row(s) affected)
```

5.4.2 String Extractors

SQL has several string extractor functions. This section briefly describes some of the more useful string extractors, such as SUBSTRING, LEFT, RIGHT, LTRIM, RTRIM, and CHARINDEX.

Suppose you want to display the names from the **Employee** table in the following format:

```
Employee Names
------------------------
Sumon, B.
Sudip, B.
Priyashi, S.
Ed, E.
Genny, G.
```

You can achieve this output by using a combination of the string functions to break down names into parts, reassemble (concatenate) those parts, and then concatenate a comma and period in their appropriate locations. Before we completely solve this particular problem, in the next few sections we will explain the string functions that you will need to get this output.

5.4.2.1 The SUBSTRING Function

The SUBSTRING function returns part of a string. Following is the format for the SUBSTRING function:

SUBSTRING(stringexpression, startposition, length)

"stringexpression" is the column that we will be using, "startposition" tells SQL Server where in the "stringexpression" to start retrieving characters from, and "length" tells SQL Server how many characters to extract. All three parameters are *required* in SQL Server 2008's SUBSTRING function. For example, consider the following:

SELECT names, SUBSTRING(names, 2, 4) AS [middle of names]
FROM Employee

This produces the following output:

```
names                   middle of names
--------------------    ---------------
Sumon Bagui             umon
Sudip Bagui             udip
Priyashi Saha           riya
Ed Evans                d Ev
Genny George            enny

(5 row(s) affected)
```

"SUBSTRING(names, 2, 4)" started from the second position in the column names and extracted four characters.

Strings in SQL Server 2008 are indexed from 1. The following query will show you what you will get if you start at position 0:

SELECT names, "first letter of names" = SUBSTRING(names, 0, 2)
FROM Employee

You will get:

```
names                   first letter of names
-------------------     ---------------------
Sumon Bagui             S
Sudip Bagui             S
Priyashi Saha           P
Ed Evans                E
Genny George            G

(5 row(s) affected)
```

In the preceding output, we got the first letter of the names because the SUBSTRING function started extracting characters beginning with position 0 (the position before the first letter) and went two character positions, which picked up the first letter in the names.

SQL Server 2008's SUBSTRING function actually allows you to start at a negative position relative to the string. For example, if you typed:

```
SELECT names, "first letter of names" = SUBSTRING(names, -1, 3)
FROM Employee
```

you would get the same output as the previous query. This is because you are starting two positions before the first character in names and going three character places, which gives you the first letter of the name.

5.4.2.2   The LEFT and RIGHT Functions

These functions return a portion of a string, starting from either the left or right side of "stringexpression." Following are the general formats for the LEFT and RIGHT functions, respectively:

```
LEFT(stringexpression, n)
RIGHT(stringexpression, n)
```

The LEFT function starts from the LEFT of the "stringexpression" column and returns n characters, and the RIGHT function starts from the right of the "stringexpression" column and returns n characters.

For example, to get the first three characters from the names column, you would enter:

```
SELECT names, LEFT(names, 3) AS [left]
FROM Employee
```

This query produces:

```
names                 left
--------------------  ----
Sumon Bagui           Sum
Sudip Bagui           Sud
Priyashi Saha         Pri
Ed Evans              Ed
Genny George          Gen

(5 row(s) affected)
```

To get the last three characters from the names column (here the count will start from the right of the column), type:

```
SELECT names, RIGHT(names, 3) AS [right]
FROM Employee
```

This query produces:

```
names                 right
--------------------  -----
Sumon Bagui           gui
Sudip Bagui           gui
Priyashi Saha         aha
Ed Evans              ans
Genny George          rge

(5 row(s) affected)
```

5.4.2.3 The LTRIM and RTRIM Functions

LTRIM removes blanks from the beginning (left) of a string. For example, if three blank spaces appear to the left of the string "Ranu", you can remove the blank spaces with the following query:

```
SELECT LTRIM('Ranu') AS names
```

This produces:

```
names
-------
Ranu

(1 row(s) affected)
```

It does not matter how many blank spaces precede the nonblank character. All leading blanks will be excised.

Similarly, RTRIM removes blanks from the end (right) of a string. For example, if blank spaces appear to the right of Ranu in the names column, you could remove the blank spaces using RTRIM, and then concatenate "Saha" with the + sign, as shown here:

SELECT RTRIM('Ranu') + 'Saha' AS names

This produces:

```
names
------------
Ranu Saha

(1 row(s) affected)
```

Notice in this example that there is a blank space before the S in Saha. The blanks are taken from Ranu*bbbb*, where *b* is a blank space. It does not matter how many *b*'s there are. To get the blank between the names, a blank has to be put back by including it before the S in Saha.

5.4.2.4   The CHARINDEX Function

The CHARINDEX function returns the starting position of a specified pattern. For example, if we wish to find the position of a space in the employee names in the Employee table, we could type:

```
SELECT names, "Position of Space in Employee Names" =
        CHARINDEX(' ',names)
FROM Employee
```

This query would give:

```
names                   Position of Space in Employee Names
--------------------    -----------------------------------
Sumon Bagui             6
Sudip Bagui             6
Priyashi Saha           9
Ed Evans                3
Genny George            6

(5 row(s) affected)
```

In Oracle, CHARINDEX is called INSTR.

Now that you know how to use some of the string extractor functions and how to concatenate, you can combine these tools to produce the following output, which will require a nesting of string functions:

```
Employee Names
-----------------------
Sumon, B.
Sudip, B.
Priyashi, S.
Ed, E.
Genny, G.

(5 row(s) affected
```

Following is the query to achieve the preceding output:

```
SELECT "Employee Names" = SUBSTRING(names, 1, CHARINDEX(' ',
       names)-1) + ', ' +
SUBSTRING(names, CHARINDEX(' ', names)+1,1) + '.'
FROM Employee
```

Here, the function CHARINDEX is said to be "nested" inside of the function SUBSTRING. In this query, we get the first name with the "SUBSTRING(names, 1, CHARINDEX(' ', names) -1)" portion. Per the second argument of the first substring function, SUBSTRING begins looking for the blank in the first position of names. "CHARINDEX(' ', names)" finds the position of the first space in the string. We need only the characters up to the first space, so we use "CHARINDEX(' ', names) –1." We then concatenate the comma and a space with "+ (', ')." Then, to extract the first character after the first space in the original names column, we use "SUBSTRING(names, CHARINDEX(' ', names)+1, 1)," followed by concatenation of a period. This last part of the operation says, "Take the string names and find the blank space in it. Add one to the position of the blank and then return one character."

To display the names in a different way, e.g., the last name, comma, and then the first initial, we could use the following query:

```
SELECT "Employee Names" = SUBSTRING(names, (CHARINDEX(' ',
       names)+1),
(CHARINDEX(' ', names))) + ', ' + SUBSTRING(names, 1, 1) + '.'
FROM Employee
```

This would produce the following output:

```
Employee Names
------------------------
Bagui, S.
Bagui, S.
Saha, P.
Eva, E.
George, G.
```

(5 row(s) affected)

In this query, we get the last name with "SUBSTRING(names, (CHARINDEX(' ', names)+1), (CHARINDEX(' ', names)))." The SUB-STRING begins at the space and picks up the rest of the characters after the space. Then a comma and a space are concatenated, and the first letter of the first name and a period are concatenated.

An interesting question arises here. All of the previous examples assume one space after the first name. What if names were entered with more spaces between them? In this case, you would have two alternatives. First, you could parse all names in the database and use UPDATE appropriately to ensure that all names had whatever form was desired, or, second, you could leave the database as is and nest more string functions such as LTRIM appropriately and remove excess spaces in the result set of the query. There is no practical limit to the number of "nestings." The multiblank exercise is left to the reader.

5.4.3 The UPPER and LOWER Functions

To produce all the output in uppercase or in lowercase, you can use the UPPER or LOWER functions. For example, to produce all the names in the Employee table in uppercase, enter:

```
SELECT UPPER(names) AS [NAMES IN CAPS]
FROM Employee
```

This produces the following output:

```
NAMES IN CAPS
--------------------
SUMON BAGUI
SUDIP BAGUI
PRIYASHI SAHA
ED EVANS
GENNY GEORGE
```

(5 row(s) affected)

To produce all the names in lowercase, you would enter:

```
SELECT LOWER(names) AS [NAMES IN SMALL]
FROM Employee
```

To further illustrate the nesting of functions, and to produce the first name followed by the first letter of the last name in all uppercase, enter:

```
SELECT "Employee Names" = UPPER(SUBSTRING(names, 1, CHARINDEX('
', names)-1)) + ', ' +
SUBSTRING(names, CHARINDEX(' ', names)+1, 1) + '.'
FROM Employee
```

This produces the following output:

```
Employee Names
----------------------
SUMON, B.
SUDIP, B.
PRIYASHI, S.
ED, E.
GENNY, G.

(5 row(s) affected)
```

5.4.4 The LEN Function

The LEN function returns the length (number of characters) of a desired string excluding trailing blanks. For example, to list the lengths of the full names (including any spaces) in the Employee table, type:

```
SELECT names, LEN(names) AS [Length of Names]
FROM Employee
```

This produces the following output:

```
names                  Length of Names
--------------------   ---------------
Sumon Bagui            11
Sudip Bagui            11
Priyashi Saha          13
Ed Evans               8
Genny George           12

(5 row(s) affected)
```

5.4.5 Matching Substrings Using LIKE

Often we want to use part of a string as a condition in a query. For example, consider the `Section` table (from our `Student_course` database), which has the following selection of data:

```
SECTION_ID COURSE_NUM SEMESTER YEAR INSTRUCTOR BLDG  ROOM
---------- ---------- -------- ---- ---------- ------ ------
85         MATH2410   FALL     08   KING       36     123
86         MATH5501   FALL     08   EMERSON    36     123
87         ENGL3401   FALL     08   HILLARY    13     101
88         ENGL3520   FALL     09   HILLARY    13     101
.
.
.
```

We might want to know something about math courses—courses with the prefix MATH. In this situation, we need an operator that can determine whether a substring exists in an attribute. Although we have seen how to handle this type of question with the SUBSTRING and CHARINDEX functions, another common way to handle this situation in a WHERE clause is by using the LIKE function.

Using LIKE as an "existence" match within WHERE entails finding whether a character substring exists in a string, if the string exists, the row is selected for inclusion in the result set. We could use SUBSTRING and/or CHARINDEX for this, but LIKE is a powerful, common, and flexible alternative used in WHERE clauses. This existence type of the LIKE query is quite useful when the position of the character string sought may be in various places in the substring. SQL Server 2008 uses the wildcard character % at the beginning or end of a LIKE string when looking for the existence of substrings. For example, suppose we want to find all names that have "Smith" in our `Student` table; you would enter the following:

```
SELECT *
FROM Student
WHERE sname = 'SMITH'
```

This produces the following output:

```
STNO   SNAME                MAJOR CLASS  BDATE
------ -------------------- ----- ------ ----------
88     Smith                NULL  NULL   1979-10-15

(1 row(s) affected)
```

Note that the case (upper or lower) in the statement, "WHERE sname = 'SMITH'," does not matter because SQL Server 2008 handles it is all uppercase. Here it appears that the names were entered in mixed case. In other words, we can say that data in SQL Server 2008 is *not* case sensitive.

To count how many people have the name of "Smith," use:

```
SELECT COUNT(*) AS Count
FROM Student
WHERE sname = 'Smith'
```

This produces:

```
Count
-----------
1

(1 row(s) affected)
```

5.4.5.1   Using the Wildcard Character with LIKE

The % is SQL Server 2008's wildcard character. For example, if we wanted to find all the names from the **Student** table that contained some form of "Smith" we would use % on both ends of "Smith" and the LIKE predicate as shown here:

```
SELECT *
FROM Student
WHERE sname LIKE '%Smith%'
```

This produces the following output, showing any "Smith" pattern in **sname**:

```
STNO    SNAME                MAJOR CLASS  BDATE
------  -------------------  ----- ------ ----------
88      Smith                NULL  NULL   1979-10-15
147     Smithly              ENGL  2      1990-05-13
151     Losmith              CHEM  3      1991-01-15

(3 row(s) affected)
```

To find any pattern starting with "Smith" from the **Student** table, you would type:

```
SELECT *
FROM Student
WHERE sname LIKE 'Smith%'
```

This would produce:

```
STNO   SNAME                 MAJOR  CLASS  BDATE
------ --------------------  -----  ------ ----------
88     Smith                 NULL   NULL   1979-10-15
147    Smithly               ENGL   2      1990-05-13
```

(2 row(s) affected)

It is not necessary to use UPPER or LOWER before **sname** in the preceding query since data in SQL Server 2008 is not case sensitive.

To find the Math courses (any **course_num** starting with MATH) in the **Section** table, you could pose a wildcard match with a LIKE as follows:

```
SELECT *
FROM Section
WHERE course_num LIKE 'MATH%'
```

This would produce the following output:

```
SECTION_ID  COURSE_NUM  SEMESTER  YEAR  INSTRUCTOR  BLDG    ROOM
----------  ----------  --------  ----  ----------  ------  ------
85          MATH2410    FALL      08    KING        36      123
86          MATH5501    FALL      08    EMERSON     36      123
107         MATH2333    SPRING    10    CHANG       36      123
109         MATH5501    FALL      09    CHANG       36      123
112         MATH2410    FALL      09    CHANG       36      123
158         MATH2410    SPRING    08    NULL        36      123
```

(6 row(s) affected)

This SQL Server case insensitivity is unique; other SQL versions would require the use of UPPER or LOWER to make this query work. In the preceding query, using odd expressions such as "MaTh%" would still work in SQL Server.

5.4.5.2   Finding a Range of Characters

SQL Server 2008 allows some POSIX-compliant regular expression patterns in LIKE clauses. We will illustrate some of these extensions for pattern matching.

LIKE can be used to find a range of characters. For example, to find all grades from C to F in the **Grade_report** table, enter:

SELECT DISTINCT student_number, grade
FROM Grade_report
WHERE grade LIKE '[c-f]'
AND student_number > 100

This produces 15 rows of output:

```
student_number grade
-------------- -----
125            C
126            C
127            C
128            F
130            C
131            C
145            F
147            C
148            C
151            C
153            C
158            C
160            C
161            C
163            C
```

```
(15 row(s) affected)
```

Note that LIKE is also case insensitive.

To find all grades from the **Grade_report** table that are *not* from C to F, we use a caret (^) before the range we want to exclude, as shown here:

SELECT DISTINCT student_number, grade
FROM Grade_report
WHERE grade LIKE '[^c-f]'
AND student_number > 100

This produces the following 21 rows of output:

```
student_number grade
-------------- -----
121            B
122            B
123            A
123            B
```

125	A
125	B
126	A
126	B
127	A
127	B
129	A
129	B
132	B
142	A
143	B
144	B
146	B
147	B
148	B
155	B
157	B

(21 row(s) affected)

As another example, to find all the courses from the Section table that start with "C" but do not have "h" as the second character, we could type:

```
SELECT *
FROM Section
WHERE course_num LIKE 'C[^h]%'
```

This would give the following 10 rows of output:

SECTION_ID	COURSE_NUM	SEMESTER	YEAR	INSTRUCTOR	BLDG	ROOM
90	COSC3380	SPRING	09	HARDESTY	79	179
91	COSC3701	FALL	08	NULL	79	179
92	COSC1310	FALL	08	ANDERSON	79	179
93	COSC1310	SPRING	09	RAFAELT	79	179
96	COSC2025	FALL	08	RAFAELT	79	179
98	COSC3380	FALL	09	HARDESTY	79	179
102	COSC3320	SPRING	09	KNUTH	79	179
119	COSC1310	FALL	09	ANDERSON	79	179
135	COSC3380	FALL	09	STONE	79	179
145	COSC1310	SPRING	09	JONES	79	179

(10 row(s) affected)

5.4.5.3   Finding a Particular Character

To find a particular character using LIKE, we would place the character in brackets ([ ]). For example, if we wanted to find all the names from the Student table that begin with a B or G and end in "ill," we could type:

```
SELECT sname
FROM Student
WHERE sname LIKE '[BG]ill'
```

We would get:

```
sname
--------------------
Bill

(1 row(s) affected)
```

5.4.5.4   Finding a Single Character or Single Digit

A single character or digit can be found in a particular position in a string by using an underscore (_) for the wildcard in that position in the string. For example, to find all students with a student_number in the 130s (130..139) from the Student table, we could type:

```
SELECT DISTINCT student_number, grade
FROM Grade_report
WHERE student_number LIKE '13_'
```

This would produce the following:

```
student_number grade
-------------- -----
130            C
131            C
132            B

(3 row(s) affected)
```

5.4.5.5   Using NOT LIKE

SQL Server 2008 has a NOT LIKE function. For example, to get a listing of the nonmath courses and the courses that do not start with "C" from the Section table, we would type:

```
SELECT *
FROM Section
WHERE course_num NOT LIKE 'MATH%'
AND course_num NOT LIKE 'C%'
```

This would give the following 14 rows of output:

```
SECTION_ID COURSE_NUM SEMESTER  YEAR INSTRUCTOR BLDG   ROOM
---------- ---------- --------  ---- ---------- ------ ------
87         ENGL3401   FALL      08   HILLARY    13     101
88         ENGL3520   FALL      09   HILLARY    13     101
89         ENGL3520   SPRING    09   HILLARY    13     101
94         ACCT3464   FALL      08   RODRIGUEZ  74     NULL
95         ACCT2220   SPRING    09   RODRIQUEZ  74     NULL
97         ACCT3333   FALL      09   RODRIQUEZ  74     NULL
99         ENGL3401   FALL      09   HILLARY    13     101
100        POLY1201   FALL      09   SCHMIDT    NULL   NULL
101        POLY2103   SPRING    10   SCHMIDT    NULL   NULL
104        POLY4103   SPRING    10   SCHMIDT    NULL   NULL
126        ENGL1010   FALL      08   HERMANO    13     101
127        ENGL1011   SPRING    09   HERMANO    13     101
133        ENGL1010   FALL      09   HERMANO    13     101
134        ENGL1011   SPRING    10   HERMANO    13     101

(14 row(s) affected)
```

5.5 Conversion Functions

Sometimes data in a table is stored with one data type, and you need to have the data in another data type. For example, let us suppose that columnA of TableA is of character data type, but you need to use this column as a numeric column in order to do mathematical operations. Similarly, there are times when you have a table with numeric data types and you need characters. What do you do? SQL Server 2008 provides three functions for converting data types—CAST, CONVERT, and STR. We discuss each of these functions in the following sections.

5.5.1 The CAST Function

The CAST function is a very useful SQL Server 2008 function that allows you to change a data type when you select a column. The CAST result can then be used for:

- Concatenating strings

- Joining columns that were not envisioned as related
- Performing unions of tables (unions are discussed in Chapter 7)
- Performing mathematical operations on columns that were defined as characters but actually contain numbers that need to be calculated.

Some conversions are automatic and implicit, so using CAST may not always be necessary. For example, converting between numbers with types INT, SMALLINT, TINYINT, FLOAT, NUMERIC, etc., is done automatically and implicitly as long as an overflow does not occur. But converting numbers with decimal places to integer data types truncates values to the right of the decimal place without a warning, so you should use CAST if a loss of precision is possible.

The general form of the syntax for the CAST function is:

CAST (original_expression AS desired_datatype)

To illustrate the CAST function, we will use the Employee table that we created earlier in this chapter. In this table, names was defined as an NVAR-CHAR column, wage was defined with a SMALLMONEY data type, and hours was defined as SMALLINT. We will use CAST to change the display of the hours column to a character column so that we can concatenate a string to it, as shown in the following query:

SELECT names, wage, hours = CAST(hours AS CHAR(2)) + ' hours worked per week'
FROM Employee

This will give us:

```
names                   wage                    hours
---------------------   ---------------------   ------------------------

Sumon Bagui             10.00                   40 hours worked per week
Sudip Bagui             15.00                   30 hours worked per week
Priyashi Saha           18.00                   NULL
Ed Evans                NULL                    10 hours worked per week
Genny George            20.00                   40 hours worked per week

(5 row(s) affected)
```

CAST is a subset of the CONVERT function, and was added to SQL Server 2005 to comply with ANSI-92 specifications.

5.5.2 The STR Function

STR is a specialized conversion function that always converts from a number (for example, float or numeric) to a character data type. It allows you to explicitly specify the length of the string and the number of decimal places that should be formatted.

The general form of the syntax for the STR function is:

STR(float_expression, character_length, number_of_decimal_places)

"character_length" must include room for a decimal place and a negative sign. STR rounds a value to the number of decimal places requested.

We will illustrate the use of the STR function using the `Employee` table. In this table, the `wage` column is a SMALLMONEY column, so it displays with two decimal places. To format it to one decimal place, we can use STR. Note that we made the character length 4 in this case in order to accommodate the .0 (the decimal point and zero). The following query shows this:

SELECT names, wage = STR(wage, 4, 1), hours
FROM Employee

This produces:

```
names                wage  hours
-------------------- ----- ------
Sumon Bagui          10.0 40
Sudip Bagui          15.0 30
Priyashi Saha        18.0 NULL
Ed Evans             NULL 10
Genny George         20.0 40

(5 row(s) affected)
```

5.5.3 The CONVERT Function

Like the CAST function, the CONVERT function is also used to explicitly convert to a given data type. The CONVERT function has additional limited formatting capabilities.

The general syntax for the CONVERT function is:

CONVERT(desired_datatype[(length)], original_expression [, style])

CONVERT has an optional third parameter, "style," which is used for formatting. If "style" is not specified, it will use the default style. Since the

CONVERT function has formatting capabilities, it is widely used when displaying dates in a particular format. Examples of the use of the CONVERT function are presented in the "Default Date Formats and Changing Date Formats" section later in this chapter.

5.6 Date Functions

Since the use of dates is becoming increasingly important, SQL Server 2008 has introduced four new date data types: DATE, TIME, DATETIMEOFFSET, and DATETIME2. These new date data types were briefly introduced in Chapter 3, where we described SQL Server 2008's data types. SQL Server 2008 also provides several date functions like DAY, MONTH, YEAR, DATEADD, DATEDIFF, DATEPART, and GETDATE that can be used for extracting and manipulating dates (add dates, find differences between dates, find the day/month/year from dates, and so on).

Before we start discussing date functions, we will create a table, `DateTable`, using some different date data types. Then we will discuss default date formats and changing those formats.

5.6.1 Creating a Table with the Date Data Types

Suppose you define date data types in a table like this:

```
CREATE TABLE DateTable (birthdate DATE,
                        birthtime TIME
                        school_date DATETIME2,
                        names VARCHAR(20))
```

Data can now be entered into the `birthday`, `birthtime`, and `school_date` columns, which are of different date data types, and into the names column. Inserting dates is usually done by using an implicit conversion of character strings to dates. The following is an example of an INSERT into `DateTable`:

```
INSERT INTO DateTable
VALUES ('10-oct-01', '05:05', '12/01/2006', 'Mala Sinha')
```

Note that single quotes are required around date data types. Since date data types are not really character columns, the character strings representing the dates are implicitly converted, provided that the character string is in a form recognizable by SQL Server.

Now if you type:

```
SELECT *
FROM DateTable
```

the following appears in the `DateTable` table:

```
birthdate  birthtime         school_date           names
---------- ----------------- --------------------- --------------------
2001-10-10 05:05:00.0000000  2006-01-12 00:00:00.00 Mala Sinha

(1 row(s) affected)
```

Insert the following into the `DateTable`:

```
birthdate  birthtime         school_date           names
---------- ----------------- --------------------- --------------------
2001-10-10 05:05:00.0000000  2006-01-12 00:00:00.00 Mala Sinha
2009-10-31 06:30:00.0000000  2016-08-24 00:00:00.00 Mary Spencer
2010-04-15 05:59:00.0000000  2017-08-24 00:00:00.00 Bill Cox
2010-01-05 12:59:00.0000000  2017-08-24 00:00:00.00 Jamie White
2010-02-23 04:38:00.0000000  2017-01-09 00:00:00.00 Seema Kapoor

(5 row(s) affected)
```

5.6.2 Default Date Formats and Changing Date Formats

By default, SQL Server 2008 displays dates in the yyyy/mm/dd format. We can change the format in which SQL Server *reads in* dates by using SET DATEFORMAT. DATEFORMAT controls only how SQL Server 2008 interprets date constants that are entered by you; it does not control how date values are displayed. For example, to have SQL Server 2008 read first the day, then month, and then year, we would type:

```
SET DATEFORMAT dmy
SELECT 'Format is yyyy/mon/dd' = CONVERT(DATE, '10/2/2009')
```

And we will get:

```
Format is yyyy/mon/dd
---------------------
2009-02-10

(1 row(s) affected)
```

In SQL Server 2008, if two-digit year dates are entered, the default behavior is to interpret the year as 19yy if the value is greater than or equal to 50 and as 20yy if the value is less than 50.

5.6.3 Date Functions

In this section, we discuss some useful SQL Server 2008 date functions— DATEADD, DATEDIFF, DATEPART, YEAR, MONTH, DAY, and GETDATE.

5.6.3.1 The DATEADD Function

The DATEADD function produces a date by adding a specified number to a specified part of a date.

The date parts are: dd for day, mm for month, and yy for year.

The format for the DATEADD function is:

DATEADD(datepart, number, datetime)

For example, to add two days to the birth date of every child in `DateTable`, we would type:

SELECT names, 'Add 2 days to birthday' = DATEADD(dd, 2, birthdate)
FROM DateTable

This would give:

```
names                   Add 2 days to birthday
--------------------    ----------------------
Mala Sinha              2001-10-12
Mary Spencer            2009-11-02
Bill Cox                2010-04-17
Jamie White             2010-01-07
Seema Kapoor            2010-02-25

(5 row(s) affected)
```

You will get similar results with yy or mm as the "datepart."

5.6.3.2 The DATEDIFF Function

The DATEDIFF function returns the difference between two parts of a date. The format for the DATEDIFF function is:

DATEDIFF(datepart, datetime1, datetime2)

As an example, to find the number of months between the birth date and the school date of every child in `DateTable`, we would type:

SELECT names, 'Months between birth date and school date' =
DATEDIFF(mm, birthdate, school_date)
FROM DateTable

This would give:

```
names                   Months between birth date and school date
-------------------     -----------------------------------------
Mala Sinha              51
Mary Spencer            82
Bill Cox                88
Jamie White             91
Seema Kapoor            83
```

(5 row(s) affected)

5.6.3.3 The DATEPART Function

The DATEPART function returns the specified part of the date requested. The format for the DATEPART function is:

DATEPART(datepart, datetime)

For example, to find the year from the birth date of every child in **DateTable** we would type:

SELECT names, 'YEARS' = DATEPART(yy, birthdate)
FROM DateTable

This would give:

```
names                   YEARS
-------------------     -----------
Mala Sinha              2001
Mary Spencer            2009
Bill Cox                2010
Jamie White             2010
Seema Kapoor            2010
```

(5 row(s) affected)

5.6.3.4 The YEAR Function

The YEAR(column) function will extract the year from a value stored as a DATETIME2 data type. For example, to extract the year from the school_date column of every child in **DateTable**, type:

SELECT names, YEAR(school_date) AS [School Year]
FROM DateTable

This produces the following output:

```
names                School Year
-------------------- -----------
Mala Sinha           2006
Mary Spencer         2016
Bill Cox             2017
Jamie White          2017
Seema Kapoor         2017

(5 row(s) affected)
```

We can also use the YEAR function in date calculations. For example, if you want to find the number of years between when a child was born (`birthdate`) and when the child went to school (`school_date`) from `DateTable`, type the following query:

SELECT names, YEAR(school_date)-YEAR(birthdate) AS [Age in School]
FROM DateTable

This produces the following output:

```
names                Age in School
-------------------- -------------
Mala Sinha           5
Mary Spencer         7
Bill Cox             7
Jamie White          7
Seema Kapoor         7

(5 row(s) affected)
```

Here, YEAR(`birthdate`) was subtracted from YEAR(`school_date`).

5.6.3.5 The MONTH Function

The MONTH function will extract the month from a date. To add six months to the birth month of every child in `DateTable`, we first extract the month with MONTH(birthdate) and then add six to it, as shown in the following query:

SELECT names, birthdate, MONTH(birthdate) AS [Birth Month], ((MONTH(birthdate)) + 6) AS [Sixth month]
FROM DateTable

This produces the following output:

```
names                birthdate  Birth Month Sixth month
-------------------- ---------- ----------- -----------
Mala Sinha           2001-10-10 10          16
Mary Spencer         2009-10-31 10          16
Bill Cox             2010-04-15 4           10
Jamie White          2010-01-05 1           7
Seema Kapoor         2010-02-23 2           8

(5 row(s) affected)
```

5.6.3.6   The DAY Function

The DAY function extracts the day of the month from a date. For example, to find the day from the birth date of every child in **DateTable**, type the following query:

```
SELECT names, birthdate, DAY([birthdate]) AS [Date]
FROM DateTable
```

This produces the following output:

```
names                birthdate  Date
-------------------- ---------- -----------
Mala Sinha           2001-10-10 10
Mary Spencer         2009-10-31 31
Bill Cox             2010-04-15 15
Jamie White          2010-01-05 5
Seema Kapoor         2010-02-23 23

(5 row(s) affected)
```

5.6.3.7   The GETDATE Function

The GETDATE function returns the current system date and time.
    For example this query,

```
SELECT 'Today ' = GETDATE()
```

will return:

```
Today
-----------------------
2009-03-11 22:34:42.500

(1 row(s) affected)
```

To find the number of years between today (the current date) and the child's school date, we could use:

```
SELECT names, 'Number of years' = DATEDIFF(yy, school_date,
GETDATE())
FROM DateTable
```

This will give us:

```
names                Number of years
-------------------  ----------------
Mala Sinha           3
Mary Spencer         -7
Bill Cox             -8
Jamie White          -8
Seema Kapoor         -8


(5 row(s) affected)
```

5.6.3.8 Inserting the Current Date and Time

Using the GETDATE function, we can insert or update the current date and time in a column. To illustrate this, we will add a new record (row) to our `DateTable`, inserting the current date and time into the `birthdate` column of this row using the GETDATE function, and then add seven years to the current date for the `school_date` column of this new row. So enter:

```
INSERT INTO DateTable
VALUES (GETDATE(), '6:45', GETDATE()+YEAR(5), 'Piyali Saha')
```

Then type:

```
SELECT *
FROM DateTable
```

This produces the following output (note the insertion of the sixth row):

```
birthdate  birthtime         school_date            names
---------- ----------------  ---------------------  --------------------
2001-10-10 05:05:00.0000000  2006-01-12 00:00:00.00 Mala Sinha
2009-10-31 06:30:00.0000000  2016-08-24 00:00:00.00 Mary Spencer
2010-04-15 05:59:00.0000000  2017-08-24 00:00:00.00 Bill Cox
2010-01-05 12:59:00.0000000  2017-08-24 00:00:00.00 Jamie White
2010-02-23 04:38:00.0000000  2017-01-09 00:00:00.00 Seema Kapoor
2009-03-11 06:45:00.0000000  2014-05-24 22:38:58.07 Piyali Saha

(6 row(s) affected)
```

SUMMARY

This chapter provided an overview of the functions available in SQL Server 2008. Functions are value transformers. Ordinarily, to use a function, an argument or arguments are furnished and the function returns a value. In this chapter, we looked at several of SQL Server 2008's aggregate, row-level, and other functions. Aggregate functions operate on multiple rows, and row-level functions operate on values. We also presented a discussion on data type conversion as well as several examples of date functions.

Review Questions

1. What are functions?
2. What are aggregate functions? Give examples of aggregate functions. What is another term for "aggregate function"?
3. What are row-level functions? Give examples of row-level functions.
4. Is COUNT an aggregate function or a row-level function? Explain why. Give at least example of when the COUNT function may come in handy. Does the COUNT function take nulls into account?
5. Is AVG an aggregate function or a row-level function?
6. Would you call TOP an aggregate function? Why or why not?
7. What is the NULLIF function? Explain.
8. How are ties handled in SQL Server?
9. How does the DISTINCT function work?
10. Are string functions (for example, SUBSTRING, RIGHT, LTRIM, etc.) aggregate functions or row-level functions?
11. What is the SUBSTRING function used for?
12. What is the CHARINDEX function used for?
13. What function would you use to find the leftmost characters in a string?
14. What are the LTRIM/RTRIM functions used for?
15. What function would produce the output in all lowercase?
16. What function would you use to find the length of a string?
17. What characters or symbols are most commonly used as wildcard characters in SQL Server 2008?
18. What is the concatenation operator in SQL Server 2008?
19. What does the YEAR function do?
20. What does the MONTH function do?
21. What does the GETDATE function do?
22. What will the following query produce in SQL Server 2008?

    SELECT (' ... ..' + names) AS [names]
    FROM Employee

23. Does SQL Server allow an expression like COUNT(DISTINCT column_name)?

24. How is the ISNULL function different from the NULLIF function?

25. What function would you use to round a value to three decimal places?

26. Which functions can the WITH TIES option be used with?

27. What clause does the WITH TIES option require?

28. What is the default date format in SQL Server 2008?

29. How do dates have to be entered in SQL Server 2008?

30. What function is used to convert between data types?

31. What function is useful for formatting numbers?

32. What function is useful for formatting dates?

Chapter 5 Exercises

Unless specified otherwise, use the Student_course database to answer the following questions. Also, use appropriate column headings when displaying your output.

1. Display the count of rows in each of the tables Grade_report, Student, and Section. How many rows would you expect in the Cartesian product of all three tables? Display the count (*not* the resulting rows) of the Cartesian product of all three tables and verify your result (use SELECT COUNT(*) ...).

2. Display the count of section_ids from the Section table. Display the count of distinct section_ids from the Grade_report table. What does this information give you? (*Hint*: section_id is the primary key of the Section table.)

3. Write, execute, and print a query to list student names and grades (just two attributes) using the table alias feature. Restrict the list to students who have either A's or B's in courses with ACCT prefixes only.

Here's how to complete this problem:

a. Get the statement to work as a count of a join of the three tables Student, Grade_report, and Section. Use table aliases in the join condition. Note that *a join of n tables requires (n-1) join conditions*, so here you have to have two join conditions: one to join the Student and Grade_report tables, and one to join the Grade_report and Section tables. Note the number of rows that you get (expect no more rows than are in the Grade_report table). Why do you get this result?

      b. Modify the query and put the Accounting condition in the WHERE clause. Note the number of rows in the result—it should be a good bit less than in step a.

      c. Again, modify the query and add the grade constraints. The number of rows should decrease again. Note that if you have WHERE *x and y or z*, parentheses are optional, but then the criteria will be interpreted according to precedence rules.

The reason that we want you to start small and add conditions is that it gives you a check on what you ought to get and it allows you to output less nonsense. Your minimal starting point should be a count of the join with appropriate join conditions.

4. Using the `Student` table, answer the following questions:

      a. How many students have names like "Smith"?

      b. How many have names that contain the letter sequence "Smith"?

      c. How many student names end in "LD"?

      d. How many student names start with "S"?

      e. How many student names do not have "i" as the second letter?

      f. Would "SELECT * FROM Student WHERE sname LIKE@Smith%'" find someone whose name is:

        (i) LA SMITH

        (ii) SMITH-JONES

        (iii) SMITH JR.

        (iv) SMITH, JR

5. Using the `Course` table, answer the following questions:

      a. List the junior-level COSC courses (LIKE COSC3xxx) and the name of the courses.

      b. List all the courses except the junior-level COSC courses (use NOT LIKE).

6. Using the COUNT function, determine whether or not there are duplicate names or student numbers in the `Student` table.

7. Assume that all math courses start with MATH.

      a. How many math courses are there in the `Section` table?

      b. From the count of courses, does it appear that there are any math courses in the `Section` table that are not in the `Course` table?

      c. Using COUNT, are there any math courses in the `Course` table that are not in the `Section` table?

      d. Does it appear that there are any courses at all that are in the `Grade_report`, `Section`, or `Course` tables that are not in the others?

e. Note that a query like the following would not work:

```
SELECT g.section_id
FROM Grade_report g, Section t
WHERE g.section_id <> t.section_id
```

Explain why WHERE .. <> .. will not work to produce the desired output.

8. For every table in the Student_course database, we would like to compile the following information: attributes, number of rows, number of distinct rows, and number of rows without nulls. Find this information using different queries and compile the information in a table similar to the following:

Table	Attribute	Rows	Distinct Rows	Rows without Nulls
Student	stno		48	48
	sname		47	48
	major		8	...
	class		etc.	...
Section	section_id		etc.	...

The other tables in the Student_course database are Grade_report, Dependent, Section, Room, Course, Prereq, Department_to_major, Languages, Plants, and teststu.

Hint: You can use the following query:

```
SELECT COUNT(*)
FROM Student
WHERE sname IS NULL
```

9. Find the count, sum, average, minimum, and maximum capacity of rooms in the database. Format the output using the STR function.
   a. Where there is a null value for the capacity, assume the capacity to be 40, and find the average room size again.

10. a. Using the Student table, display the first 10 rows with an appended initial. For the appended initial, choose the letter that is halfway through the name, so if a name is Evans, the initial is A (half of the length +1). If the name is Conway, the initial is W (again, (half of the length +1)). You do not need to round up or down; just use (LEN(Name)/2)+1 as the starting place to create the initial. Use appropriate column aliases. Your result should look like similar to this (actual names may vary depending on the current database):

person#	names
1	Lineas, E.
2	Mary, R.
3	Brenda, N.
4	Richard, H.
5	Kelly, L.
6	Lujack, A.
7	Reva, V.
8	Elainie, I.
9	Harley, L.
10	Donald, A.

     b. Display the preceding output in all capital letters.

11. a. Find the names of the bottom 50% of the students, ordered by grade.

     b. Find the names of the top 25% of the seniors, ordered by grade.

     c. Now use the WITH TIES option with step b. Is there any difference in the output?

12. a. Count the number of courses taught by each instructor.

     b. Count the number of distinct courses taught by each instructor.

13. Count the number of classes each student is taking.

14. Display all the names that are less than five characters long from the Student table.

15. List all the students with student numbers in the 140s range.

16. Find all the students (the student names should be listed only once) who received A's and B's.

17. Add an asterisk (*) to the names of all juniors and seniors who received at least one A. (This question will take a few steps, and you will have to approach this problem in a step-by-step manner.)

18. In this chapter, we used a table called Employee. Add a birthdate column and an employment_date column to the Employee table. Insert values into both columns.

     a. Display the current ages of all the employees.

     b. Find the youngest employee.

     c. Find the oldest employee.

     d. Find the youngest employee at the time of employment.

     e. Find the oldest employee at the time of employment.

     f. Add five years to the current ages of all employees. Will any of the employees be over 65 in five years?

     g. List the birth months and names of all employees.

chapter

6

Query Development and Derived Structures

Topics covered in this chapter

A problem in SQL, and in all programming for that matter, is the development of long queries or statements. One way to create long queries is to begin modestly and to incrementally build or develop the query of interest. This is the approach described in this chapter, which we will illustrate by developing a few queries. And, as you will find out, often the appropriate placement of parentheses within the query is also required to get the right answer to a question.

Another way to develop queries is to use derived structures—a pseudotable, if you will. In Microsoft® SQL Server® 2008, derived structures include views (both real and inline views) and temporary tables, both of which enable us to easily manipulate partial displays of tables. The partial displays can then be connected to answer complicated database queries. This chapter discusses derived structures, focusing specifically on views and temporary tables, and illustrates how query development can be aided with the use of derived structures.

6.1 Query Development

Queries are sometimes developed after some initial experimentation, while other times they are the result of modifying previously stored queries. The best way to understand how the query building process works is to look at an example. Suppose we want to find the names of all students in the standard Student_course database who major in computer science (COSC) and have earned a grade of B in some course. To do so, we may follow these steps:

1. Enter the following query to find students who major in computer science:

```
SELECT *
FROM Student
WHERE major = 'COSC'
```

This produces the following 10 rows of output:

```
STNO   SNAME                MAJOR CLASS  BDATE
------ -------------------- ----- ------ ----------
3      Mary                 COSC  4      1988-07-16
5      Zelda                COSC  NULL   1988-02-12
8      Brenda               COSC  2      1987-08-13
14     Lujack               COSC  1      1987-02-12
17     Elainie              COSC  1      1986-08-12
31     Jake                 COSC  4      1988-02-12
121    Hillary              COSC  1      1987-07-16
128    Brad                 COSC  1      1987-09-10
130    Alan                 COSC  2      1987-07-16
142    Jerry                COSC  4      1988-03-12
```

```
(10 row(s) affected)
```

2. Then, to get the grades of those students who are computer science majors, we need to join the Grade_report table to the preceding query. The design of the Grade_report table is shown in Figure 6.1.

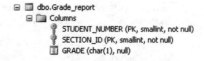

Figure 6.1   Table design of the Grade_report table

The join query now looks like the following (note the choice of columns in the SELECT statement, so that we can see the student names, majors, sections, and grades):

```
SELECT stu.sname, stu.major, g.section_id, g.grade
FROM Student stu, Grade_report g
```

WHERE stu.major = 'COSC'
AND stu.stno = g.student_number

This produces 48 rows of output (of which we show the first 15 rows):

```
sname                major section_id grade
-------------------- ----- ---------- -----
Mary                 COSC  85         A
Mary                 COSC  87         B
Mary                 COSC  90         B
Mary                 COSC  91         B
Mary                 COSC  92         B
Mary                 COSC  96         B
Mary                 COSC  101        NULL
Mary                 COSC  133        NULL
Mary                 COSC  134        NULL
Mary                 COSC  135        NULL
Zelda                COSC  90         C
Zelda                COSC  94         C
Zelda                COSC  95         B
Brenda               COSC  85         A
Brenda               COSC  92         A
  .
  .
  .


(48 row(s) affected)
```

3. To add the condition for B's, we need to add another AND clause in
the WHERE condition by adding a fifth line to the query:

SELECT stu.sname, major, section_id, grade
FROM Student stu, Grade_report g
WHERE stu.major = 'COSC'
AND stu.stno = g.student_number
AND g.grade = 'B'

This produces the following 14 rows of output:

```
sname                major section_id grade
-------------------- ----- ---------- -----
Mary                 COSC  87         B
Mary                 COSC  90         B
Mary                 COSC  91         B
```

```
Mary                  COSC  92        B
Mary                  COSC  96        B
Zelda                 COSC  95        B
Brenda                COSC  95        B
Brenda                COSC  102       B
Lujack                COSC  102       B
Lujack                COSC  145       B
Lujack                COSC  158       B
Hillary               COSC  90        B
Hillary               COSC  94        B
Hillary               COSC  95        B
```

(14 row(s) affected)

4. To get only the student names from the preceding output, we will reduce the result set by entering:

SELECT stu.sname
FROM Student stu, Grade_report g
WHERE stu.major = 'COSC'
AND stu.stno = g.student_number
AND g.grade = 'B'

This produces the following output, which is a list of all the students who are majoring in COSC and received a grade of B:

```
sname
--------------------
Mary
Mary
Mary
Mary
Mary
Zelda
Brenda
Brenda
Lujack
Lujack
Lujack
Hillary
Hillary
Hillary
```

(14 row(s) affected)

The point of this process is that it allows us to test as we go, verify that the query works up to that point, and ensure that we have a reasonable result before we move on to the next enhancement.

5. To get the final answer in a more "easy-to-read," orderly manner, we add DISTINCT (to find the distinct names) and ORDER BY (to order by names) to the query, as follows:

```
SELECT DISTINCT(stu.sname)
FROM Student stu, Grade_report g
WHERE stu.major = 'COSC'
AND stu.stno = g.student_number
AND g.grade = 'B'
ORDER BY stu.sname
```

This gives us:

```
sname
--------------------
Brenda
Hillary
Lujack
Mary
Zelda


(5 row(s) affected)
```

Actually, DISTINCT and ORDER BY do not have to be used together. When DISTINCT is used, ORDER BY is not necessary, as DISTINCT automatically orders the result set. So writing the preceding query without the ORDER BY clause would give you the same output. Try it!

The same query with the same result written using the JOIN format would look like this:

```
SELECT DISTINCT(stu.sname)
FROM Student stu JOIN Grade_report g
ON stu.stno = g.student_number
WHERE stu.major = 'COSC'
AND g.grade = 'B'
```

6.2 Parentheses in SQL Expressions

As queries get longer, they can become very ambiguous to humans without the appropriate use of parentheses. In programming languages like C, you can write a statement like this:

$$x = y + z * w$$

How is this computed? The answer depends on precedence rules. Usually in programming languages (and in SQL as well), expressions in parentheses have the highest precedence (i.e., they are calculated first). We advocate *fully* parenthesized expressions for three reasons:

- It makes the expression easier to debug.

- It tells anyone else who looks at your expression that it is written as you intended, because you explicitly and unambiguously wrote the expression in a fully parenthesized way.

- There is no guarantee that one version of SQL will behave like another.

In SQL, the precedence problem occurs when AND and OR are used in the same query. For example, what does the following query request? Does AND or OR have precedence, or is the rule "left to right"?

```
SELECT *
FROM Student
WHERE class = 3 OR class = 4 AND stno < 100
```

This query produces the following 12 rows of output:

```
STNO   SNAME                   MAJOR CLASS  BDATE
------ --------------------    ----- ------ ----------
3      Mary                    COSC  4      1988-07-16
13     Kelly                   MATH  4      1990-08-12
20     Donald                  ACCT  4      1987-10-15
24     Chris                   ACCT  4      1988-02-12
31     Jake                    COSC  4      1988-02-12
49     Susan                   ENGL  3      1990-03-11
62     Monica                  MATH  3      1990-10-14
122    Phoebe                  ENGL  3      1990-04-15
131    Rachel                  ENGL  3      1990-04-15
143    Cramer                  ENGL  3      1990-04-15
151    Losmith                 CHEM  3      1991-01-15
160    Gus                     ART   3      1988-10-15

(12 row(s) affected)
```

Although it is good to know precedence rules, you do not have to know them to write an unambiguous expression. If you use parentheses appropriately, you may make an expression clear and unambiguous without knowing precedence rules. Consider the following examples. If we type the following:

```
SELECT *
FROM Student
WHERE class = 3 OR (class = 4 AND stno < 100)
```

we get the following 12 rows of output:

```
STNO    SNAME                 MAJOR CLASS   BDATE
------  --------------------  ----- ------  ----------
3       Mary                  COSC  4       1988-07-16
13      Kelly                 MATH  4       1990-08-12
20      Donald                ACCT  4       1987-10-15
24      Chris                 ACCT  4       1988-02-12
31      Jake                  COSC  4       1988-02-12
49      Susan                 ENGL  3       1990-03-11
62      Monica                MATH  3       1990-10-14
122     Phoebe                ENGL  3       1990-04-15
131     Rachel                ENGL  3       1990-04-15
143     Cramer                ENGL  3       1990-04-15
151     Losmith               CHEM  3       1991-01-15
160     Gus                   ART   3       1988-10-15
```

```
(12 row(s) affected)
```

The preceding query has the parentheses around the AND operator, the result of which is that the AND is performed first. Since we got the same answer with no parentheses, it is evident that AND has precedence over OR. The following query has the parentheses around the OR clause, meaning the OR is performed first:

```
SELECT *
FROM Student
WHERE (class = 3 OR class = 4) AND stno < 100
```

This results in the following seven rows of output:

STNO	SNAME	MAJOR	CLASS	BDATE
3	Mary	COSC	4	1988-07-16
13	Kelly	MATH	4	1990-08-12
20	Donald	ACCT	4	1987-10-15
24	Chris	ACCT	4	1988-02-12
31	Jake	COSC	4	1988-02-12
49	Susan	ENGL	3	1990-03-11
62	Monica	MATH	3	1990-10-14

(7 row(s) affected)

Here, since the answer is different from the unparenthesized expression, it is further evidence that AND has precedence over OR. However, as the preceding two queries also demonstrate, appropriate placement of parentheses eliminates any ambiguity in queries that contain both OR and AND.

6.2.1 Operator Precedence

In SQL Server 2008, when complex expressions use multiple operators, precedence rules determine the sequence in which the operations are performed. The order of execution can obviously affect the resulting value significantly, as you saw in the example in the preceding section. While we can usually control precedence with parentheses, it is important to learn, or at least have a reference to the order of precedence.

Operators have the following precedence (the following list is shown from the highest level of precedence to the lowest level):

- * (Multiply), / (Divide), % (Modulo)

- \+ (Add), + (Concatenate), – (Subtract)

- =, >, <, >=, <=, != (Not equal to), !>, !<

- NOT

- AND

- BETWEEN, IN, LIKE, OR

- = (Assignment)

6.2.2   Data Type Precedence

When an operator combines two expressions of different data types, the data type precedence rules specify which data type is converted to the other. The data type with the lower precedence is converted to the data type with the higher precedence. Below we list the precedence order for SQL Server 2008 data types, shown from the highest level of precedence to the lowest level of precedence:

- SQL_VARIANT
- DATETIME2
- SMALLDATETIME
- FLOAT
- REAL
- DECIMAL
- MONEY
- SMALLMONEY
- BIGINT
- INT
- SMALLINT
- TINYINT
- BIT
- NTEXT
- TEXT
- IMAGE
- UNIQUEIDENTIFIER
- NVARCHAR
- NCHAR
- VARCHAR
- CHAR
- BINARY

This means that, if a number of an INT data type is multiplied by a number that is of a FLOAT data type, the result would be a FLOAT data type. To illustrate this, we will use the `Employee` table that we created in Chapter 5. The design of the `Employee` table is shown in Figure 6.2.

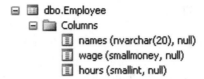

Figure 6.2   Table design of the `Employee` table

Note that the data type of the hours column is SMALLINT. But if we multiply this column (hours) by .75 (a FLOAT), we get a FLOAT data type in the result set, as shown in the following output:

```
SELECT names, hours, 'Hours * .75' = hours * .75
FROM Employee
```

This gives us:

```
names                   hours  Hours * .75
--------------------    ------ ------------------------------------
Sumon Bagui             40     30.00
Sudip Bagui             30     22.50
Priyashi Saha           NULL   NULL
Ed Evans                10     7.50
Genny George            40     30.00

(5 row(s) affected)
```

6.3 Derived Structures

Derived structures may become necessary as the queries get larger and we have to use a more step-by-step approach to find a result. Derived structures help us to build queries on top of other queries. In this section, we discuss two of the most commonly used derived structures—views and temporary tables.

6.3.1 Views

In SQL, a *view* (also called a *virtual table*) is a mechanism to procure a restricted subset of data that is accessible in ways akin to ordinary tables. We use the word "akin" because some operations on views (such as some updates and deletes) may be restricted, whereas they otherwise would be allowed if performed on the underlying structure itself.

A view serves several purposes:

■ It helps to develop a query in a step-by-step manner.
■ It can be used to restrict a set of users from seeing part of the database in a multiuser system. This can be considered a security feature.
■ Views do not occupy much disk space, since they have no data of their own.
■ Views provide a layer of abstraction to data, facilitating backward compatibility, and horizontal and vertical partitioning of data.
■ Views provide a seamless way to combine data from multiple sources.

- When you use a view for queries, you use it just as you would use the underlying table(s).
- Views can be used to create other views or queries.

Views are typically a way of building queries on top of other queries.

6.3.1.1 Creating Views

A view can be regarded as a result set that itself can be queried. The SELECT statement used to create a view can employ one or more underlying tables and/or other views in the current or other databases.

The general SQL syntax used to create a view is:

```
CREATE VIEW view_name AS
SELECT ...
```

The following example creates a view called `namemaj`, which is a view of students' names and majors from the `Student` table. To create the view, `namemaj`, enter the following in the SQL query editor pane:

```
CREATE VIEW namemaj AS
SELECT sname, major
FROM Student
```

and then execute this query in the regular way. To view `namemaj`, click on **Views** in the Object Explorer, as shown in Figure 6.3:

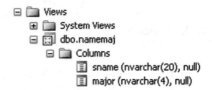

Figure 6.3 Viewing the `namemaj` view

A view is a stored SELECT statement. Each time a view is accessed, the SELECT statement in the view is run.

6.3.1.2 Using Views

The new view can be used just like a table in the FROM clause of any SELECT statement, as shown here:

```
SELECT *
FROM namemaj
```

This will give 48 rows of output, of which we show the first few rows:

```
sname                    major
-------------------      -----
Lineas                   ENGL
Mary                     COSC
Zelda                    COSC
Ken                      POLY
Mario                    MATH
Brenda                   COSC
Romona                   ENGL
Richard                  ENGL
  .
  .
  .

(48 row(s) affected)
```

Just like an ordinary table, a view can be filtered and used in a SELECT statement. For example, type the following query:

```
SELECT n.major AS [Major], n.sname AS [Student Name]
FROM namemaj AS n, Department_to_major AS d
WHERE n.major = d.dcode
AND d.dname LIKE 'COMP%'
```

This produces the following output:

```
Major Student Name
----- --------------------
COSC  Mary
COSC  Zelda
COSC  Brenda
COSC  Lujack
COSC  Elainie
COSC  Jake
COSC  Hillary
COSC  Brad
COSC  Alan
COSC  Jerry

(10 row(s) affected)
```

6.3.1.3   ORDER BY in Views

SQL Server 2008 does not allow you to use the ORDER BY clause when creating views. For example, if we try to create an ordered view called `namemaj1`, as follows:

```
CREATE VIEW namemaj1 AS
SELECT sname, major
FROM Student
ORDER BY sname
```

we will get this error message:

```
Msg 1033, Level 15, State 1, Procedure namemaj1, Line 5
The ORDER BY clause is invalid in views, inline functions,
derived tables, subqueries, and common table expressions,
unless TOP or FOR XML is also specified.
```

Other versions of SQL, such as Oracle, allow the use of the ORDER BY clause when creating views.

However, an ORDER BY clause can be used in the FROM clause after the view has been created, as shown here:

```
SELECT *
FROM namemaj
ORDER BY major
```

The preceding query produces 48 rows, of which we show the first few:

```
sname                major
-------------------- -----
Smith                NULL
Thornton             NULL
Lionel               NULL
Sebastian            ACCT
Harrison             ACCT
Francis              ACCT
Donald               ACCT
Chris                ACCT
Gus                  ART
Benny                CHEM
Losmith              CHEM
Jake                 COSC
  .
  .
  .

(48 row(s) affected)
```

6.3.1.4 SELECT INTO in Views

You cannot use a SELECT INTO statement when creating a view because it is a combined data definition language (DDL) and data manipulation language (DML) statement, as shown in the following query:

```
CREATE VIEW new_view AS
SELECT * INTO new_view
FROM Employee
```

You will get this error message:

```
Msg 156, Level 15, State 1, Procedure new_view, Line 2
Incorrect syntax near the keyword 'INTO'.
```

You can, however, issue a SELECT INTO statement in the FROM clause, as shown here:

```
CREATE VIEW new_view AS
SELECT *
FROM namemaj
WHERE major = 'MATH'
```

You will get:

```
Command(s) completed successfully.
```

And now if you type:

```
SELECT * INTO copy_of_new_view
FROM new_view
```

you will get:

```
(7 row(s) affected)
```

Actually, new_view is not a view at all. It is a table because of the SELECT .. INTO statement. So we have created a view, accessed the view, and created another table that is a copy of the view. If you type:

```
SELECT *
FROM copy_of_new_view
```

you will get the following seven rows:

```
sname                major
-------------------- -----
Mario                MATH
Kelly                MATH
Reva                 MATH
Monica               MATH
Sadie                MATH
Stephanie            MATH
Jake                 MATH
```

```
(7 row(s) affected)
```

If you access the Object Explorer, you will see the views and tables that were created in this section.

6.3.1.5 Column Aliases in Views

Column aliases can be used instead of column names in views. For example, enter the following to create a view called **namemaj2** with column aliases:

```
CREATE VIEW namemaj2 AS
SELECT sname AS [name], major AS [maj]
FROM Student
WHERE major = 'COSC'
```

Then enter:

```
SELECT *
FROM namemaj2
```

This produces the following 10 rows of output, with the column aliases in the column headings:

```
name                 maj
-------------------- ----
Mary                 COSC
Zelda                COSC
Brenda               COSC
Lujack               COSC
Elainie              COSC
Jake                 COSC
Hillary              COSC
Brad                 COSC
Alan                 COSC
Jerry                COSC
```

```
(10 row(s) affected)
```

To use the column aliases in a query, the name of the view or table alias (in this case, a view alias) has to precede the column alias, as shown in this query:

```
SELECT namemaj2.[name], namemaj2.[maj]
FROM namemaj2
WHERE namemaj2.[name] LIKE 'J%'
```

This query produces the following output:

```
name                 maj
-------------------- ----
Jake                 COSC
Jerry                COSC
```

```
(2 row(s) affected)
```

The same query could also be written as follows, where n is the table (view) alias:

```
SELECT n.[name], n.[maj]
FROM namemaj2 AS n
WHERE n.[name] LIKE 'J%'
```

6.3.1.6 Data in Views

A view consists of a set of named columns and rows of data, just like a real table; however, a view has no data of its own. Data is stored only in the underlying table or tables used to create the view, and not in the view itself. As view data is used, the view is dynamically produced from the underlying table. Views depend on the underlying tables and act like a filter on those.

When data in the original table is changed, the view is automatically updated. Therefore, the view is always up to date. And when data is changed through a view, the original (underlying) table is also automatically updated.

6.3.1.6.1 Changing Data in Views To demonstrate how changing data through a view automatically updates the original table, begin with the following Employee table, which we created and used in Chapter 5:

```
names                   wage                    hours
--------------------    --------------------    ------
Sumon Bagui             10.00                   40
Sudip Bagui             15.00                   30
Priyashi Saha           18.00                   NULL
Ed Evans                NULL                    10
Genny George            20.00                   40
```

(5 row(s) affected)

1. Create a view called `Employee_view` from the `Employee` table, as follows:

```
CREATE VIEW Employee_view AS
SELECT names
FROM Employee
```

2. To output the entire contents of the view, type the following query:

```
SELECT *
FROM Employee_view
```

This produces the following output:

```
names
--------------------
Sumon Bagui
Sudip Bagui
Priyashi Saha
Ed Evans
Genny George
```

(5 row(s) affected)

3. To update the data in the `Employee_view` view, use the following UPDATE query:

```
UPDATE Employee_view
SET names = 'Mala Saha'
WHERE names LIKE 'Priya%'
```

4. Now, to view the contents of the `Employee_view` view, type:

```
SELECT *
FROM Employee_view
```

This produces the following output (note that the third name has changed):

```
names
--------------------
Sumon Bagui
Sudip Bagui
Mala Saha
Ed Evans
Genny George

(5 row(s) affected)
```

5. Then view the contents of the underlying table by selecting all rows in the table (and note that the third name in this table has changed):

```
SELECT *
FROM Employee
```

This now gives:

```
names                 wage                  hours
-------------------- --------------------- ------
Sumon Bagui           10.00                 40
Sudip Bagui           15.00                 30
Mala Saha             18.00                 NULL
Ed Evans              NULL                  10
Genny George          20.00                 40

(5 row(s) affected)
```

If a row were added or deleted from the **Employee_view** view, the same change would also appear in the underlying table.

When adding, changing, or deleting data in views, you should always be very careful because you may not want to change the original underlying table.

6.3.1.6.2   Changing Data in Tables If data is changed in the original table, such as **Employee**, the same data in all the views related to this underlying table also gets changed.

6.3.1.7   Deleting Views

A view can be deleted with the DROP VIEW command. For example, to delete the view called `Employee_view`, you would type:

DROP VIEW Employee_view

6.3.2   Temporary Tables

Temporary tables involve extra storage as well as extra programming effort, but temporary tables are useful for doing work on a "picture of data" in the database. They are useful for doing tasks that require multiple passes so you avoid doing repetitive work. As the name implies, no permanent storage of the temporary structure is anticipated; when the use of the temporary data is over, the table is deleted. One might think of temporary tables as stored views, but the data is static and not reflective of updates to the original table or tables. As with views, temporary tables may also allow you to develop SQL queries in a step-by-step manner and may be used to simplify complex queries.

In SQL Server 2008, temporary tables reside in the default temporary database, `tempdb`. Every time SQL Server 2008 is stopped and restarted, a new copy of `tempdb` is built. Thus, temporary tables are automatically destroyed when the user who created them disconnects from SQL Server 2008.

6.3.2.1   Creating Temporary Tables

In SQL Server 2008, temporary tables are created in the same way that permanent tables are created; that is, with a CREATE TABLE or a SELECT INTO statement. However, temporary table names have to begin with either # or ##.

A fundamental principle of database theory is that data is supposed to be shared. In most production databases, users share data. One person creates and maintains some set of tables and other users do the same for other data. What a particular user creates and maintains is said to be "local" to that user. If data is to be shared, it is said to be "global."

A user may allow global data to be seen by others—that is, after all, the point of global data.

SQL Server 2008 has two types of temporary tables—local temporary tables and global temporary tables. We will discuss these types of tables in the following sections.

6.3.2.1.1   Creating Local Temporary Tables   Local temporary tables are created with # in front of the table name and are only visible to the user who is currently connected to the database. Temporary tables are deleted when the user disconnects from this instance of SQL Server. Local temporary tables are local to the session in which they are created. This means that they are not visible in any other session, not even to one from the same host or login.

You cannot have foreign key constraints on temporary tables. We will discuss foreign key constraints in Chapter 11.

The general SQL Server 2008 syntax for creating a local temporary table is:

```
SELECT column_name, ... , column_name INTO #local_temporary_tablename
FROM permanent_tablename
WHERE ...
```

As an example of how to create a local temporary table, #Temp1, enter the following SELECT query:

```
SELECT s.sname, s.stno, d.dname, s.class INTO #Temp1
FROM Student s, Department_to_major d
WHERE s.major = d.dcode
AND (s.class = 1 OR s.class = 2)
AND s.major = 'COSC'
```

You will get:

```
(6 row(s) affected)
```

This creates a local temporary table called #Temp1. You can use #Temp1 as a regular table for this session. To view the data in #Temp1, type the following:

```
SELECT *
FROM #Temp1
```

This produces the following six rows of output:

sname	stno	dname	class
Brenda	8	Computer Science	2
Lujack	14	Computer Science	1
Elainie	17	Computer Science	1
Hillary	121	Computer Science	1
Brad	128	Computer Science	1
Alan	130	Computer Science	2

```
(6 row(s) affected)
```

You can view the local temporary table from the `tempdb` database under System Databases in the Object Explorer. From the Object Explorer, click **Databases**, **System Databases**, **tempdb**, and then **Temporary Tables**. You will see the temporary table, `#Temp1`, as shown in Figure 6.4.

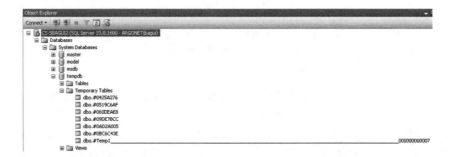

Figure 6.4   Viewing the local temporary table from the Object Explorer

As you can see in Figure 6.4, in SQL Server 2008, the local temporary table that you create is appended by a system-generated suffix—a 12-digit number with leading zeros. The local temporary table name that you provide cannot be more than 116 characters, which allows 128 characters for the complete name of the local temporary table. This is done because SQL Server allows a number of sessions to create a local temporary table with the same name without the names colliding with each other.

6.3.2.1.2   Creating Global Temporary Tables   Global temporary tables are created with a prefix of ##. Global temporary tables can be accessed by anyone who logs into the database as long as the creator of the global temporary table is still logged on. The global temporary table will be dropped automatically when the session that created it ends and when all other processes that reference it have stopped referencing it. Therefore, even though the process that created the table may have ended, it will be alive if another process is using it.

The general SQL Server syntax for creating a global temporary table is:

```
SELECT column_name, ... , column_name INTO
       ##global_temporary_tablename
FROM permanent_tablename
WHERE ...
```

As an example of creating a global temporary table, type the following SELECT statement query:

```
SELECT s.sname, s.stno, d.dname, s.class INTO ##Temp1
FROM Student s, Department_to_major d
WHERE s.major = d.dcode
AND (s.class = 1 OR s.class = 2)
AND s.major = 'COSC'
```

You will get:

```
(6 row(s) affected)
```

This query creates a global temporary table called **##Temp1**. You can use **##Temp1** as a regular table for this session. To view the data in **##Temp1**, type the following:

```
SELECT *
FROM ##Temp1
```

You will get the same output as you did for the local temporary table.

A global temporary table can also be viewed from the `tempdb` option of the Object Explorer. From the Object Explorer, click **Databases**, **System Databases**, **tempdb**, and then **Temporary Tables**; you will see the global temporary table, **##Temp1**, as shown in Figure 6.5

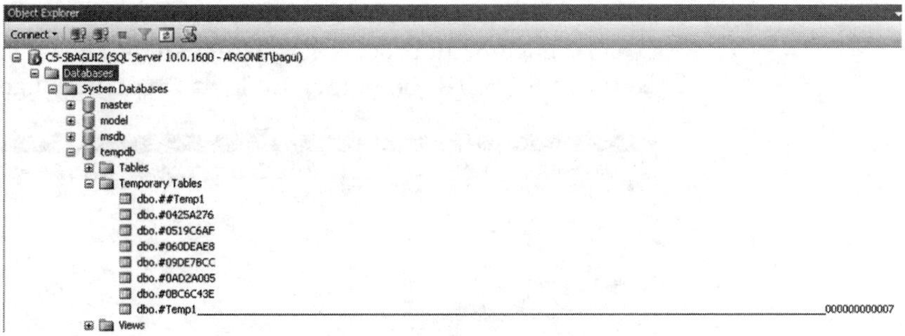

Figure 6.5   Viewing the global temporary table from the Object Explorer

Unlike views, updating data in local or global temporary tables does not change the data in the underlying original table.

You will note that, unlike the local temporary table, the global temporary table does not have a system-generated suffix attached to its name. In fact, when creating global temporary tables, you have to be careful that the same name does not already exist, so as to prevent interference between tables in any one session. There can be only one instance of a global temporary table with any particular name.

For example, if you type the following query and try to create another global temporary table called **##Temp1**:

SELECT s.sname, s.stno, d.dname, s.class INTO ##Temp1
FROM Student s, Department_to_major d
WHERE s.major = d.dcode
AND (s.class = 1 OR s.class = 2)
AND s.major = 'MATH';

you will get the following error message:

```
Msg 2714, Level 16, State 6, Line 1
There is already an object named '##Temp1' in the database.
```

6.3.2.2 Deleting Temporary Tables

If you want to delete a temporary table (local or global) before ending a session, you can use the DROP TABLE statement, just as you would to delete a permanent table.

For example, with the following query:

DROP TABLE ##Temp1

you will get the message:

```
Command(s) completed successfully.
```

To view this change (DROP), select **Temporary Tables** (from the Object Explorer) again, and then select **Refresh**, as shown in Figure 6.6. You will see that the global temporary table **##Temp1** no longer exists.

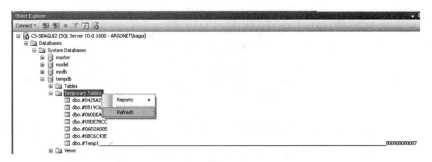

Figure 6.6 Global temporary table dropped from Object Explorer

6.4 Query Development with Derived Structures

In this section, we will discuss how derived structures such as views and temporary tables can be used in query development.

To illustrate this process, we will list from our **Student_course** database the name, student number, and department name of students who are freshman or sophomores and computer science majors.

In Step 1, we will develop a query, and in Step 2, we will show how to use this query with derived structures. Option 1 in Step 2 shows how the query can be turned into a view; Option 2 shows how the query can be turned into an inline view, and Option 3 shows how the query can be used to create a temporary table.

Step 1: Developing a Query Step by Step

1. The first step is to see which columns we need and in which tables these columns are found. We need student names (**sname**) and numbers (**stno**), which are found in the **Student** table. Department names (**dname**) are found in the **Department_to_major** table. To find the department names that correspond to the student majors, we have to combine the **Student** and **Department_to_major** tables. To combine these two tables, we will join the tables where major from the **Student** table joins with **dcode** from the **Department_to_major** table as follows (since the statements eventually will be filtered by class, we will include class in the result set):

```
SELECT s.sname, s.stno, d.dname, s.class
FROM Student s, Department_to_major d
WHERE s.major = d.dcode
```

After you type the query and run it, you will get the following 45 rows of output (of which we show the first few rows here):

```
sname                 stno   dname                 class
--------------------  -----  --------------------  ------
Lineas                2      English               1
Mary                  3      Computer Science      4
Zelda                 5      Computer Science      NULL
Ken                   6      Political Science     NULL
Mario                 7      Mathematics           NULL
Brenda                8      Computer Science      2
Romona                9      English               NULL
Richard               10     English               1
Kelly                 13     Mathematics           4
  .
  .
  .
```

(45 row(s) affected)

2. To find all the freshmen and sophomores (class 1 and 2) in the **Student** table, add "AND (s.class = 1 OR s.class = 2)" to the end of the previous query, as follows:

```
SELECT s.sname, s.stno, d.dname, s.class
FROM Student s, Department_to_major d
WHERE s.major = d.dcode
AND (s.class = 1 OR s.class = 2)
```

Running this query produces 21 rows of output (of which the first few rows are shown here):

```
sname                   stno   dname                   class
-------------------     ------ --------------------    ------
Lineas                  2      English                 1
Brenda                  8      Computer Science        2
Richard                 10     English                 1
Lujack                  14     Computer Science        1
Reva                    15     Mathematics             2
Elainie                 17     Computer Science        1
Harley                  19     Political Science       2
Lynette                 34     Political Science       1
.
.
.

(21 row(s) affected)
```

3. Now that we have the department names of all the freshmen and sophomores, we need to find the computer science majors from this group, so we add "AND s.major = 'COSC'" to the previous query as follows:

```
SELECT s.sname, s.stno, d.dname, s.class
FROM Student s, Department_to_major d
WHERE s.major = d.dcode
AND (s.class = 1 OR s.class = 2)
AND s.major = 'COSC'
```

This produces the following output (six rows), which finally gives us the student name, student number, and department name of students who are freshman or sophomores and computer science majors:

```
sname                 stno   dname                  class
-------------------   ------ --------------------   ------
Brenda                8      Computer Science       2
Lujack                14     Computer Science       1
Elainie               17     Computer Science       1
Hillary               121    Computer Science       1
Brad                  128    Computer Science       1
Alan                  130    Computer Science       2
```

(6 row(s) affected)

Note that in each case where we add more filtering in the WHERE clause, the number of rows declines. If the number of rows does not decline, it may indicate a problem.

Step 2: Using a Derived Structure

This step shows how the query developed in Step 1 can be turned into a view (Option 1), inline view (Option 2), or temporary table (Option 3). Each one of these derived structures will produce the same end results, so as you develop your own queries, you may use whichever derived structure you become most comfortable with and/or is most appropriate.

Derived structures are also very useful when you wish to use nested functions.

Option 1: Turning Your Query into a View

To create a view called stu_view using the previous query, enter:

```
CREATE VIEW stu_view AS
SELECT s.sname, s.stno, d.dname, s.class
FROM Student s, Department_to_major d
WHERE s.major = d.dcode
AND (s.class = 1 OR s.class = 2)
AND s.major = 'COSC'
```

You can now select from the view by typing:

```
SELECT *
FROM stu_view
WHERE sname LIKE 'BR%'
```

This produces the following output, which includes all the names in the view stu_view that start with "Br":

sname	stno	dname	class
Brenda	8	Computer Science	2
Brad	128	Computer Science	1

(2 row(s) affected)

Remember that the view always reflects the database as it is. The view takes up no extra storage in the database since no data is stored in a view.

Option 2: Using an Inline View

You can also place a query in the FROM clause of a SELECT statement and hence create what is called an *inline view*. An inline view exists only during the execution of a query. The main purpose of an inline view is to simplify the development of a "one-time" query. In a typical development scenario, a person would probably devise a SELECT statement, test it, examine the result, wrap it in parentheses, and continue with the development by using the inline view.

You would follow these general steps to develop an inline view:

1. Develop a query:

```
SELECT column1, column2, ...
FROM TableName
WHERE ...
```

2. Wrap the results in parentheses and make it into an inline view (an alias is required on the inline view); here we use v:

```
SELECT *
FROM (SELECT column1, column2, ...  FROM TableName
WHERE ... ) v
```

3. Then display the columns in the inline view:

```
SELECT v.column1, v.column2
FROM (SELECT column1, column2, ...  FROM TableName
WHERE ... ) v
```

You could then proceed to make the preceding query an inline view and add more complexity as needed. The beauty of creating a query in steps is that you may examine each step using COUNTs and TOPs to see if you're going in the right direction.

The part of the query that contains "(SELECT ... FROM ... WHERE)" v, is called an inner query because it is inside of the first SELECT. The first SELECT is called the outer query.

Let's look at an example of an inline view for our sample problem. In this example, we create the same view as the above previous view, only inline; that is, we create the view on the fly, give it an alias, v, and use it just as we would use a stored table or view, as follows:

```
SELECT v.sname, v.dname, v.class
FROM (SELECT s.sname, s.stno, d.dname, s.class
FROM Student AS s, Department_to_major AS d
WHERE s.major = d.dcode
AND (s.class = 1 OR s.class = 2)
AND s.major = 'COSC') AS v
```

This produces the following six rows of output:

```
sname                  dname                 class
-------------------    ------------------    ------
Brenda                 Computer Science      2
Lujack                 Computer Science      1
Elainie                Computer Science      1
Hillary                Computer Science      1
Brad                   Computer Science      1
Alan                   Computer Science      2

(6 row(s) affected)
```

In the final result set of the outer query, the column names reference the names used in the inline view result set that is aliased as v.

Option 3: Using a Global Temporary Table

One final example will show how to accomplish the same result using a temporary table. To create a global temporary table called ##Temp2 using the query developed in Step 1, enter:

```
SELECT s.sname, s.stno, d.dname, s.class INTO ##Temp2
FROM Student s, Department_to_major d
WHERE s.major = d.dcode
AND (s.class = 1 OR s.class = 2)
AND s.major = 'COSC'
```

Once you run or execute your query, you have created a global temporary table called ##Temp2.

Now if you type:

```
SELECT *
FROM ##Temp2
```

you should get the following six rows of output, which should be exactly the same as you received when using the other options:

```
sname                   stno   dname                   class
--------------------    ------ --------------------    ------
Brenda                  8      Computer Science        2
Lujack                  14     Computer Science        1
Elainie                 17     Computer Science        1
Hillary                 121    Computer Science        1
Brad                    128    Computer Science        1
Alan                    130    Computer Science        2

(6 row(s) affected)
```

The SQL programmer should weigh the programming effort (individual and team), storage costs and query efficiency when choosing which structure—views or temporary tables—is appropriate.

SUMMARY

In this chapter, we provided an overview of different derived structures available in SQL Server. Each of these derived structures has its own advantages and disadvantages. These include overall storage considerations, global versus local creation, ease of access, and data security. Having seen the different derived structures, any of them alone or in combination may make your work easier or more efficient. Oftentimes it is not easy to formulate a query all at once. The derived structures will help you formulate your queries in a more systematic, step-by-step manner, allowing you to check yourself as you go along.

Review Questions

1. Which has precedence—AND or an OR?
2. Why do we need derived structures?
3. What is a view?
4. List some advantages of using views.
5. List some advantages of using temporary tables.
6. Can temporary tables replace views in all cases?

7. What is the difference between a view and a temporary table?

8. What is the difference between a local temporary table and a global temporary table?

9. If data is changed in a view, is it changed in the original table?

10. If data is changed in a local temporary table, does it automatically change the data in the original table?

11. If data is changed in a global temporary table, does it automatically change the data in the original table?

12. What happens to a local temporary table after the session has been ended?

13. What happens to a global temporary table after the session has been ended?

14. Which type of temporary table has a system-generated suffix attached to it? What does this suffix mean?

15. Why are inline views helpful?

16. In SQL Server, is the ORDER BY clause allowed during the creation of a view?

17. Is SELECT INTO allowed in a view? Why or why not?

18. Where is the data stored in a view?

19. How do you delete views?

20. How do you delete temporary tables?

21. Do you need to delete a local temporary table? Why or why not?

22. Which operators have the highest and lowest precedence?

23. In SQL Server, if a column of FLOAT data type were divided by a column of REAL data type, what data type would the resulting column have? (*Hint*: Refer to the section on data type precedence.)

24. Is an ORDER BY clause necessary when you use DISTINCT? Why or why not?

Chapter 6 Exercises

Unless specified otherwise, use the Student_course database to answer the following questions. Also, use appropriate column headings when displaying your output.

1. Develop and execute a query to find the names of students who had HERMANO as an instructor and earned a grade of B or better in the class. Develop the query by first finding sections where HERMANO was the instructor. Save this query then edit the query and modify it to join the Section table with the Grade_report table. Then add the grade constraint.

2. Using the Student table, create a duplicate table called Stutab that contains all rows from the Student table. (*Hint*: Look at the design of the Student table to see the columns and their definitions.) Create the Stutab table with CREATE TABLE. Insert data into Stutab using the INSERT INTO.. SELECT option.

Using the newly created Stutab table:

a. List student names and majors of the juniors and seniors.

b. List student names of the COSC majors.

c. Create a view (call it vstu) that contains student names and majors for the COSC majors.

d. List the student names and majors from vstu in descending order by name.

e. Modify a row in your view of your table so that a student changes his or her major.

f. Display the view. Did modifying the vstu view also change the parent table, Stutab?

g. Try to modify the view again, but this time change the major to COMPSC (an obviously invalid column in the Stutab table because the column was defined as four characters). Can you do it? What happens?

h. Using Stutab, create a local temporary table (call it #stutemp) that contains student names and majors for the COSC majors.

i. List the student names and majors from #stutemp in ascending order by name.

j. Modify a row in #stutemp so that a student changes his or her major.

k. Display the local temporary table. Did modifying your local temporary table, #stutemp, also change the parent table, Stutab?

l. Try to modify the local temporary table again, but this time change the major to COMPSC (an obviously invalid column in the Stutab table because the column was defined as four characters). Can you do it? What happens?

m. Using Stutab, create a global temporary table (call it ##gstutemp) that contains student names and majors for the COSC majors.

n. List the student names and majors from ##gstutemp in ascending order by name.

o. Modify a row in ##gstutemp so that a student changes his or her major.

p. Display the global temporary table. Did modifying your global temporary table, ##gstutemp, also change the parent table, Stutab?

q. Try to modify the global temporary table again, but this time change the major to COMPSC (an obviously invalid column in the Stutab table because the column was defined as four characters). Can you do it? What happens?

r. Create an inline view (call it `invstu`) that contains student names and majors for COSC majors.

3. Perform an experiment to determine the precedence in a query with three conditions linked by AND and OR. Does AND, OR, or left to right take precedence?

Run this query:

```
SELECT *
FROM Student
WHERE stno < 100 AND major = 'COSC' OR major = 'ACCT'
```

Then run the following two queries and determine which one gives you the same output as the preceding nonparenthesized statement:

```
SELECT *
FROM Student
WHERE (stno < 100 AND major = 'COSC') OR major = 'ACCT'
```

and:

```
SELECT *
FROM Student
WHERE stno < 100 AND (major = 'COSC' OR major = 'ACCT')
```

What happens if you put the OR first instead of the AND and run the query without parentheses?

4. Develop a query to find the instructor name and course name for computer science courses (use the `Section` table).

a. Convert your query into a view.

b. Convert the query into an inline view with column aliases and test it.

c. Include an ORDER BY clause outside of the inline view in the main query and run your query again.

Topics covered in this chapter

In Chapter 4, we looked at how data can be retrieved from multiple tables using joins. In this chapter we will discuss how data can be retrieved from multiple tables using set operations available in Microsoft® SQL Server® 2008. We will also look at the IN and NOT .. IN predicates that can be used as workarounds for operations like MINUS that are not available in SQL Server 2008. In the final section of this chapter we will examine the UNION operation in comparison with the JOIN operation, and show how the UNION operation can be used to get the results of some joins.

7.1   Introducing Set Operations

A *set* is a collection of objects. In a relational database, a table is regarded as a set of rows. Elements in a mathematical set are not ordered—elements are either in the set or they are not. Similarly, in a relational database, rows are not assumed to be stored in any particular order. In mathematical sets, there are no duplicate elements. In relational database tables, there are not supposed to be duplicate rows; however, if a primary key is not defined for a table, spurious duplicate rows can occur.

Set operations are used in SQL to retrieve data from multiple sets and include a binary union, binary intersection, and binary set difference. A *binary union* is a set operation on two sets, the result of which contains all the elements of both sets. A *binary intersection* generates values in common between two sets. And a *binary set difference* generates values in one set less than those contained in another set.

Three explicit set operations are used in some versions of SQL—UNION, INTERSECT, and MINUS (for set difference). SQL Server 2008 allows the explicit use of the UNION and INTERSECT operations. Since the MINUS set operation is not directly available in SQL Server 2008, we will illustrate the MINUS operation by using the very common IN and NOT .. IN predicates, which enable us to accomplish the same result as using INTERSECT and MINUS.

The format of a set statement in SQL Server is as follows:

set OPERATOR set

where OPERATOR is either UNION or INTERSECT and "set" is a result set defined by a SELECT.

First, we look at examples of the UNION operator; the INTERSECT operator will be discussed later in the chapter.

The following is the syntax for the general form of a UNION:

```
SELECT *
FROM TableA
UNION
SELECT *
FROM TableB
```

Set statements allow us to combine two distinct sets of data (two result sets) only if we ensure "union compatibility." What is "union compatibility"?

7.1.1 Union Compatibility

Union compatibility, the commonly used SQL terminology for *set compatibility*, means that when using set operations, the two sets (in this case, the result sets of two SELECTs) being unioned have to have the same number of similar columns and the columns have to have compatible data types. Next, we will explain what "compatible data types" means, and we will return to the issue of "similar columns" in a later section.

So, what does "compatible" mean? The data types of the columns of the two sets being unioned do not necessarily have to be exactly the same, meaning they may differ in length and even type, but they have to be "well-matched." For union compatibility, the three basic data types are numeric, string, and dates. All numeric columns are compatible with one another, all string columns are compatible with one another, and all date columns are compatible with one another. SQL will convert integers, floating-point numbers, and decimals into a numeric data type to make them compatible with one another. So, any numeric column (such as integers) can be unioned with any other numeric column (such as decimals). Likewise, any fixed-length character column and any variable-length character column will be converted to a character data type and take on the larger size of the character columns being unioned. Similarly, date columns will be combined to a date data type.

Union compatibility can happen in several ways:

■ By unioning two tables or views that have identical columns (which implies the same domains as well)
■ By taking two subsets from a table and combining them
■ By using two views from two tables with the columns chosen so that they are compatible.

For the data type precedence rules, refer to the "Data Type Precedence" section in Chapter 6.

7.2 The UNION Operation

In SQL Server 2008, a binary union is performed with the UNION set operation. A UNION takes output from two (or more) queries and returns all rows from the result sets as a single result set (removing the duplicates). In this section, we illustrate how a UNION works; although there are other ways to retrieve this information, we are showing the UNION alternative.

Suppose we want to find the names of all students who are computer science (COSC) majors along with all students who are MATH majors from the Student table. We can write the following query that uses the UNION set operator:

```
SELECT sname
FROM Student
WHERE major = 'COSC'
UNION
SELECT sname
FROM Student
WHERE major = 'MATH'
```

The two sets being unioned have to have the same number of columns in the result sets of the SELECT clauses.

While executing the UNION, SQL first executes the first part of the query:

```
SELECT sname
FROM Student
WHERE major = 'COSC'
```

This virtually produces the following 10 rows of output:

```
sname
--------------------
Mary
Zelda
Brenda
Lujack
Elainie
Jake
Hillary
```

```
Brad
Alan
Jerry
```

```
(10 row(s) affected)
```

Then SQL executes the second part of the query:

```
SELECT sname
FROM Student
WHERE major = 'MATH'
```

This part virtually produces the following seven rows of output:

```
sname
--------------------
Mario
Kelly
Reva
Monica
Sadie
Stephanie
Jake
```

```
(7 row(s) affected)
```

SQL then combines the two virtual sets of results (the UNION operation), which includes throwing out any duplicates (an extra "Jake" in this case), leaving us with the following 16 rows of output:

```
sname
--------------------
Alan
Brad
Brenda
Elainie
Hillary
Jake
Jerry
Kelly
Lujack
Mario
Mary
Monica
Reva
```

```
Sadie
Stephanie
Zelda
```

```
(16 row(s) affected)
```

Prior to SQL Server 7, SQL Server always returned the result of a UNION in sorted order. This was because the UNION eliminated duplicate rows using an internal sorting strategy. The ordering was simply a byproduct of the sorting to eliminate duplicates. Newer versions of SQL Server, however, have several alternative internal strategies available for removing duplicates, so there is no guarantee of any particular order when you use UNION. If you would like to order the output, you should explicitly use ORDER BY at the end of your last SELECT statement.

The maximum number of rows possible when a UNION is used is the sum of the number of rows in the two result sets (or tables) in the two SELECT clauses.

7.2.1 Similar Columns in Unions

Earlier we discussed that for a union to be successful there has to be union compatibility—the two sets being unioned have to have similar columns. So what does "similar columns" mean?

If we wrote the earlier UNION example like this:

```
SELECT major
FROM Student
WHERE major = 'COSC'
UNION
SELECT sname
FROM Student
WHERE major = 'MATH'
```

we would get an output, but would the output be valid? The answer is NO. Why? You are trying to union majors and student names. These are not similar columns (though the data types of the two columns are compatible), and it does not make sense to union two columns with different semantics. So, before performing a union operation, you have to be very careful that you union like columns, and not "apples and oranges."

7.2.2 Unioning Constants or Variables

In SQL Server 2008, a group of SELECT statements can also be used to union constants or variables. You may want to use this technique to experiment with the UNION or other set operations. A union of number sets is shown below:

```
SELECT col1=100, col2=200
UNION
SELECT col1=400, col2=500
UNION
SELECT col1=100*3, col2=200*3
UNION
SELECT 900, 400
```

This will produce:

```
col1           col2
-----------    -----------
100            200
300            600
400            500
900            400
```

```
(4 row(s) affected)
```

Note that the output here happens to be sorted by the first column.

7.3 The UNION ALL Operation

UNION ALL works almost exactly like UNION but does not expunge duplicates nor sort the results. UNION ALL is more efficient in execution because it does not have to deal with sorting and row removal. Occasionally you may need to keep duplicates (just to keep all occurrences or records) in a UNION operation, which would suggest the use of UNION ALL.

The following is the same query previously shown for UNION but using UNION ALL instead of UNION:

```
SELECT sname
FROM Student
WHERE major = 'COSC'
UNION ALL
SELECT sname
FROM Student
WHERE major = 'MATH'
```

This query results in 17 unsorted rows, including one duplicate, Jake (whereas using UNION produced 16 rows with no duplicates):

```
sname
--------------------
Mary
Zelda
Brenda
Lujack
Elainie
Jake
Hillary
Brad
Alan
Jerry
Mario
Kelly
Reva
Monica
Sadie
Stephanie
Jake

(17 row(s) affected)
```

This result set is not sorted and contains two occurrences of Jake.

7.4 Handling UNION and/or UNION ALL Situations with an Unequal Number of Columns

As was mentioned earlier, in order to successfully UNION or UNION ALL result sets, the result sets being unioned have to have the same number of columns. But what if all the queries being used in the UNION or UNION ALL do not return the same number of columns and you still want to union them?

If we want to union two sets that do not have the same number of columns, we have to use NULL (or other) values in the columns as placeholders. For example, from our **Student_course** database, creating a union of the **Course** table and the **Prereq** table with all the columns would not be possible under normal circumstances because the **Course** table has four columns and the **Prereq** table has only two. We will give an example using UNION ALL. To perform this UNION ALL operation, we would have to place NULL values or some other values in the columns that will be empty, as follows (this example uses NULL as a placeholder):

```
SELECT c.*, NULL PREREQ
FROM Course c
WHERE c.credit_hours = 4
UNION ALL
SELECT NULL, p.course_number, NULL, NULL, p.prereq
FROM Prereq p
```

This produces the following 18 rows of output:

COURSE_NAME	COURSE_NUMBER	CREDIT_HOURS	OFFERING_DEPT	PREREQ
INTRO TO COMPUTER SC	COSC1310	4	COSC	NULL
DATA STRUCTURES	COSC3320	4	COSC	NULL
ADA - INTRODUCTION	COSC5234	4	COSC	NULL
CALCULUS 1	MATH1501	4	MATH	NULL
SOCIALISM AND COMMUN	POLY4103	4	POLY	NULL
POLITICS OF CUBA	POLY5501	4	POLY	NULL
NULL	ACCT3333	NULL	NULL	ACCT2220
NULL	CHEM3001	NULL	NULL	CHEM2001
NULL	COSC3320	NULL	NULL	COSC1310
NULL	COSC3380	NULL	NULL	COSC3320
NULL	COSC3380	NULL	NULL	MATH2410
NULL	COSC5234	NULL	NULL	COSC3320
NULL	ENGL1011	NULL	NULL	ENGL1010
NULL	ENGL3401	NULL	NULL	ENGL1011
NULL	ENGL3520	NULL	NULL	ENGL1011
NULL	MATH5501	NULL	NULL	MATH2333
NULL	POLY2103	NULL	NULL	POLY1201
NULL	POLY5501	NULL	NULL	POLY4103

```
(18 row(s) affected)
```

We can also use other values (instead of NULL) as placeholders, as shown in the following:

```
SELECT c.*, COU_NUM = 'XXXXXXXXXXXX'
FROM Course c
WHERE c.credit_hours = 4
UNION ALL
SELECT 'XXXXXXXXXXXX', p.course_number, 00000000000,
       'XXXXXXXXXXXX', p.prereq  FROM Prereq p
```

This gives the same output as the previous query, but this time we have used a series of X's and 0's as placeholders instead of NULL (we still have 18 rows of output):

COURSE_NAME	COURSE_NUMBER	CREDIT_HOURS	OFFERING_DEPT	COU_NUM
INTRO TO COMPUTER SC	COSC1310	4	COSC	XXXXXXXXXXXX
DATA STRUCTURES	COSC3320	4	COSC	XXXXXXXXXXXX
ADA - INTRODUCTION	COSC5234	4	COSC	XXXXXXXXXXXX
CALCULUS 1	MATH1501	4	MATH	XXXXXXXXXXXX
SOCIALISM AND COMMUN	POLY4103	4	POLY	XXXXXXXXXXXX
POLITICS OF CUBA	POLY5501	4	POLY	XXXXXXXXXXXX
XXXXXXXXXXXX	ACCT3333	0	XXXXXXXXXXXX	ACCT2220
XXXXXXXXXXXX	CHEM3001	0	XXXXXXXXXXXX	CHEM2001
XXXXXXXXXXXX	COSC3320	0	XXXXXXXXXXXX	COSC1310
XXXXXXXXXXXX	COSC3380	0	XXXXXXXXXXXX	COSC3320
XXXXXXXXXXXX	COSC3380	0	XXXXXXXXXXXX	MATH2410
XXXXXXXXXXXX	COSC5234	0	XXXXXXXXXXXX	COSC3320
XXXXXXXXXXXX	ENGL1011	0	XXXXXXXXXXXX	ENGL1010
XXXXXXXXXXXX	ENGL3401	0	XXXXXXXXXXXX	ENGL1011
XXXXXXXXXXXX	ENGL3520	0	XXXXXXXXXXXX	ENGL1011
XXXXXXXXXXXX	MATH5501	0	XXXXXXXXXXXX	MATH2333
XXXXXXXXXXXX	POLY2103	0	XXXXXXXXXXXX	POLY1201
XXXXXXXXXXXX	POLY5501	0	XXXXXXXXXXXX	POLY4103

`(18 row(s) affected)`

NULL does not have a data type so it can be used as a placeholder for both numeric and character columns. But when using other values as placeholders, the data types have to match. Hence, we used 'XX' (with the single quotes) for the character columns, and 000's (without quotes) for the numeric columns.

7.5   The IN and NOT .. IN Predicates

Although SQL Server 2008 does not have the MINUS (difference) operator per se, it does have an IN predicate and a corresponding NOT .. IN predicate that enables us to create set differences. We will look at these predicates from a set point of view. If we find the objects from set A and remove the objects that are in set B, we have found the difference of set A and B $(A - B)$.

Here are some examples:

Set A = (dog, cat, bird, monkey)

Set B = (cat, monkey, deer)

$A - B$ = (dog, bird)

$B - A$ = (deer)

A INTERSECT B = (cat, monkey)

A UNION B = (dog, cat, deer, bird, monkey)

Notice there are no duplicates in a set and there is no particular order.

7.5.1 Using IN

The following is a simple example of an IN predicate with constants in a SELECT statement:

```
SELECT sname, class
FROM Student
WHERE class IN (3,4)
```

In this example, "IN (3, 4)" is called a *subquery-set*, where (3, 4) is the set in which we are testing membership. This query says: "Find all student names from the **Student** table where the class is in the set (3, 4)." It produces the following 17 rows of output:

```
sname                class
-------------------- ------
Mary                 4
Kelly                4
Donald               4
Chris                4
Jake                 4
Susan                3
Monica               3
Phoebe               3
Holly                4
Rachel               3
Jerry                4
Cramer               3
Harrison             4
Francis              4
Losmith              3
Gus                  3
Benny                4
```

```
(17 row(s) affected)
```

The preceding query produces the same output as the following query:

```
SELECT sname, class
FROM Student
WHERE class = 3 OR class = 4
```

In other words, "IN(3,4)" means belonging to either set 3 *or* set 4, as shown by "WHERE class = 3 OR class = 4."

7.5.1.1 Using IN As a Subquery

We can expand the IN predicate's subquery-set part to be an actual query. For example, consider the following query that gives us the names of students who have a grade of "A":

```
SELECT Student.sname
FROM Student
WHERE Student.stno IN
(SELECT g.student_number
FROM Grade_report g
WHERE g.grade = 'A')
```

Subqueries will be discussed at length in the next chapter.

Note the following about this query:

- "WHERE Student.stno" references the `stno` column in the `Student` table.
- "g.student_number" is the student number column in the `Grade_report` table.
- `stno` in the `Student` table and `student_number` in the `Grade_report` table have the same domain.

You must retrieve information from the same domains for purposes of union compatibility. Here, although we are not performing a UNION operation, we are performing a set operation and hence we require union compatibility. Recall that this query has two parts to it—an inner query, which is the subquery in parentheses, and an outer query, "SELECT Student.sname ...." View this query as first forming the set of student numbers from the `Grade_report` table that have an A. You can think of the inner query being completed first. Then imagine that the outer query is executed using the inner query as the list of student numbers from which the overall result set is formed.

The preceding query produces the following 14 rows of output:

```
sname
--------------------
Lineas
Mary
Brenda
Richard
Lujack
Donald
Lynette
Susan
```

```
Holly
Sadie
Jessica
Steve
Cedric
Jerry

(14 row(s) affected)
```

You could view the preceding query as a result derived from the *intersection* of the sets A and B, where set A is the set of student numbers in the student set (from the **Student** table) and set B is the set of student numbers in the grade set (from the **Grade_report** table) that have A's.

To make this command behave like a set operator (as if it were an INTERSECT operator), you can add the qualifier DISTINCT to the result set as follows:

```
SELECT DISTINCT (Student.sname)
FROM Student
WHERE Student.stno IN
(SELECT DISTINCT (g.student_number)
FROM Grade_report g
WHERE g.grade = 'A')
```

This produces the following 14 rows of output:

```
sname
--------------------
Brenda
Cedric
Donald
Holly
Jerry
Jessica
Lineas
Lujack
Lynette
Mary
Richard
Sadie
Steve
Susan

(14 row(s) affected)
```

Here, SQL Server 2008 sorts the results for you and does not return duplicates.

7.5.2 The INTERSECT Operator

From a set point of view, an INTERSECT means if we find objects from set A that are also in set B (and vice versa), we have found the intersection of sets A and B. SQL Server 2008 has an INTERSECT operator.

The following query is the previous query written using an INTERSECT (but we display student numbers instead of student names):

```
SELECT s.stno
FROM Student s
INTERSECT
SELECT g.student_number
FROM Grade_report g
WHERE g.grade = 'A'
```

This gives the following 14 rows of output:

```
stno
------
2
3
8
10
14
20
34
49
123
125
126
127
129
142


(14 row(s) affected)
```

In this query, we had to display student numbers (stno) instead of the student names (sname) because of the set compatibility issue discussed earlier (there are no names in the Grade_report table). INTERSECT is a set operator, so the two sets being intersected have to have the same number of columns and the columns have to have compatible data types.

As another example of the use of the INTERSECT operator, we could enter the following to find all the students who had dependents:

```
SELECT s.stno
FROM Student s
INTERSECT
SELECT d.pno
FROM Dependent d
```

This would give the following 19 rows of output:

```
stno
------
2
10
14
17
20
34
62
123
126
128
132
142
143
144
145
146
147
153
158
```

```
(19 row(s) affected)
```

Though the INTERSECT operator gives us the right answer, in some ways the IN as a subquery (discussed earlier) is better to use since, when SQL Server 2008 performs the INTERSECT, it selects sets based on what is mentioned in the SELECT statement. So, for example, if we wanted the student names in addition to the student numbers, and we typed:

```
SELECT s.stno, s.sname
FROM Student s
INTERSECT
SELECT d.pno, relationship
FROM Dependent d
```

this query would not work. Why? Because although the relationship attribute is compatible with s.sname, the semantics are different. You would
get:

```
stno    sname
------  --------------------

(0 row(s) affected)
```

Here we would have to use an IN with a subquery as discussed earlier:

```
SELECT s.stno, s.sname
FROM Student AS s
WHERE (s.stno IN
(SELECT pno
FROM Dependent AS d))
```

This gives us the following 19 rows of output:

```
stno    sname
------  --------------------
2       Lineas
10      Richard
14      Lujack
17      Elainie
20      Donald
34      Lynette
62      Monica
123     Holly
126     Jessica
128     Brad
132     George
142     Jerry
143     Cramer
144     Fraiser
145     Harrison
146     Francis
147     Smithly
153     Genevieve
158     Thornton

(19 row(s) affected)
```

7.5.3 Using **NOT .. IN**

If you use the NOT .. IN predicate in your query, your query may perform poorly on large tables. The reason is that when NOT .. IN is used, no indexing can be used, because the NOT .. IN part of the query has to test the set with *all* values to find out what is *not* in the set. For smaller tables, no difference in performance will likely be detected. Nonetheless, we discuss how to use the NOT .. IN predicate in this section to understand the logical negative of the IN predicate, which will help to complete your overall understanding of the SQL language. Instead of using NOT .. IN, it is often preferable from a performance standpoint on large tables to use NOT EXISTS or outer join techniques, both of which are discussed elsewhere in this book.

Indexing is discussed in detail in Chapter 11.

Sometimes the NOT .. IN predicate may seem to more easily describe the desired outcome or may be used for a set difference. For an example, consider the following query:

```
SELECT sname, class
FROM Student
WHERE class IN (1, 3, 4)
```

This produces the following 28 rows of output:

```
sname                 class
--------------------  ------
Lineas                1
Mary                  4
Richard               1
Kelly                 4
Lujack                1
Elainie               1
Donald                4
Chris                 4
Jake                  4
Lynette               1
Susan                 3
Monica                3
Hillary               1
Phoebe                3
Holly                 4
Steve                 1
Brad                  1
Rachel                3
```

```
George          1
Jerry           4
Cramer          3
Fraiser         1
Harrison        4
Francis         4
Losmith         3
Lindsay         1
Gus             3
Benny           4
```

(28 row(s) affected)

Compare the preceding query with the following query:

```
SELECT sname, class
FROM Student
WHERE class NOT IN (2)
```

The output in this case is the same as for the preceding query because the **Student** table only has classes 1, 2, 3, and 4. If the results were not equal, this would indicate that some value of class was not 1, 2, 3, or 4.

As another example, suppose you want the names of students who are not computer science (COSC) or math (MATH) majors. The query would be:

```
SELECT sname, major
FROM Student
WHERE major NOT IN ('COSC', 'MATH')
```

This produces the following output (28 rows):

```
sname                major
-------------------- -----
Lineas               ENGL
Ken                  POLY
Romona               ENGL
Richard              ENGL
Harley               POLY
Donald               ACCT
Chris                ACCT
Lynette              POLY
Susan                ENGL
Bill                 POLY
```

```
Phoebe              ENGL
Holly               POLY
Jessica             POLY
Steve               ENGL
Cedric              ENGL
Rachel              ENGL
George              POLY
Cramer              ENGL
Fraiser             POLY
Harrison            ACCT
Francis             ACCT
Smithly             ENGL
Sebastian           ACCT
Losmith             CHEM
Genevieve           UNKN
Lindsay             UNKN
Gus                 ART
Benny               CHEM
```

(28 row(s) affected)

This output gave all majors other than COSC and MATH. Note that you must be very careful with the NOT .. IN predicate because if nulls are present in the data, you may get odd answers.

As an example, consider the following table called `Stumajor`:

```
name                major
------------------- --------------------
Mary                Biology
Sam                 Chemistry
Alice               Art
Tom                 NULL
```

(4 row(s) affected)

The `Stumajor` table has not been created for you. You have to create it, insert the records shown, and then run the queries that follow.

If you perform the following query:

```
SELECT *
FROM Stumajor
WHERE major IN ('Chemistry', 'Biology')
```

it produces the following output:

```
name                    major
-------------------     --------------------
Mary                    Biology
Sam                     Chemistry
```

(2 row(s) affected)

If you perform the following query:

```
SELECT *
FROM Stumajor
WHERE major NOT IN ('Chemistry', 'Biology')
```

it produces the following output:

```
name                    major
-------------------     --------------------
Alice                   Art
```

(1 row(s) affected)

The value NULL is not equal to anything. You might expect that NOT .. IN would give you "<Tom, null>," but it does not. Why? Because nulls in the selection column (here, `major`) are not matched with a NOT.. IN predicate.

7.5.3.1   Using NOT .. IN in a Subquery

NOT .. IN can also be used in a subquery. For example, assume that we have another table called `Instructor` that contains the data shown here:

```
Instructor

iname                   teaches
-------------------     --------------------
Richard                 COSC
Subhash                 MATH
Tapan                   BIOCHEM
```

(3 row(s) affected)

The `Instructor` table has not been created for you. You have to create it, insert the records shown, and then run the queries that follow.

Now, if we want to find all the departments that do not have instructors, we could type the following query:

```
SELECT *
FROM Department_to_major d
WHERE d.dcode NOT IN
(SELECT dcode
FROM Department_to_major d, Instructor i
WHERE d.dcode=i.teaches)
```

This produces the following output (six rows):

```
DCODE DNAME
----- --------------------
ACCT  Accounting
ART   Art
CHEM  Chemistry
ENGL  English
POLY  Political Science
UNKN  NULL


(6 row(s) affected)
```

Note that in this case, the NOT .. IN predicate "behaved" correctly and reported the NULL value for **dname** because the query is looking for department codes in the **Instructor** table; the null is part of the **Department_to_major** table and not involved in the subquery link.

7.6 The Difference Operation

Because SQL Server 2008 does not support the MINUS predicate, we will show the set difference operation using a NOT.. IN predicate with two examples.

Example 7.1   Suppose set A is the set of students in classes 2, 3, or 4 and set B is the set of students in class $= 2$. We could use the NOT .. IN predicate to remove the students in set B from set A (a difference operation) by typing the following query:

```
SELECT sname, class
FROM Student
WHERE class IN (2, 3, 4)
AND NOT class IN (2)
```

This produces the following output (17 rows):

```
sname                class
-------------------- ------
Mary                 4
Kelly                4
Donald               4
Chris                4
Jake                 4
Susan                3
Monica               3
Phoebe               3
Holly                4
Rachel               3
Jerry                4
Cramer               3
Harrison             4
Francis              4
Losmith              3
Gus                  3
Benny                4

(17 row(s) affected)
```

Example 7.2

To illustrate another difference operation, we will use views with the NOT .. IN predicate to give the effect of a difference operation. Suppose, for example, you wanted to find the names of those students who are not majoring in COSC or MATH but delete from that set those students who have made an A in some course.

First, using the NOT .. IN predicate, we will create a view (view1) of the names and majors of the students who are not COSC or MATH majors using the following query:

```
CREATE VIEW view1 AS
SELECT sname, major
FROM Student
WHERE major NOT IN ('COSC', 'MATH')
```

view1 will have the same 28 rows of output as shown in the "Using NOT .. IN" section earlier in this chapter.

Then, using the IN predicate, we will create another view (`view2`) of names and majors of students who have received A's using the following query:

```
CREATE VIEW view2 AS
SELECT Student.sname, Student.major
FROM Student
WHERE Student.stno IN
(SELECT g.student_number
FROM Grade_report g
WHERE g.grade = 'A')
```

Now if we type:

```
SELECT *
FROM view2
```

we get the following 14 rows of output:

```
sname                   major
--------------------    -----
Lineas                  ENGL
Mary                    COSC
Brenda                  COSC
Richard                 ENGL
Lujack                  COSC
Donald                  ACCT
Lynette                 POLY
Susan                   ENGL
Holly                   POLY
Sadie                   MATH
Jessica                 POLY
Steve                   ENGL
Cedric                  ENGL
Jerry                   COSC

(14 row(s) affected)
```

Then, to find those students who are not majoring in COSC or MATH, and remove from that set those who made an A in some course, the difference operation could be approached using the NOT .. IN predicate as follows, using the views we just created:

```
SELECT sname
FROM view1
WHERE sname NOT IN
(SELECT sname
FROM view2)
```

This produces the following output (19 rows):

```
sname
--------------------
Ken
Romona
Harley
Chris
Bill
Phoebe
Rachel
George
Cramer
Fraiser
Harrison
Francis
Smithly
Sebastian
Losmith
Genevieve
Lindsay
Gus
Benny

(19 row(s) affected)
```

This query has the same effect as `view1 – view2` (all students who are not majoring in COSC or MATH students who made an A in some course).

7.7   The Union and the Join

In this section, we discuss some differences between the operations UNION and JOIN. Although the UNION operation and the JOIN operation are similar in that they both combine two tables or sets of data, the approaches used by the two operations are different. We will first present an example of when a JOIN may be used versus when a UNION may be used, and then we will discuss other differences between the two operations.

7.7.1 Using a JOIN versus Using a UNION

A JOIN is very commonly used in queries. As we discussed in Chapter 4, joins (specifically equi-joins) involve creating a result set based on tables where the tables are linked via some common column. The UNION operator is mostly used to combine two sets of information where the genesis of the information is not as straightforward as in a join. Consider the following two examples.

Example 7.3	*A straightforward join operation:*

Suppose we wanted to find the names of students who took accounting courses. This is a straightforward join example. This type of query would involve joining the Student, Section, and Course tables and selecting the student names from the result set. Remember that JOIN is a binary operation and so we can join the Student table to the Grade_report table first, and then join that result to the Section table. (We could join the Section table to the Grade_report table and then join that result to the Student table as well.) Then, we can join that combined result to the Course table—so this ends up becoming a four table join with the Grade_report table acting like a bridge between the Student and Section tables. The JOIN query would be:

```
SELECT DISTINCT(sname)
FROM Course c JOIN (Section se JOIN
(Student s JOIN Grade_report g
ON s.stno = g.student_number)
ON se.section_id = g.section_id)
ON c.course_number = se.course_num
AND c.course_name LIKE 'ACC%'
```

This would give the following 20 rows of output:

```
sname
--------------------
Alan
Bill
Brad
Brenda
Cedric
```

```
Chris
Donald
Hillary
Holly
Jessica
Kelly
Ken
Mario
Monica
Phoebe
Romona
Sadie
Steve
Susan
Zelda

(20 row(s) affected)
```

Note that we had to use DISTINCT in this query since the result of a JOIN gives duplicates.

This query could also be answered using subqueries, which will be discussed in Chapter 8, but the point is that it is easy to see the relationship between the four tables.

Example 7.4	*A not-so-straightforward query:*

Suppose we wanted to find the names of the students who take accounting courses and combine them with the names of students who also major in subjects that use overhead projectors in the courses they take. With our Student_course database, this could be done using a join, but it would involve finding a join path through most of the database. For a much larger database, it might be very impractical to consider such a large join. It would be easier to first find the set of names of students who take accounting courses (call this set A) and then find students who major in subjects that use projectors (set B), then union sets A and B. The UNION approach allows us to simplify the problem and check intermediate results, so we will present this problem using a UNION. Further, each part of the problem can be done with joins or subqueries as needed for efficiency and then the results finally unioned. Set operations allow us to create sets of results any way we can and then combine the result sets using set operations; UNION is a set operation.

The first step in creating this query is to do the parts individually. That is, first find the set of names of students who take accounting courses (this is the first half of the query before the UNION). Once this is done, then we do the second part individually, that is, find the students who major in subjects that use projectors. Once we have the results for both parts, we UNION the two results. We will not need the DISTINCT clause here since UNION does not keep the duplicates. The following query illustrates this UNION approach:

```
SELECT sname
FROM Course c JOIN (Section se JOIN
(Student s JOIN Grade_report g
ON s.stno = g.student_number)
ON se.section_id = g.section_id)
ON c.course_number = se.course_num
AND c.course_name LIKE 'ACC%'
UNION
SELECT sname
FROM Student s JOIN
(Department_to_major d
JOIN (Course c JOIN
(Room r JOIN Section se
ON r.room = se.room)
ON se.course_num = c.course_number)
ON c.offering_dept = d.dcode)
ON s.major = d.dcode
AND r.ohead = 'Y'
```

This produces 30 rows (of which we show the first few rows):

```
sname
--------------------
Alan
Bill
Brad
Brenda
Cedric
Chris
Cramer
.
.
.


(30 row(s) affected)
```

7.7.2 Differences between the UNION and the JOIN

In this section, we will summarize our JOIN/UNION discussion with two abstract tables containing three rows each of symbolic data. Relations or tables are *sets of rows*.

We will first show the union. If we have two tables, `TableA` and `TableB`:

ColumnA	ColumnB	ColumnC
X1	Y1	Z1
X2	Y2	Z2
X3	Y3	Z3

Table 7.1 TableA

ColumnA	ColumnB	ColumnC
X4	Y4	Z4
X5	Y5	Z5
X6	Y6	Z6

Table 7.2 TableB

Then, a UNION operation would be:

SELECT * FROM TableA
UNION
SELECT * FROM TableB

Giving **TableC**:

ColumnA	ColumnB	ColumnC
X1	Y1	Z1
X2	Y2	Z2
X3	Y3	Z3
X4	Y4	Z4
X5	Y5	Z5
X6	Y6	Z6

Table 7.3 TableC

Using a similar set of diagrams, the JOIN operation could be shown as follows (joining `TableA` and `TableD` into `TableE`):

ColumnA	ColumnB	ColumnC
X1	Y1	Z1
X2	Y2	Z2
X3	Y3	Z3

Table 7.4   TableA

ColumnA	ColumnD	ColumnE
X1	D1	E1
X2	D2	E2
X3	D3	E3

Table 7.5   TableD

SELECT *
FROM TableA a JOIN TableD d
ON a.ColumnA = d.ColumnA

that gives **TableE**:

ColumnA	ColumnB	ColumnC	ColumnA	ColumnD	ColumnE
X1	Y1	Z1	X1	D1	E1
X2	Y2	Z2	X2	D2	E2
X3	Y3	Z3	X3	D3	E3

Table 7.6   TableE

The major differences between UNIONs and JOINs are:

- In a UNION, all the rows in the resulting tables (sets) being unioned have to be compatible; in a JOIN, only the joining columns of the tables being joined have to be compatible—the other columns may be different.
- In a UNION, no "new" or "other" columns can be conveniently added to the result set; in a JOIN, new columns can be added to the result set easily.
- In a UNION, the number of columns in the result set has to be the same as the number of columns in the sets being unioned; in a JOIN, the number of columns in the result set may vary.

7.8 A UNION Used to Implement a Full Outer Join

From Chapter 4, you will recall that the outer join adds rows to the result set that would otherwise be dropped from an inner join of both tables due to the join condition. Remember that an "inner join" (aka, equi-join, ordinary join, or regular join) combines two tables by finding common values on some column(s) common to the two tables. In a left or right outer join, we are saying, "We want all the rows from one table and only the joined rows from the other." In SQL Server 2008, the outer joins are in two classes—left and right, depending on how the query is written. A "full outer join" means that we want all rows from both tables being joined, and "fill in those rows where a join does not produce a result with nulls." In SQL Server 2008, a UNION can also be used to achieve this full outer join.

Some SQL products do not directly support the full outer join, but SQL Server 2008 directly supports it.

In SQL Server 2008, you can create a full outer join by writing a union of the left outer join and the right outer join, like this:

```
SELECT with right outer join
UNION
SELECT with left outer join
```

The order of the left outer join and the right outer join does not matter and can be reversed. To illustrate the workings of the UNION version of the full outer join, let us again use the table called **Instructor** created earlier in this chapter:

```
iname                teaches
-------------------  -------------------
Richard              COSC
Subhash              MATH
Tapan                BIOCHEM
```

If we want to get a listing of all instructors and the names of the departments for which they teach (which will be done by a regular equi-join) plus a listing of the rest of the instructors, regardless of whether they belong to a department, plus a listing of the rest of the departments, regardless of whether they have instructors, we would write the following query to achieve the full outer join effect with a UNION:

```
SELECT *
FROM Department_to_major AS d LEFT JOIN Instructor AS I
ON d.dcode=i.teaches
UNION
```

```
SELECT *
FROM Department_to_major AS d RIGHT JOIN Instructor AS I
ON d.dcode=i.teaches
```

This produces the following output (nine rows):

```
DCODE DNAME                  iname                teaches
----- --------------------   -------------------- --------------------
NULL  NULL                   Tapan                BIOCHEM
ACCT  Accounting             NULL                 NULL
ART   Art                    NULL                 NULL
CHEM  Chemistry              NULL                 NULL
COSC  Computer Science       Richard              COSC
ENGL  English                NULL                 NULL
MATH  Mathematics            Subhash              MATH
POLY  Political Science      NULL                 NULL
UNKN  NULL                   NULL                 NULL
```

```
(9 row(s) affected)
```

First, the LEFT JOIN was done, outer joining the department_to_major table and the Instructor table (so all the rows of the department_to_major table were added to the result set). Then, a RIGHT JOIN was done, again joining the department_to_major table to the Instructor table (but this time all the rows of the Instructor table were added to the result set). Finally, a UNION of the two result sets was performed, creating the effect of a full outer join (where the rows from both the tables were added back after the join).

SUMMARY

In this chapter, we explored all common set operations available in SQL Server 2008. The UNION and INTERSECT operations may be done directly with SQL Server 2008. When we cannot directly perform a set operation, we can use IN or NOT .. IN; SQL Server 2008 does not have an explicit MINUS operator, so we showed how to use the IN and NOT .. IN predicates to get the effect of that type of query. Oftentimes queries can be approached in more than one way. In several places, we showed how the same queries could be approached without the use of set operators. In some cases, sets are intuitively more appealing and actually less complicated than very large joins.

Review Questions

1. What are the major differences between the UNION operation and the JOIN operation?

2. What is the major difference between the UNION operation and the UNION ALL operation?

3. What major set operator does SQL Server 2008 not have? How can these problems be resolved?

4. What does union compatibility mean?

5. What data types are union-compatible?

6. What is the maximum number of rows that can result from a UNION of two tables—one with five rows and the other with six rows?

7. What is the maximum number of rows that can result from a JOIN of two tables—one with five rows and the other with six rows?

8. How can a UNION be used to implement an outer join? Explain.

9. What is a full outer join? Does SQL Server 2008 directly support a full outer join?

10. Do you need the same number of columns to perform a union?

11. Do you need the same data types to perform a union?

12. Do you need the same number of columns to perform a join?

13. From the examples given in the chapter, what does the UNION ALL appear to do?

14. If a VARCHAR column were unioned with a CHAR column, what would the resulting column be? (*Hint*: Refer to the "Data Type Precedence" section in Chapter 6.)

15. What does set compatibility mean?

16. What is the maximum number of rows that can result from an INTERSECT of two tables—one with five rows and the other with six rows?

17. Do you need the same number of columns to perform an INTERSECT operation?

18. Do you need the same data types to perform an INTERSECT operation?

Chapter 7 Exercises

Unless specified otherwise, use the Student_course **database to answer the following questions. Also, use appropriate column headings when displaying your output.**

1. In this exercise, you'll test the UNION statement. Having seen how the UNION statement works, demonstrate some permutations to see what

will work "legally" and what won't. First, create two tables:

```
Table1          Table2
 A    B      A    B    C    D
 x1   y1     x2   y2   z2   w2
 r1   s1     r2   s2   T2   u2
```

Make the type of the A and B columns CHAR(2). Let the type of column C in Table2 be VARCHAR(2) and column D in Table2 be VARCHAR(3).

Try the following statements and note the results:

SELECT * FROM Table1 UNION SELECT * FROM Table2

SELECT * FROM Table1 UNION SELECT A, B FROM Table2

SELECT * FROM Table1 UNION SELECT B, A FROM Table1

SELECT * FROM Table1 UNION SELECT A, C FROM Table2

SELECT * FROM Table1 UNION SELECT A, D FROM Table2

CREATE VIEW viewx AS
SELECT A, B
FROM Table2

SELECT *
FROM Table1
UNION
SELECT *
FROM viewx

Feel free to experiment with any other combinations that you deem appropriate or that you wonder about.

2. Create and print the result of a query that generates the names, class, and course numbers of students who have earned B's in computer science courses. Store this query as *Q7_2*. Then, revise *Q7_2* to delete from the result set those students who are sophomores (class = 2). Use NOT .. IN to select those students who are sophomores.

3. Find the names, grades, and course numbers of students who have earned A's in computer science or math courses. Join the Section and Grade_report tables (be careful to not create the Cartesian product). Then, UNION the set of "course numbers COSC% and A" with the set of "course numbers MATH% and A."

Hint: Start with the query to get names, grades, and course numbers for COSC% and A, and then turn this into a view. Do the same for MATH% and A, and then execute the UNION statement as follows (using your view names):

```
SELECT *
FROM view1a
UNION
SELECT *
FROM view1b
```

4. Find the names and majors of students who have made a C in any course. Make the "who have made a C in any course" a subquery for which you use IN.

5. A less obvious example of a difference query is to find a difference that is not based on simple, easy-to-get sets. Suppose that set A is the set of student names who have made A's and B's in computer science (COSC) courses. Suppose further that set B is the set of students who have taken math courses (regardless of what grade they earned).

Then, set A minus set B would contain names of students who have made A's or B's in computer science courses, less those who have taken math courses. Similarly, set B minus set A would be the set of students who took math courses, less those who made an A or a B in some COSC course.

Build these queries into set difference queries as views based on student numbers and execute them, as follows:

a. Write a query that gives the student number, name, course, and grade for each set. Save each query as $Q7\_5a$ and $Q7\_5b$.

b. Reconstruct each query into a view of just student numbers, verify that it works, and then create views to create set A and set B. Verify that you have the same number of rows in set A as you have in $Q7\_5a$, and the same number of rows in set B as you have in $Q7\_5b$.

c. Display the student numbers of students in each set difference. Show (set A minus set B) and (set B minus set A). Look at the original queries, $Q7\_5a$ and $Q7\_5b$, to verify your result.

6. Create two tables, T1 and T2, that contain a name and a salary column. In the first table, order the columns by name and then by salary. In the second table, order the columns by salary and then by name. Use the same data types for each—VARCHAR(20) and NUMBER, for example. Populate the tables with two rows each.

7. Can you UNION the two tables in the preceding question with the following query?

```
SELECT *
FROM T1
UNION
SELECT *
FROM T2
```

Why or why not? If not, can you force the union of the two tables? Illustrate how. Be sure to drop the tables when you are finished using DROP TABLE.

8. Using the `Instructor` table you created in this chapter (as well as the tables supplied in the `Student_course` database), perform the following (use the UNION or INTERSECT operator if you feel appropriate):

   a. Find all departments that have instructors. First do this using an IN predicate, and then using a regular join.
   b. Find all students who are also instructors.
   c. Find all instructors who are not students.
   d. Find all students who are not instructors.
   e. Find all students as well as all instructors.

9. Using the `Student` table, find all the students who major in math and are seniors. (*Hint*: Use the INTERSECT operator for this.)

Optional Exercise

10. **De Morgan's Theorem.** In the binary case, De Morgan's Theorem tells us that $[\text{not}(A \text{ and } B)] = [\text{not}(A) \text{ or not}(B)]$. For example, suppose A is the set of rows where students are juniors and B is the set of rows where students are females. And suppose you were asked the question, "Find the students who are not (female and juniors)." Clearly this is the set $[\text{not}(A \text{ and } B)]$. You can answer this question by finding the set of students who are not juniors $[\text{not}(A)]$ and then OR-ing this with the set of students who are not females $[\text{not}(B)]$. At times it is easier to find one or the other of the results via a query, and the point here is that the two methods of finding a result are equivalent.

   Question: Find the result set for all sections that are offered in building 13 and call this set A. Find the result set for all sections that are offered in building 36 and call this set B. Construct the SQL to find the following result sets:

a. The result of set A OR set B (use "WHERE building = 13 OR building = 36").

b. The result of the complement of a: NOT(set A OR set B).

c. The result of NOT(set A) AND NOT(set B).

d. The count of all rows in the Section table.

Does the count in d = a + b? Is the result of c the same as the result of b? Explain why or why not in each case (*Hint*: You may apply De Morgan's Theorem, which states that NOT(set A or set B) = NOT(set A) and NOT(set b).

chapter

8

Joins Versus Subqueries

Topics covered in this chapter

The purpose of this chapter is to demonstrate the use of subqueries. Subqueries may often be used as alternatives to joins. There are two main issues to consider in choosing between subqueries and joins (and other techniques for combining tables). First, you must consider how to get the information. By understanding the limitations of joins and subqueries (as well as sets and other table-combining techniques), you will broaden your choices regarding how to get information from a database. Second, you must also consider performance. You usually have a choice of how to get multitable information—joins, sets, subqueries, views, and so forth. In larger databases, you need to be flexible and consider other choices if a query performs poorly and/or if the query is done often.

Although set operations logically are also viable choices for retrieving data from multiple tables, set operations (discussed in Chapter 7) are less common and usually less efficient than joins and subqueries.

8.1   The IN Subquery

Suppose that a query requests a list of names and student numbers of students who have made A's or B's in any course. Student names are in the Student table in our Student_course database and grades are in the Grade_report table. You can complete this query as either a subquery or a join. As a subquery with an IN clause, it will take the following form:

```
SELECT Student.sname, Student.stno
FROM Student
WHERE "link to Grade_report"
   IN ("link to Student" subquery involving Grade_report)
```

In this format, the part of the query that contains:

```
SELECT Student.sname, Student.stno
FROM Student
WHERE "link to Grade_report"
```

is said to be the "outer query." The part of the query that contains:

```
("link to Student" subquery involving Grade_report)
```

is the "inner query."

The link between the Student table and the Grade_report table is the student number. In the Student table, the appropriate column is stno, and in the Grade_report table it is student_number. When using a link between tables with the IN subquery, the linking column is all that can be mentioned in the WHERE .. IN predicate and in the result set of the inner subquery. Thus, the statement with a subquery is as follows:

```
SELECT Student.sname, Student.stno
FROM Student
WHERE Student.stno
   IN (SELECT gr.student_number
     FROM Grade_report gr
     WHERE gr.grade = 'B'OR gr.grade = 'A')
       ORDER BY Student.stno
```

The part of the query *before* the IN is often called the *outer query*. The part of the query *after* the IN is called the *inner query*.

This produces 31 rows of output (of which we show the first few rows here):

```
sname                 stno
--------------------  ------
Lineas                2
Mary                  3
Zelda                 5
Ken                   6
Mario                 7
Brenda                8
Richard               10
Kelly                 13
Lujack                14
Reva                  15
Harley                19
Donald                20
Chris                 24
   .
   .
   .

(31 row(s) affected)
```

8.2 The Subquery as a Join

An alternate way to perform the preceding query would be to use a join instead of a subquery, as follows:

```
SELECT Student.sname, Student.stno
FROM Student, Grade_report gr
WHERE Student.stno = gr.student_number
AND (gr.grade = 'B' OR gr.grade = 'A')
```

This produces 67 rows of output (of which we show the first few rows here):

```
sname                 stno
--------------------  ------
Lineas                2
Lineas                2
Lineas                2
```

```
Lineas            2
Mary              3
Mary              3
Mary              3
Mary              3
Mary              3
Mary              3
Zelda             5
Ken               6
Mario             7
Brenda            8
  .
  .
  .
```

(67 row(s) affected)

Now the question is—why does the join have 67 rows of output instead of the 31 rows of output produced by the subquery?

When the join version is used to combine tables, any **Student-Grade_report** row that has equal student numbers and a grade of A or B is selected. Thus, you may expect many duplicate names in the output. To get the result without duplicates, add the qualifier DISTINCT to the join query as follows:

SELECT DISTINCT Student.sname, Student.stno
FROM Student, Grade_report AS gr
WHERE Student.stno = gr.student_number
AND (gr.grade = 'B'OR gr.grade = 'A')

This produces 31 rows of output (of which we show the first few rows here):

```
sname               stno
------------------- ------
Lineas              2
Mary                3
Zelda               5
Ken                 6
Mario               7
Brenda              8
Richard             10
Kelly               13
Lujack              14
Reva                15
```

```
Harley              19
Donald              20
Chris               24
    .
    .
    .
```

(31 row(s) affected)

When DISTINCT is used, internal sorting is performed before the result set is displayed. Such internal sorting could decrease response time for a query if tables were much larger than those in our sample database.

In the subquery version of the query, duplication of student number/name combinations does not occur in the result set. This is because you are setting up a set of student numbers (the subquery) from which you will choose rows in the outer query based on student number. A given student number either is in the subquery set or is not in the set. The student number (stno) is unique in the **Student** table and hence no duplicate rows can result.

The question of which is more efficient, the join or the subquery, depends on which SQL and database you are using. Without using extra tools, one way to test alternatives is to try the queries on the data or a subset of the data. Database systems such as Microsoft® SQL Server® 2008 provide ways (tools) to find out how queries are executed.

In thinking through the way to answer queries, it may be advantageous to use a stepwise approach. The question asks us to find a list of names and student numbers of students who have made A's or B's in any course. The immediate temptation is to go for the names and student numbers. In that case, you might start with this query:

```
SELECT sname, stno
FROM Student
```

Then, you begin to qualify the names you want to see by adding a WHERE clause.

However, if you looked at this question another way, you might first envision finding courses where A's and B's were assigned. You could start with this query:

```
SELECT *
FROM Grade_report
WHERE grade = 'A' OR grade = 'B'
```

This would give you a result set that contained all the columns in the Grade_report table. Then, you would begin to pare down the result set, wrap the query in parentheses, and use it as a subquery. In either case, you are successfully completing part of the query, then using that part to complete the overall question. Both approaches are acceptable because you view intermediate results and use the results to eventually answer the overall question.

Query writing does not have to be a "write one big query," all or none process. Writing queries in parts and testing intermediate results is good practice.

8.3   When the Join Cannot Be Turned into a Subquery

When a column from a table needs to be in the result set, that table has to be in the outer query. If two tables are being used, and if columns from both tables have to be in the result set, a join is necessary. But if the result set does not need the columns from more than one table, then the join can be turned into a subquery. The other tables can be included such that the filtering conditions can be in the subquery (or inner query), and the table that has the needed result set columns is in the outer query.

Consider this example: Our original query (the first query discussed in this chapter), requested the list of names and numbers of students who made A's or B's in any course. Student names and numbers are both in the Student table; the Grade_report table is only needed as a filter, so we could write this either as a subquery or a join.

Now, if this original query had also asked for output from the Grade_report table, such as, "list the names, numbers, *and* grades of all students who have made A's or B's," then the query would be asking for information from both the Student and Grade_report tables. In this case, you would have to join the two tables to get the information; you could not just query the Grade_report table because the Grade_report table has no student names in it. Similarly, the Student table contains no grades. So you would not be able to write this question as a subquery. Refer again to the original query example:

```
SELECT Student.sname, Student.stno
FROM Student
WHERE Student.stno
  IN (SELECT gr.student_number
    FROM Grade_report gr
    WHERE gr.grade = 'B'OR gr.grade = 'A')
      ORDER BY Student.stno
```

This query asks only for information from the **Student** table (student names and numbers). Although the query uses the **Grade_report** table, nothing from the **Grade_report** table is in the outer result set. Again, the **Grade_report** table is only needed as a filter (to get the student numbers of those who have A's and B's); hence we were able to write this part as a subquery.

The following join query asks for information from both the **Student** and **Grade_report** tables (a result set that lists both names and grades of all students who have made A's or B's in any course):

```
SELECT DISTINCT Student.sname, gr.grade
FROM Student, Grade_report gr
WHERE Student.stno = gr.student_number
AND (gr.grade = 'B' OR gr.grade = 'A')
```

This produces 41 rows of output (of which we show the first few rows here):

```
sname                    grade
-------------------      -----
Brenda                   A
Brenda                   B
Cedric                   A
Cedric                   B
Chris                    B
Cramer                   B
Donald                   A
Fraiser                  B
Francis                  B
George                   B
Harley                   B
Hillary                  B
.
.
.

(41 row(s) affected)
```

If information from a table is needed in a result set, that table cannot be buried in a subquery—it must be in the outer query.

8.4   More Examples Involving Joins and IN

The purpose of this section is to further demonstrate several queries that will and will not allow the use of the subquery. As we have discussed, some joins can be expressed as subqueries, whereas others cannot. Further, all subqueries with the IN predicate can be reformed as a join. How do you know whether you can use a subquery? It depends on the desired result set. Some more examples will help clarify this point.

Example 8.1   Find the names of all the departments that offer a course with INTRO in the title. As with the formation of all queries, we first have to ask ourselves, "Where is the data we need to answer this question?" To formulate our query, we need to use the Course table (to find the course names) and the Department_to_major table (to find the names of the departments).

Begin by viewing the column names in the tables.

If you have forgotten how to view the column names of a table, refer to Figure 1.20.

Figure 8.1 shows the column names of the Course table.

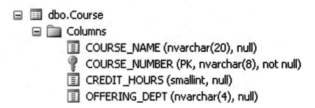

Figure 8.1   Column names of the Course table

Figure 8.2 shows the column names of the Department_to_major table.

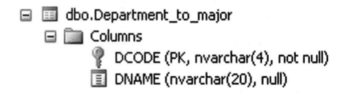

Figure 8.2   Column names of the Department_to_major table

Our query needs a department name (dname) from the Department_to_major table. We also need course information from the Course table because our query depends on a course name; however, no course information appears in the result set. We did not ask for the names of the courses, just that they have INTRO in the title. The result set only asks for department names. We can find this result by using a subquery, with the Department_to_major table in the outer query because all the information in the result set is contained in the Department_to_major table. The query would be as follows:

```
SELECT d2m.dname
FROM Department_to_major d2m
```

```
WHERE d2m.dcode
    IN (SELECT Course.offering_dept
        FROM Course
        WHERE Course.course_name LIKE '%INTRO%')
```

This produces the following output:

```
dname
--------------------
Chemistry
Computer Science
Political Science

(3 row(s) affected)
```

Example 8.2   List the student name, student major code, and section identifier of students who earned C's in courses taught by Professor Hermano (HERMANO).

First, we determine which tables are needed. We want to find the student name and major code and a section identifier for courses taken, so we need the Student and Grade_report tables for the result set. The name and major code are in the Student table. The section identifier is in Grade_report table. We will need to use the Section table for a filter because the Section table contains the instructor name. The instructor name is not requested in the result set. Again, it is a good idea to look at the column names in each of the tables first.

Figure 8.3 shows the column names of the Student table.

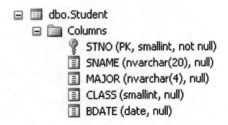

Figure 8.3   Column names of the Student table

Figure 8.4 shows the column names of the Grade_report table.

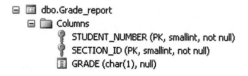

Figure 8.4 Column names of the `Grade_report` table

Figure 8.5 shows the column names of the `Section` table.

Figure 8.5 Column names of the `Section` table

After we have determined which tables we need and we know where the requested columns are, we can begin to construct the query. The result set part of the query (the outer query) must contain the **Student** and **Grade_report** tables. The rest of the query can contain any other tables that we need to locate the columns. The resulting query may look like this (a combination of a join and a subquery):

```
SELECT s.sname, s.major, g.section_id
FROM Student s, Grade_report g
WHERE g.student_number = s.stno
AND g.grade = 'C'
AND g.section_id IN
   (SELECT t.section_id
   FROM Section t
   WHERE t.instructor LIKE 'HERMANO')
```

This produces the following output:

```
sname                  major section_id
--------------------   ----- ----------
Richard                ENGL  126


(1 row(s) affected)
```

Since all IN-type subqueries can be written as joins, the preceding query could have been done as a three-table join, as follows:

```
SELECT s.sname, s.major, t.section_id
FROM Student s, Grade_report g, Section t
WHERE s.stno = g.student_number
AND g.section_id =t.section_id
AND g.grade='C'
AND t.instructor LIKE 'HERMANO'
```

| Example 8.3 | List the name and major code of students who earned C's in courses taught by Professor King (KING). |

Where is the data we need to answer this question? We need student names and major codes in the result set, and we need the Grade_report and Section tables for filtering conditions. (You viewed the columns available in each of these tables in the preceding example.) Next, we need to determine where the result set columns are located. In this example, they are all in the Student table.

Because the only table needed in the outer query is the Student table, we can structure the query in any of the following ways:

1. Student join Grade_report join Section   [three-table join]

2. Student Subquery (Grade_report join Section)   [Student outer, with a join in the subquery]

3. Student join Grade_report Subquery (Section)   [Similar to Example 2 but with a join in the outer query]

4. Student (Subquery Grade_report (Subquery Section))   [A three-level subquery]

Each of these queries should produce the same result set with different efficiencies. We'll study them further in the exercises at the end of the chapter.

8.5 Using Subqueries with Operators

In this section, we will look at examples that demonstrate the use of subqueries with comparison operators. These examples are based on the Room table, which has the following data:

BLDG	ROOM	CAPACITY	OHEAD
13	101	85	Y
36	123	35	N
58	114	60	NULL
79	179	35	Y
79	174	22	Y
58	112	40	NULL
36	122	25	N
36	121	25	N
36	120	25	N
58	110	NULL	Y

In previous chapters, we have seen SELECTs with equality WHERE conditions like the following:

```
SELECT *
FROM Room
WHERE capacity = 25
```

In this example, 25 is a constant and = is a comparison operator. The constant can be replaced by a subquery, and the operator can be any of the comparison operators (=, <>, <, >, <=, or >=). For example, we could devise a query to tell us which classrooms have a below-average capacity by computing the average in a subquery and using a comparison operator like this:

```
SELECT *
FROM Room
WHERE capacity <
    (SELECT AVG(capacity)
    FROM Room)
```

This query produces the following six rows of output, showing six rooms with below-average capacity:

BLDG	ROOM	CAPACITY	OHEAD
36	120	25	N
36	121	25	N
36	122	25	N
36	123	35	N

| 79 | 174 | 22 | Y |
| 79 | 179 | 35 | Y |

Warning: Null value is eliminated by an aggregate or other SET operation.

(6 row(s) affected)

The only problem with using subqueries in this fashion is that *the subquery must return only one row.* If an aggregate function is applied to a table in the subquery in this fashion, you will always get only one row—even if there is a WHERE clause that excludes all rows, the subquery returns one row with a null value. For example, if we were to change the preceding query to the following and force multiple rows in the subquery:

```
SELECT *
FROM Room
WHERE capacity <
    (SELECT AVG(capacity)
    FROM Room
    WHERE bldg = 99)
```

we would get:

```
BLDG    ROOM    CAPACITY OHEAD
------  ------  -------- -----
```

(0 row(s) affected)

The result is "0 rows(s) affected" because there is no bldg = 99. If we were to change the query to the following:

```
SELECT *
FROM Room
WHERE bldg =
    (SELECT bldg
    FROM Room
    WHERE capacity > 10)
```

we would get the following error message:

```
BLDG   ROOM   CAPACITY OHEAD
------ ------ -------- -----
```

Msg 512, Level 16, State 1, Line 1
Subquery returned more than 1 value. This is not permitted
when the subquery follows =, !=, <, <=, >, >= or when the
subquery is used as an expression.

When using comparison operators, only single values are acceptable from
the subquery. Again, to ensure we get only one row in the subquery and
hence a workable query, we can use an aggregate with no GROUP BY or
HAVING clause (discussed in Chapter 9).

As with all queries, the caveat to audit the result is always applicable.

SUMMARY

In this chapter, we examined the subquery. We gave examples of situations
where subqueries were allowable and where they were not. If all requested
information is found in one table, then that table can be the outer query
with filtering done in subqueries. The link between outer and inner queries
is based on a common column. The inner query can be thought of as being
completed first and forming a set from which the outer query chooses rows.

We also showed subqueries written as joins. We looked into situations
where joins could be rewritten as subqueries and where they could not. In
building queries, it may be advantageous to write a subquery, look at the
result, formulate the result set in an appropriate way, and then proceed to
use the result set in an IN clause for an outer query. Query writing does
not have to be a "write one big query," all-or-none process. Writing queries
in parts and testing intermediate results is sound practice.

Review Questions

1. What is a subquery?
2. Which part of the query/subquery is considered the "inner query," and
   which part is considered the "outer query"?
3. Can a subquery always be done as a join? Why or why not?
4. When writing a query that will have a subquery, how do you determine
   which table or tables will go in the outer query?
5. Which predicate usually can be reformulated into a join?
6. When using operators, are many values acceptable from a result of a
   subquery?
7. What can you do to ensure a working subquery?

Chapter 8 Exercises

Unless specified otherwise, use the Student_course database to answer the following questions. Also, use appropriate column headings when displaying your output.

Use the techniques from this chapter to construct and execute the following queries:

1. Find the student numbers of students who have earned A's or B's in courses taught in the fall semester. Do this in two ways, first using a subquery and then using a join.

2. Find all students who took a course offered by the Accounting (ACCT) department. List the student name and student number, the course name, and the grade in that course. (*Hint*: Begin with Department_to_major and use an appropriate WHERE clause). Note that this cannot be done with a multilevel subquery. Why?

3. For all students who are sophomores (class = 2), find their names and the names of the departments that include the students' majors.

4. Find the names of the departments that offer courses at the junior or senior levels (either one) but not at the freshman level. The course level is the first digit after the prefix; for example, AAAA3yyy is a junior course.

    Hint: Begin by creating the outer query—the names of departments that offer courses at the junior or senior levels. Save this query as *q8_4*. Then, construct the subquery—a list of departments that offer courses at the freshman level. Save the subquery as a view. Examine both lists of departments. When you have the outer query and the subquery results, recall the original query that you saved (*q8_4*) and add the subquery. Check your result with the department lists you just generated. Redo the last part of the experiment with your view. You should get the same result.

5. Find the names of courses that are prerequisites for other courses. List the course number and name, and the course number and name of the prerequisite.

6. List the names of instructors who teach courses that have other than three-hour credits. Do the problem in two ways, once with IN and once with NOT .. IN.

7. Create a table called Secretary with the columns dcode (of data type CHAR(4)) for department code and name (of data type VARCHAR(20)) for the secretary name. Insert records into the table so you have:

```
Secretary
dCode      name
-----      ---------
ACCT       Beryl
COSC       Kaitlyn
ENGL       David
HIST       Christina
BENG       Fred
HINDI      Chloe
```

a. Create a query that lists the names of departments that have secretaries (use IN and the **Secretary** table in a subquery with the **Department_to_major** table in the outer query). Save this query as *q8_7a*.

b. Create a query that lists the names of departments (using the **Department_to_major** table) that do not have secretaries (use NOT .. IN). Save this query as *q8_7b*.

c. Add one more row to the **Secretary** table that contains "<null,'Brenda'>" (which you could do, for example, in a situation in which you have hired Brenda but have not yet assigned her to a department).

d. Recall *q8_7a* and rerun it. Recall *q8_7b* and rerun it.

   The behavior of NOT..IN when nulls exist may surprise you. If nulls may exist in the subquery, then NOT .. IN either should not be used (Chapter 10 shows how to use another predicate, NOT EXISTS, which is a workaround to this problem) or should include "AND whatever IS NOT NULL." If you use NOT .. IN in a subquery, you must either ensure that nulls will not occur in the subquery or use some other predicate (such as NOT EXISTS). Perhaps the best advice is to avoid NOT .. IN unless you cannot figure out another way to solve a problem.

e. To see a correct answer, add the phrase "WHERE dcode IS NOT NULL" to the subquery in the IN and NOT .. IN cases and run them again.

   Do *not* delete the **Secretary** table, as we will revisit this problem in Chapter 10.

8. Devise a list of course names that are offered in the fall semester in rooms where the capacity is equal to or above the average room size.

Aggregation and GROUP BY

Topics covered in this chapter

An aggregate function extracts information in aggregate form—such as generating a count of rows or an average, minimum, or maximum. Aggregate functions operate on multiple rows. The SQL construction GROUP BY is a SELECT statement clause that is designed to be used in conjunction with aggregation (discussed in Chapter 5) to group data of similar types. We will first discuss using GROUP BY on one column, and then on two. Then we will look at how to use GROUP BY in conjunction with the ORDER BY, HAVING, and WHERE clauses. Finally, we will discuss aggregation with subqueries and the complexities that nulls present in aggregate functions and other queries. We will also illustrate why auditing results involving aggregation is good practice. First, we will present a SELECT in modified BNF showing the GROUP BY, HAVING, and ORDER BY clauses.

9.1   A SELECT in Modified BNF

BNF, short for *Backus Naur Form*, is used to describe syntax rules. A general form (in modified BNF) of the SELECT statement for SQL Server, with FROM, WHERE, GROUP BY, HAVING, and ORDER BY, would be:

SELECT result-set
[FROM Tables]
[WHERE row-filter]
[GROUP BY column names]
[HAVING after-filter on groups]
[ORDER BY column names]

The "[..]" notation means optional.

Our examples will show which of these SELECT options to use with one another and why we need GROUP BY and HAVING. Further, note the order of the options. FROM comes first, then WHERE (if present), then GROUP BY (if present).

9.2   The GROUP BY Clause

GROUP BY is used in conjunction with aggregate functions to group data on the basis of the same values in a column. GROUP BY will return one row for each *value* of the column that is grouped. You can use GROUP BY to group by one column or multiple columns.

As an example of how to use GROUP BY for one column, the following statement shows how you can use the aggregate function COUNT to extract the number of **class** groups from the **Student** table:

```
SELECT class, COUNT(*) AS [count]
FROM Student
GROUP BY class
```

This produces the following five rows of output, which is grouped by one column, `class`:

```
class   count
------  -----------
NULL    10
1       11
2       10
3       7
4       10


(5 row(s) affected)
```

This type of statement gives you a new way to retrieve and organize aggregate data. Other aggregate functions have a similar syntax.

The GROUP BY clause has to contain at least the attributes/expressions you are aggregating.

If a GROUP BY clause contains a two-column specification, the result is aggregated and grouped by two columns. For example, the following query provides the count of `class` and `major` from the `Student` table:

```
SELECT class, major, COUNT(*) AS [count]
FROM Student
GROUP BY class, major
```

This produces the following output (24 rows), which is grouped by `class` within `major`:

```
class   major  count
------  -----  -----------
NULL    NULL   3
2       ACCT   1
4       ACCT   4
3       ART    1
3       CHEM   1
4       CHEM   1
NULL    COSC   1
1       COSC   4
2       COSC   2
4       COSC   3
```

```
NULL    ENGL    1
1       ENGL    3
2       ENGL    2
3       ENGL    4
NULL    MATH    2
2       MATH    3
3       MATH    1
4       MATH    1
NULL    POLY    2
1       POLY    3
2       POLY    2
4       POLY    1
NULL    UNKN    1
1       UNKN    1
```

(24 row(s) affected)

The sequence of the columns in a GROUP BY clause has the effect of ordering the output. If we change the order of the GROUP BY, like this:

SELECT class, major, COUNT(*) AS [count]
FROM Student
GROUP BY major, class

Our result will look like this:

```
class   major count
------  ----- -----------
NULL    NULL  3
NULL    COSC  1
NULL    ENGL  1
NULL    MATH  2
NULL    POLY  2
NULL    UNKN  1
1       COSC  4
1       ENGL  3
1       POLY  3
1       UNKN  1
2       ACCT  1
2       COSC  2
2       ENGL  2
2       MATH  3
2       POLY  2
3       ART   1
```

```
3       CHEM   1
3       ENGL   4
3       MATH   1
4       ACCT   4
4       CHEM   1
4       COSC   3
4       MATH   1
4       POLY   1
```

```
(24 row(s) affected)
```

Here, the output is grouped by major within class. As can be seen in these examples, the last column in the GROUP BY is the first ordering attribute. In the preceding example, the last line was "GROUP BY major, class," and the result set is ordered by class and then major within class.

A statement like the following will cause a syntax error because it says that you are to count both class and major, but GROUP BY class only:

```
SELECT class, major, COUNT(*)
FROM Student
GROUP BY class
```

This query would give you the following error message:

```
Msg 8120, Level 16, State 1, Line 1
Column 'Student.MAJOR' is invalid in the select list because
it is not contained in either an aggregate function or the
GROUP BY clause.
```

To be syntactically and logically correct, you must have all the nonaggregate columns of the result set in the GROUP BY clause.

For example, let's take a look at the data in the Room table:

BLDG	ROOM	CAPACITY	OHEAD
13	101	85	Y
36	123	35	N
58	114	60	NULL
79	179	35	Y
79	174	22	Y
58	112	40	NULL
36	122	25	N
36	121	25	N
36	120	25	N
58	110	NULL	Y

The following query would be improper because you must GROUP BY ohead to SUM capacities for each ohead value:

SELECT ohead, SUM(capacity)
FROM Room

ohead, an attribute in the Room table (in our Student_course database), is short for rooms with overhead projectors.

This query would produce a similar error message as the previous query:

Msg 8120, Level 16, State 1, Line 1
Column 'Room.OHEAD' is invalid in the select list because it
is not contained in either an aggregate function or the GROUP
BY clause.

If you SELECT attributes *and* use an aggregate function, you must GROUP BY the nonaggregate attributes. The correct version of the previous statement is as follows:

SELECT ohead, SUM(capacity) AS [sum]
FROM Room
GROUP BY ohead

This produces the following three rows of output:

```
ohead sum
----- -----------
NULL  100
N     110
Y     142
Warning: Null value is eliminated by an aggregate or other
SET operation.

(3 row(s) affected)
```

This is the sum of room capacities for rooms that have no overhead projectors (N), rooms that have overhead projectors (Y), and rooms in which the overhead projector capability is unknown (NULL).

Observe that in the Room table, some rooms have null values for ohead, and the null rows are summed and grouped along with the nonnull rows.

9.2.1 GROUP BY and ORDER BY

To control and enhance the display of a GROUP BY clause, you can combine it with an ORDER BY clause. Consider the following example:

SELECT class, major, COUNT(*) AS [count]
FROM Student
GROUP BY class, major

The output for this query was presented earlier.

    This result set can also be ordered by any other column from the result set using ORDER BY. For example, the following query orders the result set in descending order by COUNT(*):

SELECT class, major, COUNT(*) AS [count]
FROM Student
GROUP BY class, major
ORDER BY COUNT(*) DESC

This produces the following output (24 rows):

```
class   major  count
------  -----  -----------
4       ACCT   4
1       COSC   4
3       ENGL   4
2       MATH   3
4       COSC   3
1       ENGL   3
NULL    NULL   3
1       POLY   3
2       POLY   2
NULL    POLY   2
2       COSC   2
2       ENGL   2
NULL    MATH   2
3       MATH   1
4       MATH   1
NULL    ENGL   1
2       ACCT   1
3       ART    1
3       CHEM   1
4       CHEM   1
NULL    COSC   1
4       POLY   1
NULL    UNKN   1
1       UNKN   1
```

(24 row(s) affected)

9.2.2 GROUP BY and DISTINCT

When a SELECT clause includes all the columns specified in a GROUP BY clause, the use of the DISTINCT function is unnecessary because the GROUP BY clause will group rows in such a way that the column or columns that are grouped will not have duplicate values.

9.3 The HAVING Clause

The GROUP BY and HAVING clauses are used together. The HAVING clause is used as a final filter (rather than as a conditional filter) on the output of a SELECT statement. The WHERE clause is a conditional filter. The query has to be grouped before the HAVING clause can be applied. For example, consider the following statement, which displays the count of students in various classes (classes of students = 1, 2, 3, 4, corresponding to freshman, sophomore, and so on):

```
SELECT class, COUNT(*) AS [count]
FROM Student
GROUP BY class
```

This produces the following output:

```
class   count
------  -----------
NULL    10
1       11
2       10
3       7
4       10


(5 row(s) affected)
```

If you are only interested in classes that have more than a certain number of students in them, you could use the following statement to "final filter" the preceding result set:

```
SELECT class, COUNT(*) AS [count]
FROM Student
GROUP BY class
HAVING COUNT(*) > 9
```

This produces the following four rows of output:

```
class   count
------  -----------
NULL    10
1       11
2       10
4       10
```

(4 row(s) affected)

As is evident here, the HAVING clause only makes sense after the result is aggregated and grouped.

9.3.1 HAVING and WHERE

Whereas HAVING, which comes after a GROUP BY, is a final filter in a SELECT statement, the WHERE clause, which excludes rows from a result set, is a conditional filter. Consider the following two queries:

```
SELECT class, COUNT(*) AS [count]
FROM Student
GROUP BY class
HAVING class = 3
```

```
SELECT class, COUNT(*) AS [count]
FROM Student
WHERE class = 3
GROUP BY class
```

Both queries produce the same result set:

```
class   count
------  -----------
3       7
```

(1 row(s) affected)

In a typical implementation, the first of these two queries is less efficient because the query engine has to complete the query before removing rows "WHERE class = 3" from the result. In the second version, the rows "WHERE class = 3" are filtered from the result set before the grouping takes place. WHERE is not always a substitute for HAVING, but when it can be used instead of HAVING, it should be. Notice that in the example:

```
SELECT class, COUNT(*) AS [count]
FROM Student
GROUP BY class
HAVING COUNT(*) > 9
```

HAVING and WHERE are not interchangeable because the grouping has to take place before the HAVING could have an effect. You cannot know in advance what the counts for each class are until they are counted.

Consider the following query, its meaning, and the processing that is required to finalize the result set:

```
SELECT class, major, COUNT(*) AS [count]
FROM Student
WHERE major = 'COSC'
GROUP BY class, major
HAVING COUNT(*) > 2
```

This produces the following output:

```
class   major count
------  ----- -----------
1       COSC  4
4       COSC  3
```

```
(2 row(s) affected)
```

In this example, all computer science (COSC) majors (per the WHERE clause) will be grouped and counted and then displayed only if "COUNT(*) > 2." The query might erroneously be interpreted as "Group and count all COSC majors by class, but only if there are more than two in a class." This interpretation is wrong, because SQL applies the WHERE, then applies the GROUP BY, and, finally, filters with the HAVING criterion.

9.4　GROUP BY and HAVING: Aggregates of Aggregates

A normal GROUP BY has an aggregate and a column that are grouped like this:

```
SELECT COUNT(stno) AS [count of student no], class
FROM Student
GROUP BY class
```

This produces a result set of five rows of counts by `class`:

```
count of student no class
------------------- ------
10                    NULL
11                    1
10                    2
7                     3
10                    4
```

(5 row(s) affected)

While you must have `class` or some other attribute in the GROUP BY, you do not have to have the `class` in the result set. Consider the following query, which generates the same numeric information as the previous query but does not report the `class` in the result:


```
SELECT COUNT(stno) AS [count of student no]
FROM Student
GROUP BY class
```


This produces the following five rows of output:


```
count of student no
-------------------
10
11
10
7
10
```

(5 row(s) affected)

This previous example may seem contradictory to the preceding discussion, but it is not. You must have all the nonaggregate columns from the result set in the GROUP BY, but you do not have to have the columns in the result set that you are grouping.

This last example may prove useful when a grouped result is needed in a filter. For example, how would you find the class with the least students? *Hint*: Remember that a query can be wrapped in parentheses and then used as a subquery—an inline view. One way to find the class with the least students would be to start like this:

```
SELECT MIN(x.c)
FROM
   (SELECT COUNT(stno) AS c
   FROM Student
   GROUP BY class) x
```

This would give:

```
-----------
7
```

```
(1 row(s) affected)
```

The next several sections will explore this and other ways to aggregate and use the result.

9.4.1 Aggregation and Grouping in SQL Server 2008

Microsoft® SQL Server® 2008 will not allow you to handle aggregation and grouping by nesting aggregates. For example, suppose you want to find the class with the smallest number of students. You might try the following query:

```
SELECT MIN(COUNT(stno))
FROM Student
GROUP BY class
```

Though it may seem logical, this query will not work in SQL Server 2008. It will give you the following error message:

```
Msg 130, Level 15, State 1, Line 1
Cannot perform an aggregate function on an expression
containing an aggregate or a subquery.
```

The MIN function is an aggregate function, and aggregate functions operate on rows within tables. In this case, the query is asking MIN to operate on a table of counted classes that have not yet been calculated. The point is that SQL Server 2008 does not handle this mismatch of aggregation and grouping.

This mismatch of aggregation and grouping can be handled by other SQL versions such as Oracle.

To work around this aggregation and grouping mismatch in SQL Server 2008, you can use derived structures such as temporary tables, inline views, or regular views (derived structures were covered in Chapter 6). Using either a temporary table or an inline view is the most logical way to solve this problem, and these two choices are described in the following sections.

9.4.1.1 Aggregation and Grouping Handled with a Global Temporary Table

This section shows how we can handle the mismatch of aggregation and grouping (described in the preceding section) using a global temporary table.

The following steps describe how to use a global temporary table to find the class with the smallest number of students:

1. Display the counts of classes, grouped by `class`:

   ```
   SELECT COUNT(stno) AS [count of students]
   FROM Student
   GROUP BY class
   ```

   This produces the following five rows of output:

   ```
   count of students
   -----------------
   10
   11
   10
   7
   10


   (5 row(s) affected)
   ```

2. To find the smallest number of students in a class, first count the students grouped by `class` and put this result in `##Temp1` (a global temporary table)—shown in the first of the following queries. Then find the smallest number of students in a class from the global temporary table, `##Temp1`, with "SELECT MIN(count) AS [MINIMUM COUNT] FROM ##Temp1," and use this information in a subquery with a HAVING clause as follows:

   ```
   SELECT (COUNT([stno] )) AS [count] INTO ##Temp1
   FROM Student
   GROUP BY [class]

   SELECT COUNT(stno) AS [count of stno], class
   FROM Student
   GROUP BY class
   HAVING COUNT(stno) =
   (SELECT MIN(count) AS [Minimum count]
   ```

FROM ##Temp1)

This produces the desired output (the class with the smallest number of students):

```
count of stno class
------------- ------
7             3
```

(1 row(s) affected)

Instead of the global temporary table, we could have used a view or an inline view. The inline view is shown next.

9.4.1.2   Aggregation and Grouping Handled with an Inline View

As described in Chapter 6, you can put a query in the FROM clause of a SELECT statement to create an inline view. An inline view exists only during the execution of a query.

The following steps describe how to use an inline view to find the class with the smallest number of students:

1. Count the stno in the FROM clause of the SELECT statement as follows:

```
SELECT 'Min of Count'= MIN(in_view.c)
FROM
   (SELECT c = COUNT(stno)
FROM Student
GROUP BY class) AS in_view
```

Because SQL Server 2008 cannot directly find aggregates of aggregates, in the preceding query we give a name to the count in the inline view, "c", to temporarily store the aggregate result in the inline view, "in_view". We then operate on the inline view as though it were a table and find the smallest value for c.

The preceding query produces the following output:

```
Min of Count
------------
7
```

(1 row(s) affected)

2. To find out which class has the least students, you can write the final query using the preceding query as a subquery with a HAVING clause in the outer part of the final query, as follows:

```
SELECT class, "Count of Class" = COUNT(*)
FROM Student
GROUP BY class
HAVING COUNT(*) =
(SELECT MIN(c)
FROM (SELECT COUNT(stno) AS [c]
FROM Student
GROUP BY class) AS in_view)
```

This produces the desired output:

```
class  Count of Class
------ --------------
3      7
```

```
(1 row(s) affected)
```

So, although SQL Server 2008 does not handle a mismatch of aggregation and HAVING, you can use your knowledge of temporary tables and inline views to work around the problem. This problem may also be solved using regular views. It is also noteworthy to see the process of query development in that some problems require using small queries and building from them to a final result.

Once again, Chapter 6 covers the advantages and disadvantages of using each of the derived structures.

9.5   Auditing in Subqueries

In this section, we consider a potential problem with using aggregation with subqueries. As with Cartesian products and joins, aggregation hides details and should always be audited. The two tables that follow will be used to illustrate this problem.

Table `GG` is similar to the `Grade_report` table and contains a student section identifier (`ssec`), grades (`gd`), and student names (`sname`):

GG

ssec	gd	sname
100	A	Brenda
110	B	Brenda
120	A	Brenda
200	A	Brenda
210	A	Brenda
220	B	Brenda
100	A	Richard
100	B	Doug
200	A	Richard
110	B	Morris

Tables GG and SS have not been created for you. You have to create them, insert the records shown, and then run the queries that follow. You could also create a similar table using "set rowcount 10" and executing an appropriate query on Grade_report.

Table SS is similar to the Section table and contains a section identifier (sec) and an instructor name (iname):

SS

sec	iname
100	Jones
110	Smith
120	Jones
200	Adams
210	Jones

Now suppose that you want to find out how many A's each instructor awarded. You might start with a join of the GG and SS tables. A normal equi-join would be as follows:

```
SELECT *
FROM GG, SS
WHERE GG.ssec = SS.sec
```

This would produce the following output (nine rows):

ssec	gd	sname	sec	iname
100	A	Brenda	100	Jones
100	A	Richard	100	Jones
100	B	Doug	100	Jones
110	B	Brenda	110	Smith
110	B	Morris	110	Smith
120	A	Brenda	120	Jones
200	A	Brenda	200	Adams
200	A	Richard	200	Adams
210	A	Brenda	210	Jones

(9 row(s) affected)

In addition, the following query tells you that there are six A's in the GG table:

```
SELECT COUNT(*) AS [Count of A's]
FROM GG
WHERE gd = 'A'
```

giving:

```
Count of As
------------
6
```

(1 row(s) affected)

Now, if you want to find out which instructors gave the A's, you would type this query:

```
SELECT SS.iname
FROM SS, GG
WHERE SS.sec = GG.ssec
  AND GG.gd = 'A'
```

You get the following six rows of output:

```
iname
----------------
Jones
Jones
Jones
Adams
```

```
Adams
Jones
```

(6 row(s) affected)

Now, to find how many A's each instructor gave, include a COUNT and GROUP BY as follows:

```
SELECT SS.iname AS [iname] , COUNT(*) AS [count]
FROM SS, GG
WHERE SS.sec = GG.ssec
 AND GG.gd = 'A'
GROUP BY SS.iname
```

This produces the following output:

```
iname              count
---------------    -----------
Adams              2
Jones              4
```

(2 row(s) affected)

This shows that instructor Adams gave two A's and instructor Jones gave four A's. So far, so good. You should note that the final count/grouping has the same number of A's as the original tables—the sum of the counts equals 6. Now, if you had devised a count query with a sub-SELECT, you could get an answer that looks correct but in fact is not. For example, consider the following subquery version of the preceding join query:

```
SELECT SS.iname AS [iname] , COUNT(*) AS [count]
FROM SS
WHERE SS.sec IN
  (SELECT GG.ssec
  FROM GG
  WHERE GG.gd = 'A')
GROUP BY SS.iname
```

This produces the following output:

```
iname              count
---------------    -----------
Adams              1
Jones              3
```

(2 row(s) affected)

The reason you get this output is that the second query is counting names of instructors and whether an A is present in the set of courses that this instructor teaches—not how many A's are in the set, just whether any exist. The previous join query gives you all the A's in the joined table and hence gives the correct answer to the question, "How many A's did each instructor award?" The sub-SELECTed query answers a different question: "In how many sections did the instructor award an A?"

The point in this example is that if you are using SELECT and COUNT, it is a very good idea to audit your results often. If you want to count the number of A's by instructor, begin by first counting how many A's there are. Then, you can construct a query to join and count. You should be able to total and reconcile the number of A's to the number of A's by instructor. The fact that the result makes sense is very useful in determining (albeit not proving) correctness.

9.6 Nulls Revisited

Nulls present a complication with regard to aggregate functions and other queries because nulls are never equal to, less than, greater than, or not equal to any value. Using aggregates by themselves on columns that contain nulls will ignore the null values. For example, suppose you have the following table called `Sal`:

```
name             salary
---------------  ----------
Joe              1000
Sam              2000
Bill             3000
Dave             NULL

(4 row(s) affected)
```

Table `Sal` has not been created for you. You will have to create it to run the queries that follow.

Now consider the following query:

```
SELECT COUNT(*) AS [?] , AVG(salary) AS [average] , SUM(salary) AS
[sum] , MAX(salary) AS [max] , MIN(salary) AS [min]
FROM Sal
```

This produces the following output:

```
count         average      sum          max          min
-----------   -----------  -----------  -----------  -----------
4             2000         6000         3000         1000
```
Warning: Null value is eliminated by an aggregate or other
SET operation.

(1 row(s) affected)

COUNT(*) counts all rows, but AVG, SUM, etc., ignore the nulled salary
rows in computing the aggregate. Counting columns indicates the presence
of nulls. If you count using the following query:

SELECT COUNT(name) AS [Count of Name]
FROM Sal

you will get:

```
Count of Name
-------------
4
```

(1 row(s) affected)

If you use the salary column:

SELECT COUNT(salary) AS [Count of salary]
FROM Sal

you get:

```
Count of salary
---------------
3
```
Warning: Null value is eliminated by an aggregate or
other SET operation.

(1 row(s) affected)

This indicates that you have a null salary. If you want to include nulls in
the aggregate, and have a rational value to substitute for a value that is
not known (a big assumption), you can use the ISNULL function.

The ISNULL function was introduced and discussed in Chapter 5.

ISNULL returns a value if the value is NULL. ISNULL has the form
"ISNULL(column name, value if null)," which is used in place of the column
name. For example, if you type the following:

```
SELECT name, ISNULL(salary, 0) AS [salary]
FROM Sal
```

you will get the following output:

```
name             salary
---------------- -----------
Joe              1000
Sam              2000
Bill             3000
Dave             0
```

(4 row(s) affected)

If you type the following:

```
SELECT COUNT(ISNULL(salary,0)) AS [Count of salary]
FROM Sal
```

you will get:

```
Count of salary
---------------
4
```

(1 row(s) affected)

The "Count of salary" is now 4, instead of the 3 that you received earlier when the ISNULL function was not used.

If you type the following:

```
SELECT AVG(ISNULL(salary, 0)) AS [Average of salary]
FROM Sal
```

you will get:

```
Average of salary
-----------------
1500
```

(1 row(s) affected)

The "Average of salary" is now 1500, instead of the 2000 that you had received earlier because the zero value for the null is used in the calculation. Changing the NULL values to a real value may be misleading when aggregates are used.

One final note on aggregation: What seems almost contradictory to these examples is that when grouping is added to a query, nulls in the grouped column are included in the result set. So, if the `Sal` table contained columns like this:

```
name              salary       job
--------------- ----------- ----------
Joe               1000         Programmer
Sam               2000         NULL
Bill              3000         Plumber
Dave              NULL         Programmer
```

```
(4 row(s) affected)
```

and if you ran a query like this:

```
SELECT SUM(salary) AS [Sum of salary], job
FROM Sal
GROUP BY job
```

you would get the following output:

```
Sum of salary job
------------- ----------
2000          NULL
3000          Plumber
1000          Programmer
Warning: Null value is eliminated by an aggregate or other
SET operation.
```

```
(3 row(s) affected)
```

The aggregate ignores values that are null, but grouping will compute a value for the nulled column value!

SUMMARY

In this chapter, we introduced the GROUP BY and HAVING clauses in SELECT statements. GROUP BY involves reporting aggregation within a column's values. HAVING is a final filter in a SELECT and is used to filter results that have been aggregated and grouped. We gave several examples of using grouped aggregate results to answer questions we had not considered before this chapter, e.g., "Which class has the smallest number of students?" We also discussed why it is always important to audit your queries and the results for correctness. Aggregation hides details (like nulls) and queries that have not been audited should always be viewed suspiciously.

Review Questions

1. What do aggregate functions do?
2. How does the GROUP BY clause work?
3. What is the difference between GROUP BY and ORDER BY?
4. What is the HAVING clause used for?
5. Can the WHERE clause always be considered a substitute for the HAVING clause? Why or why not?
6. Do functions of functions have to be handled in a special way in Server SQL 2008?
7. Will nulls in grouped columns be included in a result set?
8. How do aggregate functions treat nulls?
9. Does the sequence of the columns in a GROUP BY clause have an effect on the end result?
10. When would it not make sense to use the GROUP BY and DISTINCT clauses functions together?
11. Is GROUP BY affected by nulls?
12. Which comes first in a SELECT statement—ORDER BY or GROUP BY? Why?
13. The GROUP BY and _____ clauses are used together.

Chapter 9 Exercises

Unless specified otherwise, use the `Student_course` database to answer the following questions. Also, use appropriate column headings when displaying your output.

1. Display a list of courses (course names) that have prerequisites and the number of prerequisites for each course. Order the list by the number of prerequisites.
2. How many juniors (class = 3) are there in the **Student** table?
3. Group and count all MATH majors by class and display the count if there are two or more in a class. (Remember that class here refers to freshman, sophomore, and so on, and is recorded as 1, 2, and so on.)
4. Print the counts of A's, B's, and so on from the **Grade_report** table.

  a. Using temporary tables (local or global), print the lowest count of the grades (that is, if there were 20 A's, 25 B's, and 18 C's, you should print the lowest count of grades as C) from the Grade_report table.

  b. Using inline views, print the highest count of the grades (that is, if there were 20 A's, 25 B's, and 18 C's, you should print the highest count of grades as B) from the Grade_report table.

  c. Why would you not want to use views for this problem?

5. Print the counts of course numbers offered in descending order by count. Use the Section table only.

6. Create a table with names and number-of-children (NOC). Insert five or six rows into this table. Use COUNT, SUM, AVG, MIN, and MAX on the NOC attribute in one query and check that the numbers you get are what you expect.

7. Create a table of names, salaries, and job locations. Insert at least 10 rows into this table and no fewer than three job locations. (There will be several employees at each location.) Find the average salary for each job location with one SELECT.

8. Print an ordered list of instructors and the number of A's they assigned to students. Order the output by number of A's (lowest to highest). You can (and probably will) ignore instructors that assign no A's.

9. Create a table called Employees with a name, a salary, and a job title. Include exactly six rows. Make the salary null in one row, the job title null in another, and both the salary and the job title null in another. Use this data:

```
Name        Salary  Title
---------   ------  ----------
Mary        1000    Programmer
Brenda      3000
Stephanie           Artist
Alice
Lindsay     2000    Artist
Christina   500     Programmer
```

  a. Display the table.
  b. Display the count, sum, maximum, minimum, and average salary.
  c. Display the count, sum, maximum, minimum, and average salary, counting salary as 0 if no salary is listed.
  d. Display the average salary grouped by job title.
  e. Display the average salary grouped by job title when the null salary is counted as 0.

    f. Display the average salary grouped by job title when salary is counted as 0 if it is null and include a value when there is no job title.

10. Find the instructor and the section where the highest number of A's were awarded.

11. Find the COUNT of the number of students by `class` who are taking classes offered by the computer science (COSC) department. Perform the query in two ways: once using a condition in the WHERE clause and once filtering with a HAVING clause. (*Hint*: These queries need a five-table join.)

    Delete (DROP) all of your "scratch" tables (the ones you created just for this exercise—`Employees`, `NOC`, and any others you may have created).

chapter

10

Correlated Subqueries

Topics covered in this chapter

A *correlated subquery* is a subquery whose information is referenced by the main, outer query such that the inner query may be thought of as being executed repeatedly. In this chapter, we will look in detail at these correlated subqueries. We will discuss existence queries (EXISTS) and correlation as well as NOT EXISTS. We will also take a look at SQL's universal and existential qualifiers. Before discussing correlated subqueries in detail, however, we need to make sure that we understand what a noncorrelated subquery is.

10.1 Noncorrelated Subqueries

A *noncorrelated subquery* is a subquery that is independent of the outer query. In other words, the subquery could be executed on its own. The following is an example of a query that is *not* correlated:

```
SELECT s.sname
FROM Student s
WHERE s.stno IN
(SELECT gr.student_number
FROM Grade_report gr
WHERE gr.grade = 'A')
```

The first part of the preceding query (the first three lines) is the main, outer query, and the second part (the part in parentheses) is the subquery (also referred to as an *inner, nested,* or *embedded query*). To demonstrate that this subquery is an independent entity, you could run it by itself:

```
SELECT gr.student_number
FROM Grade_report gr
WHERE gr.grade = 'A'
```

This would produce the following output (17 rows):

```
student_number
--------------
2
3
8
8
10
14
20
34
49
123
125
126
127
129
129
142
142

(17 row(s) affected)
```

The preceding subquery is thought of as being evaluated first, creating the set of student numbers that have A's. Then, the subquery's result set is used to determine which rows in the main query will be SELECTed. For discussion purposes in this chapter, we will call this internal execution scenario the "uncorrelated execution pattern." The full query results in the following output (14 rows):

```
sname
--------------------
Lineas
Mary
Brenda
Richard
Lujack
Donald
Lynette
Susan
Holly
Sadie
Jessica
Steve
Cedric
Jerry

(14 row(s) affected)
```

10.2 Correlated Subqueries

As stated at the beginning of the chapter, a *correlated subquery* is a subquery whose information is referenced by the main, outer query such that the inner query may be thought of as being executed repeatedly.

Correlated subqueries present a different execution scenario to the data manipulation language (DML) than do ordinary, noncorrelated subqueries. The correlated subquery cannot stand alone, as it depends on the outer query; therefore, completing the subquery prior to execution of the outer query is not an option. The efficiency of the correlated subquery varies; it may be worthwhile to test the efficiency of correlated subqueries versus joins or sets.

One situation in which you cannot avoid correlation is the "for all" query, which is discussed later in this chapter.

To illustrate how a correlated subquery works, the following is an example of the noncorrelated subquery from the previous section revised as a correlated subquery:

```
SELECT s.sname
FROM Student s
WHERE s.stno IN
(SELECT gr.student_number
FROM Grade_report gr
WHERE gr.student_number = s.stno  − inner query tied to outer query
 AND gr.grade = 'A')
```

This produces the following output (14 rows), which is the same as the output of the noncorrelated subquery (shown earlier):

```
sname
--------------------
Lineas
Mary
Brenda
Richard
Lujack
Donald
Lynette
Susan
Holly
Sadie
Jessica
Steve
Cedric
Jerry

(14 row(s) affected)
```

In this example, the inner query (the part in parentheses) references the outer one—observe the use of **s.stno** in the WHERE clause of the inner query. Rather than thinking of this query as creating a set of student numbers that have A's, each row from the outer query can be considered to be SELECTed individually and tested against all rows of the inner query one at a time until it is determined whether or not a given student number is in the inner set and whether or not that student earned an A.

This query was illustrated with and without correlation. You might think that a correlated subquery is less efficient than doing a simple subquery because the simple subquery is done once, whereas the correlated subquery is done once for each outer row. However, the internal handling of how the query executes depends on the version of SQL and the optimizer for that database engine.

The correlated subquery acts like a nested DO loop in a programming language, where the first row from the **Student** table is SELECTed and tested against all the rows in the **Grade_report** table, and then the second **Student** row is SELECTed and tested against all rows in the **Grade_report** table. The following is the DO loop in pseudocode:

```
LOOP1: For each row in Student s DO
    LOOP2: For each row in Grade_report gr DO
        IF (gr.student_number = s.stno) THEN
            IF (gr.grade = 'B') THEN TRUE
    END LOOP2;
IF TRUE, THEN Student row is SELECTed
END LOOP1
```

For future reference, we will call this the "correlated execution pattern."

10.3 Existence Queries and Correlation

Correlated queries are most often written so that the question in the inner query is one of existence. For example, suppose you want to find the names of students who have taken a computer science (COSC) class and have earned a grade of B in that course. This query can be written in several ways. For example, you can write it as a noncorrelated subquery as follows:

```
SELECT s.sname
FROM Student s
WHERE s.stno IN
(SELECT gr.student_number
FROM Grade_report gr, Section
WHERE Section.section_id = gr.section_id
AND Section.course_num LIKE 'COSC%'
AND gr.grade = 'B')
```

This produces the following output (17 rows):

```
sname
--------------------
Lineas
Mary
Brenda
Lujack
Reva
Harley
Chris
```

```
Lynette
Hillary
Phoebe
Holly
George
Cramer
Fraiser
Francis
Lindsay
Stephanie
```

```
(17 row(s) affected)
```

You can think of this query as first forming the set of student numbers of students who have made B's in COSC courses—the inner query result set. In the inner query, you must have both the **Grade_report** table (for the grades) and the **Section** table (for the course numbers). Once you form this set of student numbers (by completing the inner query), the outer query looks through the **Student** table and SELECTs only those students who are in the inner query result set.

This query could also be done by creating a double-nested subquery containing two INs, or it could be written using a three-table join.

Had we chosen to write the query with an unnecessary correlation, it might look like this:

```
SELECT s.sname
FROM Student s
WHERE s.stno IN
(SELECT gr.student_number
FROM Grade_report gr, Section
WHERE Section.section_id = gr.section_id
AND Section.course_num LIKE 'COSC%'
AND gr.student_number = s.stno
AND gr.grade = 'B')
```

The output of this query would be the same as the previous one, but the way the query executes internally is different—it follows the correlated execution pattern described earlier. In this case, the use of the **Student** table in the subquery is unnecessary. Although correlation is unnecessary, this example is included to show the following:

- When correlation is necessary
- How to untangle unnecessarily correlated queries
- How you might migrate your thought process toward correlation, should it be necessary

Now we will look at situations in which the correlation of a subquery *is* necessary, and, in particular, introduce a new predicate: EXISTS.

10.3.1 Using EXISTS

In situations in which the correlation of a subquery *is* necessary, you can write the correlated subquery with the EXISTS predicate, which looks like this:

```
SELECT s.sname
FROM Student s
WHERE EXISTS
(SELECT 1 FROM Grade_report gr, Section
WHERE Section.section_id = gr.section_id
AND Section.course_num LIKE 'COSC%'
AND gr.student_number = s.stno
AND gr.grade = 'B')
```

The output of this query would be the same as the output (17 rows) of both of the previous queries.

Let's dissect this query. The EXISTS predicate says, "Choose the row from the **Student** table in the outer query if the subquery is true (that is, if a row in the subquery exists that satisfies the condition in the subquery WHERE clause)." Since no actual result set need be formed in the subquery, "SELECT 1" is used as a "dummy" result set to indicate that the subquery is true (1 is returned) or false (no rows are returned). In the noncorrelated case, we linked the student number in the **Student** table to the inner query by the IN predicate as follows:

```
SELECT s.stno
FROM Student s
WHERE s.stno IN
  (SELECT "student number ...)
```

When using the EXISTS predicate, we test the **student.stno** column in a different way—we are seeking whether the subquery's WHERE is satisfied. The subquery's WHERE contains the **s.stno** link.

We have indicated that we are using EXISTS with "(SELECT 1 ...)." Using the EXISTS predicate, the subquery does not form a result set per se, but rather causes EXISTS to return a 1 if successful or return nothing if unsuccessful. We will designate the successful subquery as true, and the unsuccessful one as false. The use of "SELECT *" in the inner query is common among SQL programmers. However, from an "internal" standpoint,

"SELECT *" causes the SQL engine to check the data dictionary unnecessarily. Since the actual result of the inner query is not important, it is strongly suggested that you use "SELECT 1" (or "SELECT 'X' ..." instead of "SELECT * ..." so that a constant is selected instead of some "sensible" entry. "SELECT 'X'" ... or "SELECT 1 ..." is simply more efficient.

The EXISTS predicate forces us to correlate the query. To illustrate that correlation is usually necessary with EXISTS, consider the following query:

```
SELECT s.sname
FROM Student s
WHERE EXISTS
(SELECT 'X' FROM Grade_report gr, Section t
 WHERE t.section_id = gr.section_id
AND t.course_num LIKE 'COSC%'
AND gr.grade = 'B')
```

This produces 48 rows of output (of which we show the first few rows):

```
sname
--------------------
Lineas
Mary
Zelda
Ken
Mario
Brenda
Romona
Richard
Kelly
Lujack
Reva
 .
 .
 .


(48 row(s) affected)
```

This query uses EXISTS but has no correlation. This syntax infers that for each student row, we test the joined **Grade_report** and **Section** tables to see whether there is a course number like COSC and a grade of B (which, of course, there is). We unnecessarily ask the subquery question over and over again. The result from this latter, uncorrelated EXISTS query is the same as the following:

```
SELECT s.sname
FROM Student s
```

The point is that the correlation is usually necessary when we use EXISTS.

Consider another example in which a correlation could be used. Suppose we want to find the names of all students who have three or more B's. A first pass at a query might be something like this:

```
SELECT s.sname
FROM Student s WHERE "something" IN
(SELECT "something"
FROM Grade_report
WHERE "count of grade = 'B'" > 2)
```

This query can be done with a HAVING clause, as we saw in Chapter 9, but we want to show how to do this in yet another way. Suppose we arrange the subquery to use the student number (stno) from the Student table as a filter and count in the subquery only when a row in the Grade_report table correlates to that student. The query (this time with an implied EXISTS) looks like this:

```
SELECT s.sname
FROM Student s
WHERE 2 < (SELECT COUNT(*)
    FROM Grade_report gr
    WHERE gr.student_number = s.stno
    AND gr.grade = 'B')
```

This results in the following output (eight rows):

```
sname
--------------------
Lineas
Mary
Lujack
Reva
Chris
Hillary
Phoebe
Holly

(8 row(s) affected)
```

Although there is no EXISTS in this query, it is implied. The syntax of the query does not allow an EXISTS, but the sense of the query is "WHERE

EXISTS a COUNT of 2 which is less than..." In this correlated subquery, we have to examine the Grade_report table for each member of the Student table to see whether or not the student has more than two B's. We test the entire Grade_report table for each student row in the outer query.

If it were possible, a subquery without the correlation would be more desirable because it would appear simpler to understand. The overall query might be as follows:

```
SELECT s.sname
FROM Student s
WHERE s.stno IN
(subquery that defines a set of students who have made 3 B's)
```

Therefore, we might attempt to write the following query:

```
SELECT s.sname
FROM Student s
WHERE s.stno IN
 (SELECT gr.student_number
  FROM Grade_report gr
  WHERE gr.grade = 'B')
```

However, as the following 27 rows of output illustrates (of which we show only the first few rows), this query would give us only students who earned at least one B:

```
sname
--------------------
Lineas
Mary
Zelda
Ken
Mario
Brenda
Kelly
Lujack
Reva
Harley
Chris
Lynette
 .
 .
 .

(27 row(s) affected)
```

To get a list of students who have earned at least three B's, we could try the following query:

```
SELECT s.sname
FROM Student s
WHERE s.stno IN
(SELECT gr.student_number, COUNT(*)
 FROM Grade_report gr
 WHERE gr.grade = 'B'
 GROUP BY gr.student_number
 HAVING COUNT(*) > 2)
```

However, this does not work, because the subquery cannot have two columns in its result set unless the main query has two columns in the WHERE .. IN.

Here, the subquery would have to have only `gr.student_number` to match `s.stno`. So, we might try to construct a double inline view, as shown in the following query:

```
SELECT s.sname
FROM Student s
WHERE s.stno IN
 (SELECT vi.student_number
  FROM
  (SELECT gr.student_number, ct = COUNT(*)
     FROM Grade_report gr
     WHERE gr.grade = 'B'
     GROUP BY gr.student_number
     HAVING COUNT(*) > 2) AS vi)
```

The inline view was discussed in Chapter 6. This query succeeds, producing the following output (eight rows):

```
sname
--------------------
Lineas
Mary
Lujack
Reva
Chris
Hillary
Phoebe
Holly

(8 row(s) affected)
```

This query also works in Oracle, but it may fail in other SQL versions.

As you can see, there are several ways to query the database with SQL. In this case, the correlated subquery may be the easiest to see and perhaps the most efficient.

10.3.2   From IN to EXISTS

A simple example of converting from IN to EXISTS—uncorrelated to correlated (or vice versa)—would be to move the set test in the WHERE .. IN of the uncorrelated subquery to the WHERE of the EXISTS in the correlated query.

As an example, consider the following uncorrelated subquery:

```
SELECT *
FROM Student s
WHERE s.stno IN
 (SELECT g.student_number
  FROM Grade_report g
  WHERE grade = 'B')
```

This query asks the question, "What students made a B in a course?" The following is the same query written as a correlated subquery:

```
SELECT *
FROM Student s
WHERE EXISTS
 (SELECT g.student_number
  FROM Grade_report g
  WHERE grade = 'B'
  AND s.stno = g.student_number)
```

This produces 27 rows of output (of which we show the first few rows):

STNO	SNAME	MAJOR	CLASS	BDATE
2	Lineas	ENGL	1	1990-04-15
3	Mary	COSC	4	1988-07-16
5	Zelda	COSC	NULL	1988-02-12
6	Ken	POLY	NULL	1990-07-15
7	Mario	MATH	NULL	1990-08-12
8	Brenda	COSC	2	1987-08-13
13	Kelly	MATH	4	1990-08-12
14	Lujack	COSC	1	1987-02-12
15	Reva	MATH	2	1990-06-10

```
19      Harley          POLY  2       1991-04-16
24      Chris           ACCT  4       1988-02-12
34      Lynette         POLY  1       1991-07-16
121     Hillary         COSC  1       1987-07-16
122     Phoebe          ENGL  3       1990-04-15
123     Holly           POLY  4       1991-01-15
.
.
.
```

(27 row(s) affected)

This example gives you a pattern to move from uncorrelated queries to correlated ones and to test the efficiency of both kinds of queries. Both of the preceding queries produce the same output.

Let us look at this process in reverse-correlated to uncorrelated. Suppose you wanted to know the capacity of rooms to which Professor Chang is assigned. You might start by looking at the Section table like this:

```
SELECT *
FROM Section
WHERE Instructor LIKE 'CHA%'
```

This would give:

```
SECTION_ID COURSE_NUM SEMESTER YEAR INSTRUCTOR BLDG   ROOM
---------- ---------- -------- ---- ---------- ------ ------
107        MATH2333   SPRING   10   CHANG      36     123
109        MATH5501   FALL     09   CHANG      36     123
112        MATH2410   FALL     09   CHANG      36     123
```

(3 row(s) affected)

Then you realize that you need to connect the Section table to the Room table, and you decide to connect the two tables with a correlated query like this:

```
SELECT r.Capacity
FROM Room r
WHERE EXISTS
  (SELECT 1
   FROM Section s
   WHERE r.Room = s.Room
   AND s.Instructor LIKE 'CHA%')
```

Now as you look at this correlated subquery, you notice that you can un-correlate it by moving the correlation (where the outer query, Room r, is in the subquery) to an IN clause and arrive at this version:

```
SELECT r.Capacity
FROM Room r
WHERE r.Room IN
   (SELECT s.Room
    FROM Section s
    WHERE s.Instructor LIKE 'CHA%')
```

The result of both the correlated and uncorrelated versions would be:

```
Capacity
--------
35

(1 row(s) affected)
```

As you look at queries and the variations on them, you can ask yourself which is easier to modify or easier to understand. These are subjective measures. An objective measure would be, "Which of these is more efficient?" The answer depends on the SQL engine and table size. For the tables in the sample database, you will likely see no difference in efficiency. For other databases with larger tables and production queries, you should always try variations on queries to see which works best.

10.3.3 Using NOT EXISTS

As with the IN predicate, which has a NOT .. IN complement, EXISTS may also be used with NOT. In some situations, the predicates EXISTS and NOT EXISTS are vital. For example, if we ask a "for all" question, it must be answered by "existence" (actually, the lack thereof [that is, "not existence"]). In logic, the statement, "find x for all y" is logically equivalent to "do not find x where there does not exist a y." Or, there is no x for no y. Or, you cannot find an x when there is no y.

In SQL, there is no "for all" predicate. Instead, SQL uses the idea of "for all" logic with NOT EXISTS. (A word of caution, however—SQL is not simply a logic exercise, as we will see.) In this section, we look at how EXISTS and NOT EXISTS work in SQL. In the following section, "SQL Universal and Existential Qualifiers," we will address the "for all" problem.

Consider the following query:

```
SELECT s.sname
FROM Student s
WHERE EXISTS
   (SELECT 'X'
    FROM Grade_report gr
    WHERE s.stno = gr.student_number
    AND gr.grade = 'C')
```

This produces the following output (of which we show the first 10 rows):

```
sname
--------------------
Zelda
Ken
Mario
Brenda
Richard
Reva
Donald
Jake
Susan
Monica
  .
  .
  .


(24 row(s) affected)
```

The question asked here is, "Find students who made a C in some course." These 24 students have a C somewhere. For this correlated subquery, "student names" are selected in the outer query when:

■ The student is enrolled in a section ("WHERE s.stno = gr.student_number"), and
■ The same student has a grade of C (note the correlation in the WHERE clause in the inner query)

Both conditions in the subquery must be true for the student row to be selected in the outer query. When viewed from the outer query, a student is selected if the inner query is true. True means something is returned; false means nothing is returned from the subquery. Therefore, SELECT ..

EXISTS "says" SELECT .. WHERE true. The inner query is true if any row is selected in the inner query.

Now suppose we change the question a little and ask, "What students have not made a C in any course?" This question is answered in a fashion similar to the preceding query but with a NOT EXISTS in it instead of EXISTS:

```
SELECT s.sname
FROM Student s
WHERE NOT EXISTS
   (SELECT 'X'
    FROM Grade_report gr
    WHERE s.stno = gr.student_number
    AND gr.grade = 'C')
```

This produces the following 24 rows of output (of which we show the first few):

```
sname
--------------------
Lineas
Mary
Romona
Kelly
Lujack
Elainie
Harley
Chris
Lynette
Smith
  .
  .
  .

(24 row(s) affected)
```

In this query, we are still selecting with the pattern SELECT .. WHERE true because all SELECTs with EXISTS work that way. But the twist is that the subquery has to be false to be selected with NOT EXISTS. If the subquery is false, then NOT EXISTS is true and the outer row is selected.

Now, logic implies that if either s.stno <> gr.student_number or gr.grade <> 'C', then the subquery "fails"—that is, it is false for that student row. Since the subquery is false, the NOT EXISTS would return a true for that row. Unfortunately, this logic is not quite what happens. Recall that we characterized the correlated subquery (the correlated execution pattern) as follows:

```
LOOP1: For each row in Student s DO
    LOOP2: For each row in Grade_report DO
        IF (gr.student_number = s.stno) THEN
            IF (gr.grade = 'C') THEN TRUE
    END LOOP2;
IF TRUE, THEN student row is SELECTed
END LOOP1
```

Note that LOOP2 is completed before the next student is tested. In other words, just because a student number exists that is not equal, it will not cause the subquery to be false. Rather, the entire subquery table is parsed and the logic is more like this:

For a row in the outer table, ".. WHERE EXISTS s.stno = gr.student_number ... ," is there a "gr.grade = 'C'"? If, when the student numbers are equal, no C can be found, then the subquery returns no rows—it is false for that student row. So, with NOT EXISTS, we will select students who have student numbers equal in the **Grade_report** and **Student** tables but have no C in the **Grade_report** table. The point about "no C in the **Grade_report** table" can only be answered true by looking at all the rows in the inner query and finding no C for that student.

There is one more important point to be made here. The query discussed here is "Find students who have no C's in any course." You might be tempted to answer the question with a join like this:

```
SELECT *
FROM Student s, Grade_report g
WHERE s.stno = g.student_number
AND g.grade <> 'C'
```

This join query answers a different question. The query for the join is "Find students who have made grades other than C." In the former case ("Find students who have no C's") you are looking for students who have no C in their set of grades. In the latter case, you will find students who have made grades other than C, but they could have made C's as well.

The output of the preceding query would be:

STNO	SNAME	MAJOR	CLASS	BDATE	STUDENT_NUMBER	SECTION_ID	GRADE
2	Lineas	ENGL	1	1990-04-15	2	85	D
2	Lineas	ENGL	1	1990-04-15	2	102	B
2	Lineas	ENGL	1	1990-04-15	2	126	B
2	Lineas	ENGL	1	1990-04-15	2	127	A
2	Lineas	ENGL	1	1990-04-15	2	145	B

```
3        Mary             COSC  4      1988-07-16 3         85        A
3        Mary             COSC  4      1988-07-16 3         87        B
3        Mary             COSC  4      1988-07-16 3         90        B
3        Mary             COSC  4      1988-07-16 3         91        B
3        Mary             COSC  4      1988-07-16 3         92        B
3        Mary             COSC  4      1988-07-16 3         96        B
5        Zelda            COSC  NULL   1988-02-12 5         95        B
6        Ken              POLY  NULL   1990-07-15 6         95        B
7        Mario            MATH  NULL   1990-08-12 7         95        B
8        Brenda           COSC  2      1987-08-13 8         85        A
 .
 .
 .
(78 row(s) affected)
```

10.4   SQL Universal and Existential Qualifiers

In SQL, "for all" and "for each" are the universal qualifiers, whereas "there exists" is the existential qualifier. As mentioned in the preceding section, SQL does not have a "for all" predicate; however, logically, the following relationship exists:

For all x, WHERE $P(x)$ is true

is logically the same as:

There does not exist an x, WHERE $P(x)$ is not true.

A "for all" type of SQL query is less straightforward than the other queries we have used because it involves a double-nested, correlated subquery using the NOT EXISTS predicate. Take a look at the following example.

Example 10.1

To show a "for all" type of SQL query, we will use the **Languages** table in our **Student_course** database. This table has names of students who have multiple foreign-language capabilities. We begin by looking at the table by typing the following query:

```
SELECT *
FROM Languages
ORDER BY name
```

This produces the following output (18 rows):

```
NAME        LANGU
---------   -------
BRENDA      FRENCH
BRENDA      CHINESE
BRENDA      SPANISH
```

```
JOE        CHINESE
KENT       CHINESE
LUJACK     SPANISH
LUJACK     FRENCH
LUJACK     GERMAN
LUJACK     CHINESE
MARY JO    GERMAN
MARY JO    CHINESE
MARY JO    FRENCH
MELANIE    CHINESE
MELANIE    FRENCH
RICHARD    CHINESE
RICHARD    GERMAN
RICHARD    FRENCH
RICHARD    SPANISH
```

(18 row(s) affected)

Suppose we want to find out which languages are spoken by all students (for which we would ask the question, "For each language, does it occur with all students?"). Although this manual exercise would be very difficult for a large table, for our practice table we can answer the question by displaying and manually examining the table ordered by language.

To see how to use SQL to answer a question of the type, "Which languages are spoken by all students?" we will present a query and then show how it works. Following is the query to answer our question:


```
SELECT name, langu
FROM Languages x
WHERE NOT EXISTS
   (SELECT 'X'
    FROM Languages y
    WHERE NOT EXISTS
      (SELECT 'X'
       FROM Languages z
       WHERE x.langu = z.langu
       AND y.name = z.name))
```


As you will see, all the for all/for each questions follow this double-nested, correlated NOT EXISTS pattern.

This produces the following output (seven rows):

```
name       langu
---------- -------
BRENDA     CHINESE
RICHARD    CHINESE
LUJACK     CHINESE
MARY JO    CHINESE
MELANIE    CHINESE
JOE        CHINESE
KENT       CHINESE

(7 row(s) affected)
```

The Way This Query Works

To select a language spoken by all students, the query proceeds as follows:

1. Select a row in **Languages** x (outer query).
2. For that row, begin selecting each row again in **Languages y** (middle query).
3. For each of the middle query rows, we want the inner query (**Languages z**) to be true for all cases of the middle query (remember that true is translated to false by NOT EXISTS). As each inner query is satisfied (it is true), it forces the middle query to continue looking for a match—to look at all cases and eventually conclude false (evaluate to false overall). If the middle query is false, the outer query sees true because of its NOT EXISTS.

To make the middle query (y) find false, all the inner query (z) occurrences must be true (that is, the languages from the outer query must exist with all names from the middle one [y] in the inner one [z]). For an eventual "match," every row in the middle query for an outer query row must be false (that is, every row in the inner query is true).

These steps are explained in further detail in the next example, in which we use a smaller table so that the explanation is easier to understand.

Example 10.2   Suppose we have the following simpler table, **Languages1**, when attempting to answer the question "Which languages are spoken by all students?":

Languages1:

```
name                    language
-------------------     --------------------
Joe                     Hindi
Mary                    Hindi
Mary                    French
```

The Languages1 table does not exist. You will have to create it. Keep the column names and types similar to the Languages table.

This query is similar to the one used in Example 1:

```
SELECT name, language
FROM Languages1 x
WHERE NOT EXISTS
  (SELECT 'X'
   FROM Languages1 y
   WHERE NOT EXISTS
   (SELECT 'X'
    FROM Languages1 z
    WHERE x.language = z.language
    AND y.name = z.name))
ORDER BY language
```

It produces the following output:

```
name                    language
-------------------     --------------------
Joe                     Hindi
Mary                    Hindi
```

```
(2 row(s) affected)
```

The Way This Query Works

The following is a step-by-step explanation of how this query would work in the Languages1 table:

1. The row <Joe, Hindi> is selected by the outer query (x).
2. The row <Joe, Hindi> is selected by the middle query (y).
3. The row <Joe, Hindi> is selected by the inner query (z).

4. The inner query is true:

```
X.LANGUAGE = Hindi
Z.LANGUAGE = Hindi
Y.NAME = Joe
Z.NAME = Joe
```

5. Because the inner query returns a row (is true), the NOT EXISTS of the middle query translates this to false and continues with the next row in the middle query. The middle query selects <Mary, Hindi> and the inner query begins again with <Joe, Hindi> seeing:

```
X.LANGUAGE = Hindi
Z.LANGUAGE = Hindi
Y.NAME = Mary
Z.NAME = Joe
```

This is false, so the inner query selects a second row, <Mary, Hindi>:

```
X.LANGUAGE = Hindi
Z.LANGUAGE = Hindi
Y.NAME = Mary
Z.NAME = Mary
```

This is true, so the inner query is true. (Notice that **X.LANGUAGE** has not changed yet; the outer query [**X**] is still on the first row.)

6. Because the inner query returns a row (is true), the NOT EXISTS of the middle query translates this to false and continues with the next row in the middle query.

The middle query now selects <Mary, French>, and the inner query begins again with <Joe, Hindi> seeing:

```
X.LANGUAGE = Hindi
Z.LANGUAGE = Hindi
Y.NAME = Mary
Z.NAME = Joe
```

This is false, so the inner query SELECTs a second row, <Mary, Hindi>:

```
X.LANGUAGE = Hindi
Z.LANGUAGE = Hindi
Y.NAME = Mary
Z.NAME = Mary
```

This is true, so the inner query is true.

7. Because the inner query is true, the NOT EXISTS of the middle query again converts this true to false and wants to continue, but the middle query is out of rows. This means that the middle query is false.

8. Because the middle query is false, and since we are testing:

```
"SELECT distinct name, language
FROM Languages1 x
WHERE NOT EXISTS
   (SELECT 'X' FROM Languages1 y ...",
```

the false from the middle query is translated to true for the outer query and the row <Joe, Hindi> is selected for the result set. Note that "Hindi" occurs with both "Joe" and "Mary."

9. The second row in the outer query will repeat the steps from above for <Mary, Hindi>. The value "Hindi" will be seen to occur with both "Joe" and "Mary" as <Mary, Hindi> is added to the result set.

10. The third row in the outer query begins with <Mary, French>. The middle query selects <Joe, Hindi> and the inner query selects <Joe, Hindi>. The inner query sees the following:

```
X.LANGUAGE = French
Z.LANGUAGE = Hindi
Y.NAME = Joe
Z.NAME = Mary
```

This is false, so the inner query selects a second row, <Mary, Hindi>:

```
X.LANGUAGE = French
Z.LANGUAGE = Hindi
Y.NAME = Joe
Z.NAME = Mary
```

This is false, so the inner query selects a third row, <Mary, French>:

```
X.LANGUAGE = French
Z.LANGUAGE = French
Y.NAME = Joe
Z.NAME = Mary
```

This is also false. The inner query returns no rows (fails). The inner query evaluates to false, which causes the middle query to return rows (it "sees" true) because of the NOT EXISTS. Since the middle query sees true, it is finished and evaluated to true. Since the middle query evaluates to true, the NOT EXISTS in the outer query changes this to false and `X.LANGUAGE = French` fails because `X.LANGUAGE = French` did not occur with all the values of **name**.

Consider again the "for all" query presented in this example:

```
SELECT name, language
FROM Languages1 x
WHERE NOT EXISTS
  (SELECT 'X'
   FROM Languages1 y
   WHERE NOT EXISTS
   (SELECT 'X'
    FROM Languages1 z
    WHERE x.language = z.language
    AND y.name = z.name))
ORDER BY language
```

The clue as to what a query of this kind means can be found in the inner query where the outer query is tested. In the phrase that says "WHERE x.language = z. language," "x.language" is where the query is testing which *language* occurs *for all* names.

This query is a SQL realization of a relational division exercise. Relational division is a "for all" operation just like that which we have illustrated here. In relational algebra, the query must be set up into a divisor, dividend, and quotient in this pattern:

$$\text{quotient } (B) \longleftarrow \text{dividend } (A, B) \text{ divided by divisor } (A).$$

If the question is "What language for *all* names?" then the divisor, A, is names, and the quotient, B, is language. It is most prudent to set up SQL like relational algebra with a two-column table (like **Languages** or **Languages1**) for the dividend and then treat the divisor and the quotient appropriately. Our query will have the column for language, **x.language**, in the inner query, as **language** will be the quotient. We have chosen to also report **name** in the result set.

Example 10.3   Note that the preceding query is completely different from the following query, which asks, "Which *students* speak all languages?":

```
SELECT DISTINCT name, language
FROM Languages1 x
```

```
WHERE NOT EXISTS
  (SELECT 'X'
   FROM Languages1 y
   WHERE NOT EXISTS
   (SELECT 'X'
    FROM   Languages1 z
    WHERE y.language = z.language
    AND x.name = z.name))
ORDER BY language
```

This produces the following output:

```
name                  language
--------------------  --------------------
Mary                  French
Mary                  Hindi
```

(2 row(s) affected)

Note that the inner query contains "x.name," which means the question was "Which names occur for *all* languages?" or, put another way, "Which students speak all languages?" The "all" goes with languages for "x.name."

SUMMARY

In this chapter we discussed the correlated subquery, noncorrelated subquery, EXISTS, and NOT EXISTS. We have described situations where the correlation of a subquery is necessary and can be written with the EXISTS predicate. The EXISTS predicate can usually be used as another way to answer common questions that can also use joins, sets, and IN subqueries. We showed how to "translate" subqueries with IN to those with EXISTS and vice versa. The EXISTS predicate uses a true/false return set, and hence the query that follows EXISTS is written with a constant in the result set "... WHERE EXISTS (SELECT 1 or SELECT 'X' ...)."

NOT EXISTS is truly special as it allows us to ask "for all" questions. "For all" questions cannot be done another way in SQL; there is no "for all" predicate. While the logic for the "for all" query may seem difficult to follow, the good news is that if a "for all" question is posed properly, one can follow the pattern presented here to answer relational division questions (which x occurs for all y's).

Review Questions

1. What is a noncorrelated subquery?
2. Which type of subquery can be executed on its own?
3. Which part of a query is evaluated first, the query or the subquery?
4. What are correlated subqueries?
5. What does the EXISTS predicate do?
6. What are considered universal qualifiers?
7. Is correlation necessary when we use EXISTS? Why or why not?
8. Explain how the "for all" type of SQL query involves a double-nested correlated subquery using the NOT EXISTS predicate.

Chapter 10 Exercises

Unless specified otherwise, use the `Student_course` database to answer the following questions. Also, use appropriate column headings when displaying your output.

1. List the names of students who have received C's. Do this in three ways: (a) as a join, (b) as a noncorrelated subquery, and (c) as a correlated subquery. Show your results and account for any differences.
2. In the section "Existence Queries and Correlation," you were asked to find the names of students who have taken a computer science class and earned a grade of B. We noted that it could be done in several ways. One query could look like this:

```
SELECT s.sname
FROM Student s
WHERE s.stno IN
   (SELECT gr.student_number
    FROM Grade_report gr, Section
    WHERE Section.section_id = gr.section_id
    AND Section.course_num LIKE 'COSC____'
    AND gr.grade = 'B')
```

Redo this query, putting the finding of the COSC course in a correlated subquery. The query should be as follows: The **Student** table noncorrelated subquery to the **Grade_report** table, correlated EXISTS to the **Section** table.

3. In the section "SQL Universal and Existential Qualifiers," we illustrated both.

An existence query:

```
SELECT s.sname
FROM Student s
WHERE EXISTS
  (SELECT 'X'
   FROM Grade_report gr
   WHERE Student.stno = gr.student_number
   AND gr.grade = 'C')
```

and a NOT EXISTS version:

```
SELECT s.sname
FROM Student s
WHERE NOT EXISTS
  (SELECT 'X'
   FROM Grade_report gr
   WHERE Student.stno = gr.student_number
   AND gr.grade = 'C')
```

Show that the EXISTS version is the complement of the NOT EXISTS version—count the rows in the EXISTS result, the rows in the NOT EXISTS result, and the rows in the Student table. Also, devise a query to give the same result with IN and NOT .. IN.

4. a. Discover whether or not all students take courses by counting the students, and then count those students whose student numbers are in the Grade_report table and those whose student numbers are not in the table. Use IN and then NOT .. IN, and then use EXISTS and NOT EXISTS. How many students take courses and how many students do not?

   b. Find out which students have taken courses but have not taken COSC courses. Create a set of student names and courses from the Student, Grade_report, and Section tables (use the prefix COSC to indicate computer science courses). Then, use NOT .. IN to "subtract" from that set another set of names of students (who take courses) who have taken COSC courses. For this set difference, use NOT .. IN.

   c. Change NOT .. IN to NOT EXISTS (with other appropriate changes) and explain the result. The "other appropriate changes" include adding the correlation and the change of the result column in the subquery set.

5. There exists a table called Plants in the Student_course database. Find out what company or companies have plants in all cities.

6. a. Run the following query and print the result:

```
SELECT distinct name, langu
FROM Languages x
WHERE NOT EXISTS
  (SELECT 'X'
   FROM Languages y
   WHERE NOT EXISTS
     (SELECT 'X'
      FROM Languages z
      WHERE x.langu =z.langu
      AND y.name=z.name))
```

Save the query (e.g., save for all).

b. Recreate the `Languages` table under a new name (e.g., call it some other name, such as `LANG1`). To do this, first create the table and then use the INSERT statement with the subselect option "(INSERT INTO LANG1 AS SELECT * FROM Languages)."

c. Add a new person to your table who speaks only BENG.

d. Recall your SELECT from 6a. Change the table from `Languages` to `LANG1` and rerun the query.

e. How is this result different from the situation in which the new person was not in `LANG1`? Provide an explanation of why the query did what it did.

7. The `Department_to_major` table has a list of four-letter department codes with the department names. In Chapter 8, Exercise 7 (hereafter referred to as Exercise 8-7), you created a table called `Secretary`, which should now have data like this:

```
Secretary
dCode       name
-------     --------
ACCT        Beryl
COSC        Kaitlyn
ENGL        David
HIST        Christina
BENGALI     Fred
HINDI       Chloe
Null        Brenda
```

In Exercise 8-7, you did the following:

a. Create a query that lists the names of departments that have secretaries (use IN and the `Secretary` table in a subquery with the `Department_to_major` table in the outer query). Save this query as *q8_7a.*

b. Create a query that lists the names of departments (using the `Department_to_major` table) that do not have secretaries (use NOT .. IN). Save this query as *q8_7b*.

c. Add one more row to the `Secretary` table that contains "<null,'Brenda'>" (which you could do, for example, in a situation in which you have hired Brenda but have not yet assigned her to a department).

d. Recall *q8_7a* and rerun it. Recall *q8_7b* and rerun it.

We remarked in Exercise 8-7 that the NOT .. IN predicate has problems with nulls; The behavior of NOT .. IN when nulls exist may surprise you. If nulls may exist in the subquery, then NOT .. IN should not be used. If you use NOT .. IN in a subquery, you must ensure that nulls will not occur in the subquery or you must use some other predicate, such as NOT EXISTS. Perhaps the best advice is to avoid NOT .. IN.

Here, we repeat Exercise 8-7 using NOT EXISTS:

a. Reword query *q8_7a* to use EXISTS. You will have to correlate the inner and outer queries. Save this query as *q10_7aa*.

b. Reword query *q8_7b* to use NOT EXISTS. You will have to correlate the inner and outer queries. Save this query as *q10_7bb*. You should *not* have the phrase "IS NOT NULL" in your NOT EXISTS query.

Note the difference in behavior versus the original question. List the names of those departments that have and do not have secretaries. The point here is to encourage you to use NOT EXISTS in a correlated subquery rather than NOT .. IN.

Indexes and Constraints on Tables

Topics covered in this chapter

In previous chapters, we concentrated primarily on retrieving information from existing tables. This chapter revisits the creation of tables, but now focuses on how indexes and constraints can be added to tables to make the tables more efficient and to increase the integrity of the data in the tables (and hence in the database). Referential integrity constraints are also discussed.

Microsoft® SQL Server® 2008 does *not* need indexes to successfully retrieve results for a SELECT statement. But an *index* may speed up queries and searches on the indexed columns and may facilitate sorting and grouping operations. As tables get larger, the value of using proper indexes becomes much more of an issue. Indexes can be used to quickly find data that satisfies conditions in a WHERE clause, find matching rows in a JOIN clause, or efficiently maintain *uniqueness* of the key columns during inserts and updates.

Constraints are a powerful way to increase the data integrity in a database. Integrity implies believability and correctness. Any data that destroys the sense of correctness of data is said to lack integrity. For example, a constraint is used to establish relationships with other tables. A violation of integrity would be if a nonexistent referenced row were included in the relationship. The CONSTRAINT clause can be used with the CREATE TABLE or the ALTER TABLE statements to create or delete constraints, respectively.

11.1 The "Simple" CREATE TABLE

We presented a "simple" CREATE TABLE statement in earlier chapters. To refresh your memory, here is an example:

```
CREATE TABLE Test1
  (name VARCHAR(20),
   ssn CHAR(9),
   dept_number INT,
   acct_balance SMALLMONEY)
```

The following are the elements of this CREATE TABLE command:

- We created a table called `Test1`.
- "name" is a variable-length character string with a maximum length of 20.
- "ssn" (social security number) is a fixed-length character string of length 9.
- "dept_number" is an integer (which in SQL Server 2008 simply means no decimals allowed).
- "acct_balance" is a currency column.

Beyond choosing data types for columns in tables, you may need to make other choices to create an effective database. You can create indexes on tables, which then can be used to aid in the enforcement of certain validation rules. You also can use other "add-ons" called constraints, which make you enter *good* data and hence maintain the integrity of a database. In the following sections, we will explore indexes and then constraints.

Indexes cannot be created on all column types in SQL Server 2008. For example, you cannot create an index on a column that contains the TEXT, NTEXT, or IMAGE data types.

11.2 Indexes

SQL Server 2008 allows you to create several indexes on one table. In SQL Server 2008, it is the job of the query optimizer to determine which indexes will be the most useful in processing a specific query. While indexes may enhance queries in large tables, indexes will slow update operations (insert, delete, update) because every update causes a rebuild of the index. We will begin by introducing the "simple" CREATE INDEX statement.

Discussing the query optimizer is beyond the scope of this book.

11.2.1 The "Simple" CREATE INDEX

What is an index? Suppose we have a large table (say, one million rows) defined like this:

```
Inventory (product_number, description, color, quantity_on_hand,
quantity_on_order)
```

This table is organized with product_number as the primary key, but it is a large table. Every primary key has an index called a "primary index." So, if you want to find product number 357679, the database engine only has to look at the primary index to know where that row is located.

Now suppose that we routinely want to ask our database a question like, "How many red widgets do we have on hand?" Finding "red widgets" will involve looking at every row to find "widgets" and "red." We can create "secondary indexes" on description and color so that if we want to find objects in the database by description or color, the database can look up the rows for description = "widget" and color = "red" and answer questions like, "How many red widgets do we have on hand?" without looking at each and every row. Indexes are query efficiency aids used primarily on large tables that are often queried the same way.

The CREATE INDEX statement is used to create a new index on some column in an existing table. The following is the general syntax for the CREATE INDEX statement:

CREATE INDEX index_name
ON Tablename (column [ASC | DESC])

For example, if we wanted to create an index called ssn_ndx on the ssn column in descending order of ssn for the Test1 table, we would enter the following:

CREATE INDEX ssn_ndx
ON Test1 (ssn DESC)

Although the user has the option of setting the column in ascending (ASC) or descending (DESC) order, the index will be created in ascending order if DESC is not included, because ASC is the default order in indexes.

11.2.2 Viewing and Modifying Indexes

To view the index that you just created, ssn_ndx, click on the + sign beside the newly created table, Test1, and then click on the + sign beside the **Indexes** node, as shown in Figure 11.1.

Figure 11.1 Viewing the index

Now, to see if this index, `ssn_ndx`, is in ascending or descending order, right-click on the index and select **Properties**, as shown in Figure 11.2, and you will see Figure 11.3. Figure 11.3 shows that this index is in descending order and is indexed by the `ssn` column.

Figure 11.2   Accessing the properties of an index

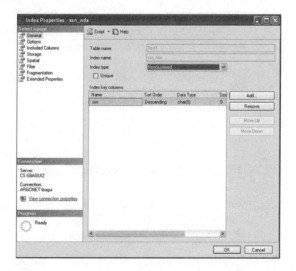

Figure 11.3   Viewing the properties of an index

In the dialog box shown in Figure 11.3, we can click **Add** to add more columns to the index key; and we can select the key and then click **Remove** to remove columns from the index key.

To prevent duplicate values in indexed columns, you must use the UNIQUE option in the CREATE INDEX statement, as follows:

```
CREATE UNIQUE INDEX ssn_ndx1
ON Test1 (ssn DESC)
```

This query will create the unique index, **ssn_ndx1**, as shown in Figure 11.4.

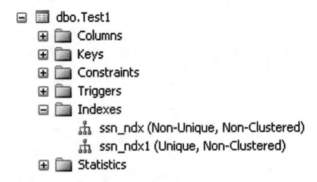

Figure 11.4   Viewing the unique index

The UNIQUE option can be used on columns that will not be a primary key in a table. A primary key is a key or field that uniquely identifies a row in a table.

The UNIQUE option will disallow duplicate entries for a column even though the column is not a primary key in a table. NULLs are allowed in nonprimary key indexes.

11.2.3   Deleting Indexes

You can use a DROP INDEX statement to delete an index in SQL. The general format of the DROP INDEX statement is as follows:

```
DROP INDEX Table_name.index_name
```

For example, to delete the index, **ssn_ndx1** created on **Test1**, you would type the following:

```
DROP INDEX Test1.ssn_ndx1
```

Unused indexes slow data modification without helping retrieval. So, if you have indexes that are not being used, you should delete (drop) them. All indexes are automatically deleted (dropped) if the table is deleted.

11.3 Constraints

As with indexes, constraints can be added to tables or included in the CRE-ATE TABLE command. As explained previously, constraints are added to give tables more integrity. In this section, we discuss some of the constraints available in SQL Server 2008: the NOT NULL, PRIMARY KEY, UNIQUE, and CHECK constraints, as well as a few referential constraints.

11.3.1 The NOT NULL Constraint

The NOT NULL constraint is an integrity constraint that allows the database creator to deny the creation of a row where a column would have a null value. Usually, a null signifies a missing data item. As discussed in previous chapters, nulls in databases present an interpretation problem—do they mean not applicable, not available, unknown, or what? If a situation in which a null is present could affect the integrity of the database, then the table creator can deny anyone the ability to insert nulls into the table for that column. To deny nulls, we can create a table with the NOT NULL constraint on a column(s) after the data type. The following example shows how to include the NOT NULL constraint using a CREATE TABLE statement:

```
CREATE TABLE Test2
(name VARCHAR(20),
 ssn CHAR(9),
 dept_number INT NOT NULL,
 acct_balance SMALLMONEY)
```

In this newly created table, `Test2`, the `dept_number` column now has a NOT NULL constraint included (the ALLOW NULLS option is not checked, as shown in the table design in Figure 11.5):

CS-SBAGUI2.St...se - dbo.Test2		
Column Name	Data Type	Allow Nulls
name	varchar(20)	☑
ssn	char(9)	☑
dept_number	int	☐
acct_balance	smallmoney	☑

Figure 11.5 Table design of `Test2`

The NOT NULL constraint can also be added to the column after the table has been created. You can check the ALLOW NULLS option of the `dept_number` column in Figure 11.5, or you can use SQL to do this.

If simply checking an option allows you to change field definitions, why do we show you how to use SQL? In other versions of SQL, there may not be a graphical user interface as easy to use as SQL Server Management Studio. Command-line SQL is the norm in most database systems and knowledge of how to use SQL and ALTER TABLE is essential to efficiently using these systems. To do this in SQL, you will have to use the ALTER TABLE command.

We will illustrate this using the `Test2` table that we just created.

Say, for example, that we want to add a NOT NULL constraint (using SQL) after the table has been created. We can use the ALTER COLUMN option within the ALTER TABLE statement, as shown in the following general syntax:

```
ALTER TABLE Tablename
ALTER COLUMN column_name column_type(size) NOT NULL
```

So, to set the `dept_number` column in `Test2` to NOT NULL, we would type the following:

```
ALTER TABLE Test2
ALTER COLUMN dept_number INTEGER NOT NULL
```

This will give us the same table design that we got in Figure 11.5.

There are three caveats to observe about the ALTER COLUMN extension of the ALTER TABLE statement:

1. The column's type and size must *always* be typed after the column name. For example, the following statement will cause SQL Server 2008 to announce a syntax error:

```
ALTER TABLE Test2
ALTER COLUMN name NOT NULL
```

You will get the following error message:

```
Msg 156, Level 15, State 1, Line 2
Incorrect syntax near the keyword 'NOT'.
```

2. If you enter the column type without the column size, the column size will reset to the default maximum size of the data type.
3. You cannot put a NOT NULL constraint on a column that already contains nulls.

11.3.2 The PRIMARY KEY Constraint

When creating a table, a PRIMARY KEY constraint will prevent duplicate values for the column(s) defined as a primary key. Internally, the designation of a primary key also creates a primary key index.

Designation of a primary key will be necessary for the referential integrity constraints that follow. The designation of a primary key also automatically puts the NOT NULL constraint in the definition of the column(s), as we will see in an example later in the chapter. A fundamental rule of relational databases is that primary keys cannot be null.

One of the following three SQL options is generally used when setting the primary key.

Option 1:

The first option is to declare the primary key while creating the table, in the CREATE TABLE statement. Here, the PRIMARY KEY constraint is added to the column upon creation:

```
CREATE TABLE Test2a
  (ssn CHAR(9) CONSTRAINT ssn_pk PRIMARY KEY,
    name VARCHAR2(20), etc.
```

ssn_pk is the name of the PRIMARY KEY constraint for the ssn column. It is conventional to name all constraints (although most people do not bother to name NOT NULL constraints).

This option would commonly be used when creating a table with one column as the primary key. But the second and third options of setting the primary key would probably be preferable, and possibly necessary, because they provide more flexibility.

Option 2:

The second option to create a primary key is called the "table format," in which the constraint(s) are added after the columns are enumerated and typed. The CREATE TABLE statement looks like the following:

```
CREATE TABLE Test2a
  (ssn CHAR(9),
    some other columns .. ,
        CONSTRAINT ssn_pk PRIMARY KEY (ssn))
```

This option is also very common and must be used in place of the first option for multicolumn primary keys.

Option 3:

The third option to create a primary key is to add the stipulation of the PRIMARY KEY post hoc by using ALTER TABLE. This option is less common than the first two because ordinarily the primary key is known and defined when the table is created. The syntax for the PRIMARY KEY addition in the ALTER TABLE command is as follows:

ALTER TABLE Tablename
ADD CONSTRAINT constraint_name PRIMARY KEY (column_name(s))

So, to make **ssn** a primary key column in **Test2**, we could type the following:

ALTER TABLE Test2
ADD CONSTRAINT ssn_pk PRIMARY KEY (ssn)

When you type in the preceding statement, you may receive the following error message:

```
Msg 8111, Level 16, State 1, Line 1
Cannot define PRIMARY KEY constraint on nullable column in
table 'Test2'.
Msg 1750, Level 16, State 0, Line 1
Could not create constraint. See previous errors.
```

This error will occur in SQL Server 2008 if you have not yet dealt with declaring the attribute NOT NULL. SQL Server does not allow you to define a primary key on a column that allows nulls. So in this ALTER TABLE scenario, if you have not already done so, you need to first make **ssn** a column that will not accept nulls as follows:

ALTER TABLE Test2
ALTER COLUMN ssn CHAR(9) NOT NULL

The design of the **Test2** table will now look like Figure 11.6:

CS-SBAGUI2.St...se - dbo.Test2		
Column Name	Data Type	Allow Nulls
▸ name	varchar(20)	☑
ssn	char(9)	☐
dept_number	int	☐
acct_balance	smallmoney	☑

Figure 11.6 New table design of **Test2**

Now we can type the following statement to create the primary key:

ALTER TABLE Test2
ADD CONSTRAINT ssn_pk PRIMARY KEY (ssn)

Figure 11.7 shows the primary key constraint that we just created (note the key icon to the left of the **ssn** column).

CS-SBAGUI2.St...se - dbo.Test2		
Column Name	Data Type	Allow Nulls
▶ name	varchar(20)	☑
⚿ ssn	char(9)	☐
dept_number	int	☐
acct_balance	smallmoney	☑

Figure 11.7   Primary key constraint

You can view this `ssn_pk` constraint from the Object Browser by clicking on the + sign beside **Test2**, and then clicking the + sign beside the **Keys** node. You will see Figure 11.8.

- □ ⊞ dbo.Test2
  - ⊞ 📁 Columns
  - ⊟ 📁 Keys
    - ⚿ ssn_pk
  - ⊞ 📁 Constraints
  - ⊞ 📁 Triggers
  - ⊞ 📁 Indexes
  - ⊞ 📁 Statistics

Figure 11.8   The `ssn_pk` constraint

11.3.2.1   Concatenated Primary Keys

In relational databases, it is sometimes necessary to define more than one column as the primary key. When more than one column makes up a primary key, it is called a *concatenated* primary key. In SQL Server 2008, however, you *cannot* directly designate a concatenated primary key (using the first option discussed in the previous section) with a statement like the following:

```
CREATE TABLE Test2a
(ssn CHAR(9) PRIMARY KEY,
 salary INT PRIMARY KEY)
```

This will give the following error message:

```
Msg 8110, Level 16, State 0, Line 1
Cannot add multiple PRIMARY KEY constraints to table 'Test2a'.
```

In SQL Server 2008, you define the concatenated primary key in the following way (using the second option):

```
CREATE TABLE Test2a
  (ssn CHAR(9),
   salary INT,
   CONSTRAINT ssn_salary_pk PRIMARY KEY(ssn, salary))
```

The table design of the **Test2a** table will now look like Figure 11.9:

CS-SBAGUI2.Stu...e - dbo.Test2a		
Column Name	Data Type	Allow Nulls
ssn	char(9)	☐
salary	int	☐

Figure 11.9 Table design of **Test2a**

Or you can create the concatenated primary key with two separate statements, first with a CREATE TABLE:

```
CREATE TABLE Test2b
  (ssn CHAR(9)     NOT NULL,
   salary INT NOT NULL)
```

and then with an ALTER TABLE:

```
ALTER TABLE Test2b
ADD CONSTRAINT ssn_salary_pk1 PRIMARY KEY (ssn, salary)
```

This will produce the same table design as was shown in Figure 11.9. It
is far more common to use the CREATE TABLE concatenated primary
key creation (the second option) because the primary key should be known
when the table is created in the first place.

We called this latter constraint **ssn_salary_pk1** since you cannot have
another constraint called **ssn_salary_pk** (which was a constraint created
for table **Test2a**).

Figure 11.10 shows the constraints created for table **Test2b**. Note that
the constraint shows up not only as a key constraint but also as an index.

Figure 11.10 Viewing the constraints of table **Test2b**

Take a look at another example of a concatenated primary key

Suppose we have a new table in our database, Grade1, which has columns student_number, section_id, and grade. Further suppose that a grade cannot be determined by either the student_number or the section_id alone. A given student_number will have multiple grades and a given section will have multiple grades as well. Hence, both a student number and a section are needed to identify a grade in the table. Because both of these columns (together) are required to uniquely identify a grade, the student_number and section_id will be the concatenated primary key of the Grade1 table.

The CREATE TABLE statement for this table would be:

```
CREATE TABLE Grade1
  (student_number CHAR(9) NOT NULL,
   section_id CHAR(9) NOT NULL,
   grade CHAR(1)
   CONSTRAINT ssn_section_pknew PRIMARY KEY(student_number, section_id))
```

The CREATE TABLE and ALTER TABLE sequence for creating the Grade1 table with the concatenated primary key is shown next. First we create the Grade1 table:

```
CREATE TABLE Grade1
  (student_number CHAR(9) NOT NULL,
   section_id CHAR(9)        NOT NULL,
   grade CHAR(1))
```

Then we define the concatenated primary key as follows:

```
ALTER TABLE Grade1 ADD CONSTRAINT snum_section_pk
     PRIMARY KEY(student_number, section_id)
```

Figure 11.11 shows the table design of the Grade1 table.

CS-SBAGUI2.Stu...e - dbo.Grade1		
Column Name	Data Type	Allow Nulls
student_number	char(9)	☐
section_id	char(9)	☐
grade	char(1)	☑

Figure 11.11 Table design of Grade1

Figure 11.12 shows the constraint `snum_section_pk`.

Figure 11.12   The `snum_section_pk` constraint

11.3.3   The UNIQUE Constraint

Similar to PRIMARY KEY, UNIQUE is another column integrity constraint. UNIQUE is different from PRIMARY KEY in three ways:

- UNIQUE keys can exist in addition to (or without) the PRIMARY KEY.
- UNIQUE does *not* necessitate NOT NULL, whereas PRIMARY KEY does.
- There can be more than one UNIQUE key in a table but only one PRIMARY KEY.

As an example of using the UNIQUE constraint, suppose that we created a table of names and occupational titles in which everyone must have a unique title. Further suppose that the table had an employee number as a primary key. The statement to create the table might look like the following:

```
CREATE TABLE Emp
  (empno INT,
   name VARCHAR(20),
   title VARCHAR(20),
   CONSTRAINT empno_pk PRIMARY KEY(empno),
   CONSTRAINT title_uk UNIQUE (title))
```

Figure 11.13 shows the table design of the newly created `Emp` table:

Column Name	Data Type	Allow Nulls
empno	int	☐
name	varchar(20)	☑
title	varchar(20)	☑

CS-SBAGUI2.St...urse - dbo.Emp

Figure 11.13   Table design of `Emp`

In Figure 11.13, we can see that both the `empno` and `title` fields will not allow nulls, as `empno` is defined as a primary key and `title` is defined as unique.

Figure 11.14 shows the `empno_pk` and `title_uk` constraints of the `Emp` table.

Figure 11.14   Showing the `empno_pk` and `title_uk` constraints

In SQL Server 2008, when you declare a PRIMARY KEY or UNIQUE constraint, internally a unique index is created just as if you had used the CREATE INDEX command. In terms of internal storage and maintenance of indexes in SQL Server 2008, there is no difference between unique indexes created using the CREATE INDEX command and indexes created using the UNIQUE constraint. In fact, an index is a type of constraint. When it comes to the query optimizer, how the index was created is irrelevant. The query optimizer makes decisions based on the presence of the unique index.

Discussing the query optimizer is beyond the scope of this book.

11.3.4   The CHECK Constraint

In addition to the NOT NULL, PRIMARY KEY, and UNIQUE constraints, we can also include a CHECK constraint on our column designs in SQL Server 2008. A CHECK constraint will disallow a value that is outside the bounds of the CHECK. Consider the following example that limits values of the `class` attribute to be between 1 and 4:

```
CREATE TABLE StudentA
  (ssn CHAR(9),
   class INT
      CONSTRAINT class_ck CHECK (class BETWEEN 1 AND 4),
   name VARCHAR(20))
```

This will give the table design shown in Figure 11.15:

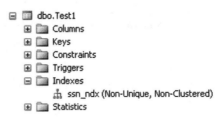

	Column Name	Data Type	Allow Nulls
▶	ssn|	char(9)	☑
	class	int	☑
	name	varchar(20)	☑

Figure 11.15   Table design of StudentA

To view the CHECK constraint, from the Object Explorer, click the + sign beside the StudentA table and then click the + sign beside **Constraints**; you will see Figure 11.16.

```
⊟ 🔲 dbo.Test1
    ⊞ 📁 Columns
    ⊞ 📁 Keys
    ⊞ 📁 Constraints
    ⊞ 📁 Triggers
    ⊟ 📁 Indexes
           🔀 ssn_ndx (Non-Unique, Non-Clustered)
    ⊞ 📁 Statistics
```

Figure 11.16   The CHECK constraint

Once this CHECK constraint has been added, we could not, for example, successfully execute the following INSERT:

INSERT INTO StudentA VALUES ('123456789', 5, 'Smith')

We would get the following error message:

```
Msg 547, Level 16, State 0, Line 1
The INSERT statement conflicted with the CHECK constraint
"class_ck". The conflict occurred in database
"Student_course", table "dbo.StudentA", column 'class'.
The statement has been terminated.
```

This error occurs because the values of the class column have to be from 1 to 4 (and we tried to insert 5). We could however, enter a null value for class, which technically does not violate the integrity constraint (unless we specify so by making class also NOT NULL).

The use of CHECK constraints is encouraged for both small and large tables.

11.3.5   Deleting a Constraint

The following is the general SQL syntax to delete any named constraint:

ALTER TABLE Tablename
DROP CONSTRAINT constraint_name

For example, in table `Test2a` we created a constraint called `ssn_salary_pk`, which made both the `ssn` and `salary` columns primary keys of the table. If we want to delete this constraint, which means making both the `ssn` and `salary` columns just regular columns (and not primary keys), we would type the following:

ALTER TABLE Test2a
DROP CONSTRAINT ssn_salary_pk

Now the table design of table `Test2a` will appear as shown in Figure 11.17 (note that `Test2a` no longer has the constraint—the primary keys are no longer marked):

CS-SBAGUI2.Stu...e - dbo.Test2a		
Column Name	Data Type	Allow Nulls
ssn	char(9)	☐
salary	int	☐

Figure 11.17   Primary keys no longer marked

Figure 11.18 also shows no constraints for table Test2a.

Figure 11.18   Constraints deleted

11.3.6 Referential Integrity Constraints

To define a relationship between two tables we can create a referential integrity constraint—a foreign key-primary key constraint. A relational database consists of relations (tables) and relationships (foreign key-primary key relationships). A referential integrity constraint is one in which a row in one table (with the foreign key) cannot exist unless a value (column) in that row refers to a primary key value (column) in another table.

A foreign key is a column in one table that is used to link that table to another table in which that column is a primary key. Relationships are implemented in relational databases through the foreign keys.

For example, suppose we have the following two tables:

Department

```
deptno   deptname
------   -----------
1        Accounting
2        Personnel
3        Development
```

Employee

```
empno   empname   dept
-----   -------   ----
100     Jones     2
101     Smith     1
102     Adams     1
104     Harris    3
```

In the `Employee` table, the values of `dept` all reference a department number (`deptno`) in the `Department` table. `deptno` in the `Department` table is the primary key of that table. `dept` in the `Employee` table is a foreign key that references `deptno` in the `Department` table. To maintain referential integrity, it would be inappropriate to enter a row in the `Employee` table that did not have an existing department number already defined in the `Department` table. Trying to insert the following row into the `Employee` table would be a violation of the integrity of the database, because department number 4 does not exist (that is, it has no integrity):

```
<105,'Walsh', 4>
```

Likewise, it would be invalid to try to change a value in an existing row (that is, perform an UPDATE) to make it equal to a value that does not exist. If, for example, we tried to change

```
<100,'Jones', 2>
```

to

```
<100,'Jones', 5>
```

this would violate database integrity because there is no department 5.

Finally, it would be invalid to delete a row in the `Department` table that contains a value for a department number that is already in the `Employee` table. For example, if:

```
<2,'Personnel'>
```

were deleted from the Department table, then the row

```
<100,'Jones', 2>
```

would refer to a nonexistent department. It therefore would be a reference or relationship with no integrity.

In each case (INSERT, UPDATE, and DELETE), we say that there needs to be a referential integrity constraint on the dept column in the Employee table referencing deptno in the Department table. When this primary key-foreign key (deptno in the Department table and dept in the Employee table), is defined, we have defined the relationship of the Employee table to the Department table.

In the INSERT and UPDATE cases discussed earlier, you would expect (correctly) that the usual action of the system would be to deny the invalid action. In SQL Server 2008, in the case of the DELETE and UPDATE commands, there is a cascade option available that will allow us to cascade the DELETE or UPDATE operations, respectively. Whereas an "ordinary" referential integrity constraint would simply disallow the deletion of a row where the referenced row would be orphaned, a cascaded delete would delete the referencing row as well. If, for example, in the previous data we deleted department 3, in a cascaded delete situation, the referencing row in the Employee table, "<104, Harris, 3>" would be deleted as well.

11.3.6.1 Defining the Referential Integrity Constraint in SQL

To establish a referential integrity constraint, it is necessary for the column that is being referenced to be first defined as a primary key. In the preceding Employee–Department example, we have to first create the Department table with a primary key. The CREATE TABLE statement for the Department table (the *referenced* table) could look like this:

```
CREATE TABLE Department
   (deptno INT,
    deptname VARCHAR(20),
    CONSTRAINT deptno_pk PRIMARY KEY (deptno))
```

The table design of the Department table would look like Figure 11.19.

CS-SBAGUI2.St...bo.Department		
Column Name	Data Type	Allow Nulls
deptno	int	☐
deptname	varchar(20)	☑

Figure 11.19 Table design of Department

The constraints for the `Department` table would look like Figure 11.20:

Figure 11.20   Constraints of the `Department` table

The `Employee` table (the *referencing* table containing the foreign key) would then be created using this statement:

```
CREATE TABLE Employee
  (empno INT CONSTRAINT empno_pk1 PRIMARY KEY,
   empname VARCHAR(20),
   dept INT CONSTRAINT dept_fk REFERENCES Department(deptno))
```

The table design of the `Employee` table would then be as shown in Figure 11.21:

CS-SBAGUI2.St... dbo.Employee		
Column Name	Data Type	Allow Nulls
empno	int	☐
empname	varchar(20)	☑
dept	int	☑

Figure 11.21   Table design of `Employee`

Now, to view the referential integrity constraints on the `Employee` table, click the + sign beside **Employee** and then click the + sign beside **Keys**, and you will see Figure 11.22.

Figure 11.22   Viewing the referential integrity constraints of the `Employee` table

From the SQL Server 2008 interface, the foreign key can be renamed, deleted or modified. Should it be necessary to modify the foreign key, you would right-click `dept_fk` under **Keys** and select **Modify**, as shown in Figure 11.23.

Figure 11.23   Modifying the foreign key

You will get the screen shown in Figure 11.24. Without actually modifying the foreign key, you can get information about the key in this screen. You can expand the **Tables And Columns Specification** option (under **General**), and you will be able to see what the foreign key base table is (that is, the table with the foreign key, which in this case is the `Employee` table), what the foreign key columns are (in this case, `dept`), what the primary/unique key base table is (that is, the table with the primary key, which in this case is `Department`), the primary key/unique key column (which in this case is `deptno`). You can change these options by clicking on the ... icon to the right of Tables And Column Specification.

The "CREATE TABLE Employee..." statement defines a column, `dept`, to be of type INT, but the statement goes further in defining `dept` to be a *foreign* key that references another table, `Department`. Again, within the `Department` table, the referenced column, `deptno`, has to be an already defined primary key.

Also note that the `Department` table has to be created first. If we tried to create the `Employee` table before the `Department` table with the referential CONSTRAINT, we would be trying to reference a nonexistent table and this would also cause an error.

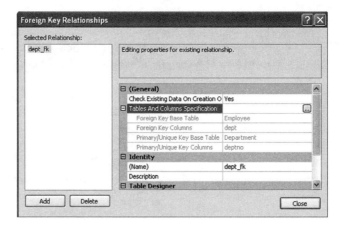

Figure 11.24   The `dept_fk` foreign key

11.3.6.2   Adding the Foreign Key after Tables Are Created

As we have seen with other constraints, the foreign key can be added after tables are created. To do so, we must first have set up the primary key of the referenced table. The syntax of the ALTER TABLE command to add a foreign key to a referencing table would look like this:

```
ALTER TABLE Employee
   ADD CONSTRAINT dept_fk
   FOREIGN KEY (dept)
   REFERENCES Department(deptno)
```

The optional name of the CONSTRAINT is `dept_fk`. The column's data types in the REFERENCES clause must agree with the column's data types in the referenced table.

11.3.6.3   DELETE and the Referential CONSTRAINT

There are a couple of options in the DELETE option of a foreign key referential constraint in SQL Server 2008—CASCADE and NO ACTION. Both of these options specify what action takes place on a row if that row has a referential relationship and the referenced row is deleted from the parent table. First we will discuss the default, which is NO ACTION, and then we will look at the CASCADE option.

11.3.6.3.1   ON DELETE NO ACTION   If the NO ACTION alternative is used in the ON DELETE option of the CREATE TABLE command, and we try to delete a row from the parent table (in this case, the Department table) that has a referencing row in the dependent table (in this case, the Employee table), then SQL Server 2008 will raise an error and the delete action on the row in the parent table will be undone. The NO ACTION option on the ON DELETE option is the default.

The ON DELETE NO ACTION option is added after the REFERENCES clause of a CREATE TABLE command. A CREATE TABLE statement with ON DELETE NO ACTION will be shown in the next example.

In order to create the following Employee table, you will need to delete the previous one.

```
CREATE TABLE Employee
  (empno INT     CONSTRAINT empno_pk2 PRIMARY KEY,
  empname VARCHAR(20),
    dept INT REFERENCES Department(deptno)
          ON DELETE NO ACTION)
```

Make sure you have created the Department table before you attempt to create this Employee table.

The referential integrity constraints of the Employee table are shown in Figure 11.25.

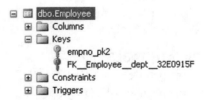

Figure 11.25   Viewing the referential integrity constraints of the Employee table

Then, to view the ON DELETE NO ACTION, right-click on FK_ Employee_dept_32E0915F and select **Modify.** (The actual name of the key was assigned by SQL Server in this case because no fk-name was given as in the "CREATE TABLE Employee ..." statement. If you do this on your computer, the actual name will likely not be FK...32E...). You will see Figure 11.26, the **Foreign Key Relationships** screen. On this screen, under the **Table Designer**, expand the **INSERT And UPDATE** Specification option, and you will see the **Delete Rule as No Action**, as shown in Figure 11.26.

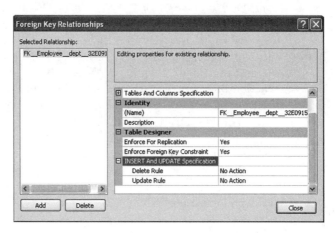

Figure 11.26   Viewing the ON DELETE NO ACTION option

11.3.6.3.2   ON DELETE CASCADE   While ON DELETE NO ACTION is the default and likely the correct choice for most database situations, there is also the ON DELETE CASCADE option. The cascade option is used in rare circumstances because much data can be automatically erased with this option. Should the ON DELETE CASCADE option be used, it can be added after the REFERENCES clause of a CREATE TABLE statement.

In order to create the following Employee table, you will need to delete the previous one.

```
CREATE TABLE Employee
   (empno INT     CONSTRAINT empno_pk3 PRIMARY KEY,
   empname VARCHAR(20),
   dept INT REFERENCES Department(deptno)
          ON DELETE CASCADE)
```

The table design of the Employee table will be similar to what was shown in Figure 11.21.

The ON DELETE CASCADE option will be included in the referential integrity constraint. To view the ON DELETE CASCADE, from the Foreign Key Relationships screen, once again expand the INSERT And UPDATE Specification option, and you will see the Delete Rule as Cascade, as shown in Figure 11.27.

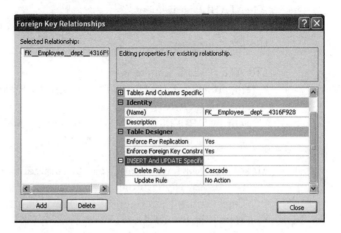

Figure 11.27 Viewing the ON DELETE CASCADE option

CASCADE will allow the deletions in the dependent table (in this case, the `Employee` table) that are affected by the deletions of the rows in the referenced table (in this case, the `Department` table). Suppose, for example, we had a `deptno = 3` in the `Department` table. Also suppose that we had employees in department 3. If we deleted department 3 in the `Department` table, then with CASCADE we would also delete all employees in the `Employee` table with `dept = 3`.

11.3.6.4 UPDATE and the Referential CONSTRAINT

Both the CASCADE and NO ACTION options are also available with the ON UPDATE option of a foreign key referential constraint in SQL Server 2008. Both these options specify what action takes place on a row if that row has a referential relationship and the referenced row is updated in the parent table. We show the syntax of these two options in the following sections.

11.3.6.4.1 ON UPDATE NO ACTION Just as with the ON DELETE option, if the NO ACTION option is used with the ON UPDATE option of the CREATE TABLE statement, and we try to update a row from the parent table (in this case, the `Department` table) that has a referencing row in the dependent table (in this case, the `Employee` table), then SQL Server

2008 will raise an error and the update action on the row in the parent table will be rolled back. The NO ACTION option on the ON UPDATE option is the default.

Just as in the ON DELETE NO ACTION option, the ON UPDATE NO ACTION option is added after the REFERENCES clause of a CREATE TABLE statement.

In order to create the following `Employee` table, you will need to delete the previous one.

```
CREATE TABLE Employee
   (empno INT CONSTRAINT empno_pk4 PRIMARY KEY,
    empname VARCHAR(20),
    dept INT REFERENCES Department(deptno)
            ON UPDATE NO ACTION)
```

Make sure you have created the `Department` table before you attempt to create this `Employee` table.

Once again, the design of the `Employee` table will be similar to what was shown in Figure 11.21.

The ON UPDATE NO ACTION option will be included in the referential integrity constraint. To view the ON UPDATE CASCADE, from the Foreign Key Relationships screen, expand the INSERT And UPDATE Specification option, and you will see the Update Rule as No Action, as shown in Figure 11.28.

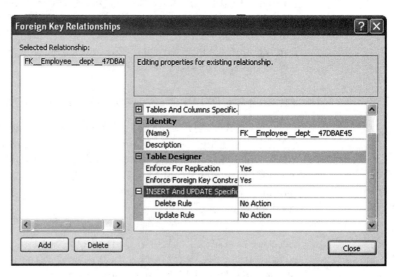

Figure 11.28 Viewing the ON UPDATE NO ACTION option

11.3.6.4.2 ON UPDATE CASCADE   The ON UPDATE CASCADE option is also added after the REFERENCES clause of a CREATE TABLE statement.

In order to create the following `Employee` table, you will need to delete the previous one.

```
CREATE TABLE Employee
  (empno INT CONSTRAINT empno_pk5 PRIMARY KEY,
   empname VARCHAR(20),
   dept INT REFERENCES Department(deptno)
           ON UPDATE CASCADE)
```

The design of the `Employee` table will be similar to what was shown in Figure 11.21.

The ON UPDATE CASCADE option will be included in the referential integrity constraint. To view the ON UPDATE CASCADE, from the Foreign Key Relationships screen, once again, expand the INSERT And UPDATE Specification option, and you will see the Update Rule as Cascade, as shown in Figure 11.29.

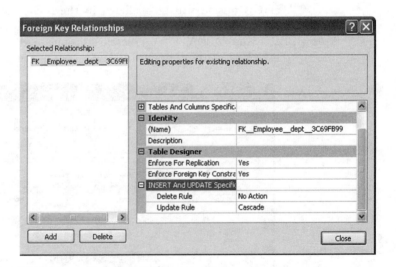

Figure 11.29   Viewing the ON UPDATE CASCADE option

When CASCADE is included in the ON UPDATE option, the row is updated in the referencing table (in this case, the `Employee` table) if that row is updated in the parent table (in this case, the `Department` table).

11.3.6.5   Using ON DELETE and ON UPDATE Together

You can also use the ON DELETE and ON UPDATE options together if needed. Both ON DELETE and ON UPDATE do not necessarily have to be set on the same option. That is, both of them do not have to be set to NO ACTION or CASCADE at the same time. You can have a NO ACTION option set for one option and a CASCADE set for the other option. For example, you may create the `Employee` table as follows:

Once again, note that before you create this `Employee` table, you must delete the previous version.

```
CREATE TABLE Employee
  (empno INT CONSTRAINT empno_pk6 PRIMARY KEY,
   empname VARCHAR(20),
   dept INT REFERENCES Department(deptno)
          ON UPDATE CASCADE
          ON DELETE NO ACTION)
```

The table design of the `Employee` table will then be similar to what was shown in Figure 11.21.

Both the ON UPDATE CASCADE option and the ON DELETE NO ACTION option will be included in the referential integrity constraint. Once again, from the Foreign Key Relationships screen, expand the INSERT And UPDATE Specification option, and you will see the Delete Rule as well as the Update Rule, as shown in Figure 11.30.

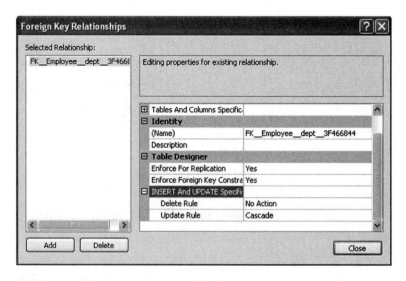

Figure 11.30   Setting ON DELETE and ON UPDATE together

So, in summary, SQL Server 2008 gives you quite a bit of flexibility in setting up your referential integrity constraints.

SUMMARY

This chapter was about indexes and integrity constraints. Indexes are actual "hidden" tables that give the location of indexed values in a table. Indexes become important when databases become large and are queried often. The creation of a primary key implicitly includes the creation of a primary key index. Secondary indexes are indexes on some value other than the primary key. Secondary indexes have to be explicitly created using a CREATE INDEX command. Secondary indexes should be considered if a database is large and if production queries on the database involve seeking the values that are indexed. Constraints can be included in the CREATE TABLE command or can be added later using ALTER TABLE.

Integrity in a database means that you can trust the data you get out of it. If, for example, part numbers are from 100 to 500, then a way is provided by SQL Server to make sure that only part numbers from 100 to 500 get into the database (a CHECK constraint). Other constraints are also very useful in ensuring integrity—NOT NULL, PRIMARY KEY, and UNIQUE. NOT NULL means that a value in a row cannot be null. PRIMARY KEY constraints ensure that all values of the primary key are unique and, at the same time, not null. A table can have only one primary key. A UNIQUE constraint ensures that a value cannot be duplicated. UNIQUE constraints differ from primary keys in that values can be null and there can be as many UNIQUE constraints as are needed be to ensure integrity.

Referential integrity means that a value in some table references a primary key usually in some other table. The point of referential integrity is that referenced values must exist or integrity is lost. The example given in the chapter defines a referential integrity constraint between an employee and a department. In the employee table, a reference to a department number is given. The constraint ensures that no employee is added into the database unless the department to which they are assigned exists.

We also illustrated constraint options and how to view, edit, and delete indexes and constraint, and we provided some caveats about ON DELETE CASCADE, which can automatically delete a lot data.

Review Questions

1. What is an index?
2. Does an index slow down updates on indexed columns?
3. What is a constraint?

4. How many indexes does SQL Server 2008 allow you to have on a table?
5. What command would you use to create an index?
6. What is the default ordering that will be created by an index (ascending or descending)?
7. When can the UNIQUE option be used?
8. What does the IGNORE NULL option do?
9. How do you delete an index?
10. What does the NOT NULL constraint do?
11. What command must you use to include the NOT NULL constraint after a table has already been created?
12. When a PRIMARY KEY constraint is included in a table, what other constraints does this imply?
13. What is a concatenated primary key?
14. How are the UNIQUE and PRIMARY KEY constraints different?
15. What is a referential integrity constraint? What two keys does the referential integrity constraint usually include?
16. What is a foreign key?
17. What does the ON DELETE CASCADE option do?
18. What does the ON UPDATE NO ACTION option do?
19. Can you use ON DELETE and ON UPDATE in the same constraint?

Chapter 11 Exercises

Unless specified otherwise, use the `Student_course` database to answer the following questions. Unless otherwise directed, name all constraints.

1. To test choices of data types, create a table with various data types like this:

```
CREATE TABLE Test3
    (name VARCHAR(20),
     ssn CHAR(9),
     dept_number INTEGER,
     acct_balance SMALLMONEY)
```

Then, insert values into the table to see what will and will not be accepted. The following data may or may not be acceptable. You are welcome to try other choices.

```
'xx','yy',2,5
'xx','yyy',2000000000,5
'xx','yyyy',2,1234567.89
```

2. a. Create an index of **ssn** in ascending order of **ssn**. Try to insert some new data in the **ssn** column. Does your **ssn** column take nulls?

b. Does your **ssn** column take duplicates? If so, how can you prevent this column from taking duplicates?

c. Include a NOT NULL constraint on the **ssn** column. Now try to insert some new data with nulls in the **ssn** column. What happens?

d. With this NOT NULL constraint, is it necessary to include the PRIMARY KEY constraint? Why or why not? Now include the PRIMARY KEY constraint and see if there is any difference in the types of values the **ssn** column.

e. Include some data with null values in the **dept_number** and **acct_balance** columns. Now include the NOT NULL constraint in the **acct_balance** column. What happens?

Delete **Test3**.

3. To test the errors generated when NOT NULL is used, create a table called **Test4**, which looks like this:

```
CREATE TABLE Test4
  (a CHAR(2) NOT NULL,
   b CHAR(3))
```

Insert some data and try to enter a null value for **a**. Acceptable input data for a null is "NULL."

4. a. Create or recreate, if necessary, **Test3**, which does not specify a primary key. Insert some data into the table with at least one duplicate **ssn**. Then, try to impose the PRIMARY KEY constraint with an ALTER TABLE statement. What happens?

b. Recreate the **Test3** table, but this time add a primary key of **ssn**. If you still have the **Test3** table from Exercise 4a, you may be able to delete *offending* rows and add the PRIMARY KEY constraint. Enter two more rows to your table—one containing a new **ssn** and one with a duplicate **ssn**. What happens?

5. Create the **Department** and **Employee** tables, as per the examples earlier in the chapter, with all the constraints (PRIMARY KEY, referential, and UNIQUE constraints). You can add the constraints at create time or you can use ALTER TABLE to add the constraints. Insert some data into the **Department** table first, with departments 1, 2, and 3. Then insert some data into the **Employee** table.

Note: Before doing these exercises, it is prudent to create two tables, called **Deptbak** and **Empbak**, to contain the data you load, because you will be deleting, inserting, dropping, recreating, and so on. You can create `Deptbak` and `Empbak` tables (as temporary tables) with the data we have been using with a query like:

```
SELECT *
INTO Deptbak
FROM Dept
```

Then, when you have added, deleted, updated, and so on and you want the original table from the start of this problem, you simply run the following commands:

```
DROP TABLE Dept
SELECT *
INTO Dept
FROM Deptbak
```

   a. Create a violation of insertion integrity by adding an employee to a nonexistent department. What happens?

   b. Create an update violation by trying to change an existing employee to a nonexistent department, and then by trying to change a referenced department number.

   c. Try to delete a department for which there is an employee. What happens? What happens if you try to delete a department to which no employee has yet been assigned?

   d. Redo this entire experiment (starting with Exercise 5a), except that this time create the `Employee` table with the ON DELETE CASCADE option. View the table design of the `Employee` table.

   e. Redo exercises 5a–5c, except that this time, create the `Employee` table with the ON DELETE NO ACTION option.

   f. Redo exercises 5a–5c, except that this time, create the `Employee` table with the ON UPDATE CASCADE option.

   g. Redo exercises 5a–5c, except that this time, create the `Employee` table with the ON UPDATE NO ACTION option.

   h. Redo exercises 5a–5c, except that this time, create the `Employee` table with the ON UPDATE NO ACTION and ON DELETE CASCADE option together. View the Foreign Key Relationships screen and the Delete and Update rules.

6. Create a table (your choice) with a PRIMARY KEY and a UNIQUE constraint. Insert some data into the table and, as you do, enter a *good* row and a *bad* row (the *bad* row violates a constraint). Demonstrate a violation of each of your constraints one at a time. Show the successes and the errors as you receive them.

7. In this chapter, the `Employee` table was referenced to (depended on) the `Department` table. Suppose that there were another table that depended on the `Employee` table, such as `Emp_Dependent`, where the `Dependent` table contained the columns `name` and `empnum`. Create the `Emp_Dependent` table. Then add the referential constraint where `empnum` references the `Employee` table, with ON DELETE CASCADE (and note that the `Employee` table also has an ON DELETE CASCADE option). You are creating a situation in which the `Emp_Dependent` table references the `Employee` table, which references the `Department` table. Will SQL Server let you do this? If so, and if you delete a row from the `Department` table, will it cascade through the `Employee` table and on to the `Emp_Dependent` table?

Appendix 1
The **Student_course**
Database

A1.1 The Student_course Database

STUDENT

STNO	NOT NULL	SMALLINT	PRIMARY KEY
SNAME		NVARCHAR(20)	
MAJOR		NVARCHAR(4)	
CLASS		SMALLINT	
BDATE		SMALLDATETIME	

DEPENDENT

PNO	NOT NULL	SMALLINT
DNAME		NVARCHAR(20)
RELATIONSHIP		NVARCHAR(8)
SEX		CHAR(1)
AGE		SMALLINT

GRADE_REPORT

STUDENT_NUMBER	NOT NULL	SMALLINT
SECTION_ID	NOT NULL	SMALLINT
GRADE		CHAR(1)
PRIMARY KEY(STUDENT_NUMBER, SECTION_ID)		

SECTION

SECTION_ID	NOT NULL	SMALLINT	PRIMARY KEY
COURSE_NUM		NVARCHAR(8)	
SEMESTER		NVARCHAR(6)	
YEAR		CHAR(2)	
INSTRUCTOR		NVARCHAR(10)	
BLDG		SMALLINT	
ROOM		SMALLINT	

DEPARTMENT_TO_MAJOR

DCODE	NOT NULL	NVARCHAR(4)	PRIMARY KEY
DNAME		NVARCHAR(20)	

COURSE

COURSE_NAME		NVARCHAR(20)	
COURSE_NUMBER	NOT NULL	NVARCHAR(8)	PRIMARY KEY
CREDIT_HOURS		SMALLINT	
OFFERING_DEPT		NVARCHAR(4)	

ROOM

BLDG	NOT NULL	SMALLINT
ROOM	NOT NULL	SMALLINT
CAPACITY		SMALLINT
OHEAD		NVARCHAR(1)
PRIMARY KEY(BLDG, ROOM)		

PREREQ

COURSE_NUMBER	NVARCHAR(8)
PREREQ	NVARCHAR(8)
PRIMARY KEY(COURSE_NUMBER, PREREQ)	

PLANTS

COMPANY   NVARCHAR(20)
PLANTLO   NVARCHAR(15)
PRIMARY KEY(COMPANY, PLANTLO)

LANGUAGES

NAME   NVARCHAR(9)
LANGU   NVARCHAR(7)
PRIMARY KEY(NAME, LANGU)

A1.2   ER Diagram of the Student_course Database

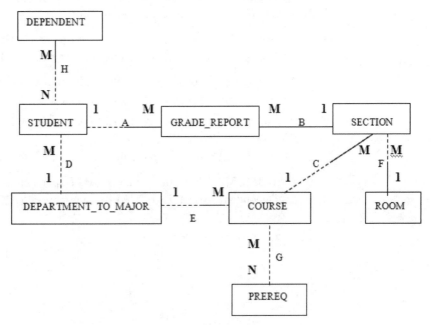

Figure A1.1   ER diagram of the Student_course database

A1.3   Brief Description of the ER Diagram

A. A Student MAY be registered in one or more (M) Grade_Reports (Grade_Report is for a specific course).

   A Grade_Report MUST relate to one and only one (1) Student.

(Students may be in the database and not registered for any courses, but if a course is recorded in the Grade_Report table, it must be related to one and only one student.)

B. A Section MUST have one or more (M) Grade_Reports (Sections only exist if they have students in them).

A Grade_Report MUST relate to one and only one (1) Section.

C. A Section MUST relate to one and only one (1) Course.

A Course MAY be offered as one or more (M) Sections.

(Courses may exist where they are not offered in a section, but a section, if offered, must relate to one and only one course.)

D. A Student MAY be related to one and only one (1) Department_to_major (A student may or may not have declared a major).

A Department_to_major may have one or more (M) Students (A department may or may not have student-majors).

E. A Course MUST be related to one and only one (1) Department_to_major.

A Department_to_major MAY offer one or more (M) Courses.

F. A Section MUST be offered in one and only one (1) Room.

A Room MAY host one or more (M) Sections.

G. A Course MAY have one or more (M) Prereq (A course may have one or more prerequisites).

A Prereq MAY be a prerequisite for one or more (N) Courses.

H. A Student MAY have one or more (M) Dependents.

A Dependent MUST be related to one or more (N) Students.

```
create table Student
(STNO SMALLINT PRIMARY KEY NOT NULL,
 SNAME NVARCHAR(20) NULL,
 MAJOR NVARCHAR(4) NULL,
 CLASS SMALLINT NULL,
 BDATE SMALLDATETIME NULL)
;
create table Grade_report
(STUDENT_NUMBER SMALLINT NOT NULL,
 SECTION_ID SMALLINT NOT NULL,
 GRADE CHAR(1)
 CONSTRAINT stno_secid PRIMARY KEY (STUDENT_NUMBER,
SECTION_ID))
;
create table Section
(SECTION_ID SMALLINT PRIMARY KEY NOT NULL,
 COURSE_NUM NVARCHAR(8),
 SEMESTER NVARCHAR(6),
 YEAR CHAR(2),
 INSTRUCTOR NVARCHAR(10),
 BLDG SMALLINT,
 ROOM SMALLINT)
;
create table Department_to_major
```

```
(DCODE NVARCHAR(4) PRIMARY KEY NOT NULL,
 DNAME NVARCHAR(20))
;
create table Plants
(COMPANY NVARCHAR(20),
 PLANTLO NVARCHAR(15))
;
create table Prereq
(COURSE_NUMBER NVARCHAR(8),
 PREREQ NVARCHAR(8)
 CONSTRAINT couno_pre PRIMARY KEY(COURSE_NUMBER, PREREQ))
;
create table Course
(COURSE_NAME NVARCHAR(20),
 COURSE_NUMBER NVARCHAR(8) PRIMARY KEY NOT NULL,
 CREDIT_HOURS SMALLINT,
 OFFERING_DEPT NVARCHAR(4))
;
create table Languages
(NAME NVARCHAR(9),
 LANGU NVARCHAR(7))
;
create table Room
 (BLDG SMALLINT NOT NULL,
 ROOM SMALLINT NOT NULL,
 CAPACITY SMALLINT,
 OHEAD NVARCHAR(1)
 CONSTRAINT bldg_room PRIMARY KEY(BLDG, ROOM))
;
create table Dependent
(PNO SMALLINT NOT NULL,
 DNAME NVARCHAR(20) NULL,
 RELATIONSHIP NVARCHAR(8) NULL,
 SEX CHAR(1) NULL,
 AGE SMALLINT NULL)
;
insert into Languages values('BRENDA','FRENCH');
insert into Languages values('BRENDA','CHINESE');
insert into Languages values('RICHARD','CHINESE');
insert into Languages values('RICHARD','GERMAN');
insert into Languages values('MARY JO','FRENCH');
insert into Languages values('RICHARD','FRENCH');
insert into Languages values('LUJACK','GERMAN');
insert into Languages values('LUJACK','CHINESE');
insert into Languages values('MARY JO','GERMAN');
insert into Languages values('MARY JO','CHINESE');
insert into Languages values('MELANIE','FRENCH');
insert into Languages values('LUJACK','FRENCH');
```

```
insert into Languages values('MELANIE','CHINESE');
insert into Languages values('BRENDA','SPANISH');
insert into Languages values('RICHARD','SPANISH');
insert into Languages values('JOE','CHINESE');
insert into Languages values('LUJACK','SPANISH');
insert into Languages values('KENT','CHINESE');
insert into course values('ACCOUNTING I','ACCT2020',3,'ACCT');
insert into course values('ACCOUNTING II','ACCT2220',3,'ACCT');
insert into course values('MANAGERIAL FINANCE',
'ACCT3333',3,'ACCT');
insert into course values('ACCOUNTING INFO SYST',
'ACCT3464',3,'ACCT');
insert into course values('INTRO TO COMPUTER SC',
'COSC1310',4,'COSC');
insert into course values('TURBO PASCAL','COSC2025',3,'COSC');
insert into course values('ADVANCED COBOL',
'COSC2303',3,'COSC');
insert into course values('DATA STRUCTURES',
'COSC3320',4,'COSC');
insert into course values('DATABASE','COSC3380',3,'COSC');
insert into course values('OPERATIONS RESEARCH',
'COSC3701',3,'COSC');
insert into course values('ADVANCED ASSEMBLER',
'COSC4301',3,'COSC');
insert into course values('SYSTEM PROJECT',
'COSC4309',3,'COSC');
insert into course values('ADA - INTRODUCTION',
'COSC5234',4,'COSC');
insert into course values('NETWORKS','COSC5920',3,'COSC');
insert into course values('ENGLISH COMP I',
'ENGL1010',3,'ENGL');
insert into course values('ENGLISH COMP II',
'ENGL1011',3,'ENGL');
insert into course values('WRITING FOR NON MAJO',
'ENGL3520',2,'ENGL');
insert into course values('ALGEBRA','MATH2333',3,'MATH');
insert into course values('DISCRETE MATHEMATICS',
'MATH2410',3,'MATH');
insert into course values('CALCULUS 1','MATH1501',4,'MATH');
insert into course values('AMERICAN CONSTITUTIO',
'POLY1201',1,'POLY');
insert into course values('INTRO TO POLITICAL S',
'POLY2001',3,'POLY');
insert into course values('AMERICAN GOVERNMENT',
'POLY2103',2,'POLY');
insert into course values('SOCIALISM AND COMMUN',
'POLY4103',4,'POLY');
insert into course values('POLITICS OF CUBA',
```

```
'POLY5501',4,'POLY');
insert into course values('TECHNICAL WRITING',
'ENGL3402',2,'ENGL');
insert into course values('FUND. TECH. WRITING',
'ENGL3401',3,'ENGL');
insert into course values('INTRO TO CHEMISTRY',
'CHEM2001',3,'CHEM');
insert into course values('ORGANIC CHEMISTRY',
'CHEM3001',3,'CHEM');
insert into course values('CALCULUS 2','MATH1502',3,'MATH');
insert into course values('CALCULUS 3','MATH1503',3,'MATH');
insert into course values('MATH ANALYSIS','MATH5501',3,'MATH');
insert into department_to_major values('ACCT','Accounting');
insert into department_to_major values('ART','Art');
insert into department_to_major values('COSC',
'Computer Science');
insert into department_to_major values('ENGL','English');
insert into department_to_major values('MATH','Mathematics');
insert into department_to_major values('POLY',
'Political Science');
insert into department_to_major values('UNKN',null);
insert into department_to_major values('CHEM','Chemistry');
insert into grade_report values(2,85,'D');
insert into grade_report values(2,102,'B');
insert into grade_report values(2,126,'B');
insert into grade_report values(2,127,'A');
insert into grade_report values(2,145,'B');
insert into grade_report values(3,85,'A');
insert into grade_report values(3,87,'B');
insert into grade_report values(3,90,'B');
insert into grade_report values(3,91,'B');
insert into grade_report values(3,92,'B');
insert into grade_report values(3,96,'B');
insert into grade_report values(3,101,null);
insert into grade_report values(3,133,null);
insert into grade_report values(3,134,null);
insert into grade_report values(3,135,null);
insert into grade_report values(8,85,'A');
insert into grade_report values(8,92,'A');
insert into grade_report values(8,96,'C');
insert into grade_report values(8,102,'B');
insert into grade_report values(8,133,null);
insert into grade_report values(8,134,null);
insert into grade_report values(8,135,null);
insert into grade_report values(10,101,null);
insert into grade_report values(10,112,null);
insert into grade_report values(10,119,null);
insert into grade_report values(10,126,'C');
```

```
insert into grade_report values(10,127,'A');
insert into grade_report values(10,145,'C');
insert into grade_report values(13,85,'B');
insert into grade_report values(13,95,'B');
insert into grade_report values(13,99,null);
insert into grade_report values(13,109,null);
insert into grade_report values(13,119,null);
insert into grade_report values(13,133,null);
insert into grade_report values(13,134,null);
insert into grade_report values(13,135,null);
insert into grade_report values(14,102,'B');
insert into grade_report values(14,112,null);
insert into grade_report values(14,91,'A');
insert into grade_report values(14,135,null);
insert into grade_report values(14,145,'B');
insert into grade_report values(14,158,'B');
insert into grade_report values(15,85,'F');
insert into grade_report values(15,92,'B');
insert into grade_report values(15,99,null);
insert into grade_report values(15,102,'B');
insert into grade_report values(15,135,null);
insert into grade_report values(15,145,'B');
insert into grade_report values(15,158,'C');
insert into grade_report values(17,112,null);
insert into grade_report values(17,119,null);
insert into grade_report values(17,135,null);
insert into grade_report values(19,102,'B');
insert into grade_report values(19,119,null);
insert into grade_report values(19,133,null);
insert into grade_report values(19,158,'D');
insert into grade_report values(20,87,'A');
insert into grade_report values(20,94,'C');
insert into grade_report values(6,201,null);
insert into grade_report values(8,201,null);
insert into grade_report values(24,90,'B');
insert into grade_report values(34,90,'B');
insert into grade_report values(49,90,'C');
insert into grade_report values(62,90,'C');
insert into grade_report values(70,90,'C');
insert into grade_report values(121,90,'B');
insert into grade_report values(122,90,'B');
insert into grade_report values(123,90,'B');
insert into grade_report values(125,90,'C');
insert into grade_report values(126,90,'C');
insert into grade_report values(127,90,'C');
insert into grade_report values(128,90,'F');
insert into grade_report values(129,90,'A');
insert into grade_report values(130,90,'C');
```

```
insert into grade_report values(131,90,'C');
insert into grade_report values(132,90,'B');
insert into grade_report values(142,90,'A');
insert into grade_report values(143,90,'B');
insert into grade_report values(144,90,'B');
insert into grade_report values(145,90,'F');
insert into grade_report values(146,90,'B');
insert into grade_report values(147,90,'C');
insert into grade_report values(148,90,'C');
insert into grade_report values(31,90,'C');
insert into grade_report values(151,90,'C');
insert into grade_report values(153,90,'C');
insert into grade_report values(155,90,'B');
insert into grade_report values(157,90,'B');
insert into grade_report values(158,90,'C');
insert into grade_report values(163,90,'C');
insert into grade_report values(161,90,'C');
insert into grade_report values(160,90,'C');
insert into grade_report values(5,90,'C');
insert into grade_report values(7,90,'C');
insert into grade_report values(9,90,'F');
insert into grade_report values(62,94,'C');
insert into grade_report values(70,94,'C');
insert into grade_report values(49,94,'C');
insert into grade_report values(5,94,'C');
insert into grade_report values(6,94,'C');
insert into grade_report values(7,94,'C');
insert into grade_report values(8,94,'C');
insert into grade_report values(9,94,'F');
insert into grade_report values(5,95,'B');
insert into grade_report values(6,95,'B');
insert into grade_report values(7,95,'B');
insert into grade_report values(8,95,'B');
insert into grade_report values(9,95,'F');
insert into grade_report values(121,95,'B');
insert into grade_report values(122,95,'B');
insert into grade_report values(123,95,'B');
insert into grade_report values(125,95,'B');
insert into grade_report values(126,95,'B');
insert into grade_report values(127,95,'B');
insert into grade_report values(128,95,'F');
insert into grade_report values(129,95,'B');
insert into grade_report values(130,95,'C');
insert into grade_report values(121,94,'B');
insert into grade_report values(122,94,'B');
insert into grade_report values(123,94,'B');
insert into grade_report values(125,94,'C');
insert into grade_report values(126,94,'C');
```

```
insert into grade_report values(127,94,'C');
insert into grade_report values(128,94,'F');
insert into grade_report values(129,94,'A');
insert into grade_report values(130,94,'C');
insert into grade_report values(24,95,'B');
insert into grade_report values(24,96,'B');
insert into grade_report values(24,97,null);
insert into grade_report values(24,98,null);
insert into grade_report values(24,99,null);
insert into grade_report values(24,100,null);
insert into grade_report values(34,98,null);
insert into grade_report values(34,97,null);
insert into grade_report values(34,93,'A');
insert into grade_report values(49,98,null);
insert into grade_report values(49,97,null);
insert into grade_report values(49,93,'A');
insert into grade_report values(123,98,null);
insert into grade_report values(123,97,null);
insert into grade_report values(123,93,'A');
insert into grade_report values(125,98,null);
insert into grade_report values(125,97,null);
insert into grade_report values(125,93,'A');
insert into grade_report values(126,98,null);
insert into grade_report values(126,97,null);
insert into grade_report values(126,93,'A');
insert into grade_report values(127,98,null);
insert into grade_report values(127,97,null);
insert into grade_report values(127,93,'A');
insert into grade_report values(142,100,null);
insert into grade_report values(143,100,null);
insert into grade_report values(144,100,null);
insert into grade_report values(145,100,null);
insert into grade_report values(146,100,null);
insert into grade_report values(147,100,null);
insert into grade_report values(148,100,null);
insert into grade_report values(142,107,null);
insert into grade_report values(143,107,null);
insert into grade_report values(144,107,null);
insert into grade_report values(145,107,null);
insert into grade_report values(146,107,null);
insert into grade_report values(147,107,null);
insert into grade_report values(148,107,null);
insert into grade_report values(142,202,null);
insert into grade_report values(143,202,null);
insert into grade_report values(144,202,null);
insert into grade_report values(145,202,null);
insert into grade_report values(146,202,null);
insert into grade_report values(147,202,null);
```

```
insert into grade_report values(148,202,null);
insert into grade_report values(142,88,null);
insert into grade_report values(143,88,null);
insert into grade_report values(144,88,null);
insert into grade_report values(145,88,null);
insert into grade_report values(146,88,null);
insert into grade_report values(147,88,null);
insert into grade_report values(148,88,null);
insert into grade_report values(142,89,'A');
insert into grade_report values(143,89,'B');
insert into grade_report values(144,89,'B');
insert into grade_report values(145,89,'F');
insert into grade_report values(146,89,'B');
insert into grade_report values(147,89,'B');
insert into grade_report values(148,89,'B');
insert into grade_report values(151,97,null);
insert into grade_report values(153,97,null);
insert into grade_report values(155,97,null);
insert into grade_report values(157,97,null);
insert into grade_report values(158,97,null);
insert into grade_report values(160,97,null);
insert into grade_report values(161,97,null);
insert into grade_report values(163,97,null);
insert into grade_report values(151,109,null);
insert into grade_report values(153,109,null);
insert into grade_report values(155,109,null);
insert into grade_report values(157,109,null);
insert into grade_report values(158,109,null);
insert into grade_report values(160,109,null);
insert into grade_report values(161,109,null);
insert into grade_report values(163,109,null);
insert into grade_report values(151,201,null);
insert into grade_report values(153,201,null);
insert into grade_report values(155,201,null);
insert into grade_report values(157,201,null);
insert into grade_report values(158,201,null);
insert into grade_report values(160,201,null);
insert into grade_report values(161,201,null);
insert into grade_report values(163,201,null);
insert into plants values('GULP OIL','PITTSBURGH');
insert into plants values('GULP OIL','GULF BREEZE');
insert into plants values('GULP OIL','MOBILE');
insert into plants values('GULP OIL','SAN FRANCISCO');
insert into plants values('GULP OIL','HONOLULU');
insert into plants values('GULP OIL','BINGHAMTON');
insert into plants values('IBN COMPUTERS','PITTSBURGH');
insert into plants values('IBN COMPUTERS','GULF BREEZE');
insert into plants values('IBN COMPUTERS','MOBILE');
```

```
insert into plants values('IBN COMPUTERS','SAN FRANCISCO');
insert into plants values('IBN COMPUTERS','HONOLULU');
insert into plants values('IBN COMPUTERS','BINGHAMTON');
insert into plants values('BO$S TIRES','PITTSBURGH');
insert into plants values('BO$S TIRES','GULF BREEZE');
insert into plants values('BO$S TIRES','MOBILE');
insert into plants values('BO$S TIRES','SAN FRANCISCO');
insert into plants values('BO$S TIRES','HONOLULU');
insert into plants values('BO$S TIRES','BINGHAMTON');
insert into plants values('BANK D$AMERICER','PITTSBURGH');
insert into plants values('BANK D$AMERICER','GULF BREEZE');
insert into plants values('BANK D$AMERICER','MOBILE');
insert into plants values('BANK D$AMERICER','SAN FRANCISCO');
insert into plants values('BANK D$AMERICER','HONOLULU');
insert into plants values('BANK D$AMERICER','BINGHAMTON');
insert into plants values('COLONEL MOTORS','PITTSBURGH');
insert into plants values('COLONEL MOTORS','GULF BREEZE');
insert into plants values('COLONEL MOTORS','SAN FRANCISCO');
insert into plants values('COLONEL MOTORS','HONOLULU');
insert into plants values('COLONEL MOTORS','BINGHAMTON');
insert into plants values('COLONEL MOTORS','TUSCALOOSA');
insert into plants values('COKE COLA','PITTSBURGH');
insert into plants values('COKE COLA','GULF BREEZE');
insert into plants values('COKE COLA','MOBILE');
insert into plants values('COKE COLA','SAN FRANCISCO');
insert into plants values('COKE COLA','HONOLULU');
insert into plants values('COKE COLA','BINGHAMTON');
insert into plants values('COKE COLA','TUSCALOOSA');
insert into plants values('WENDIES','PITTSBURGH');
insert into plants values('WENDIES','GULF BREEZE');
insert into plants values('WENDIES','MOBILE');
insert into plants values('WENDIES','SAN FRANCISCO');
insert into plants values('WENDIES','HONOLULU');
insert into plants values('WENDIES','BINGHAMTON');
insert into plants values('WENDIES','TUSCALOOSA');
insert into plants values('CAPTAIN E$S','PITTSBURGH');
insert into plants values('CAPTAIN E$S','GULF BREEZE');
insert into plants values('CAPTAIN E$S','MOBILE');
insert into plants values('CAPTAIN E$S','SAN FRANCISCO');
insert into plants values('CAPTAIN E$S','HONOLULU');
insert into plants values('CAPTAIN E$S','BINGHAMTON');
insert into plants values('CAPTAIN E$S','TUSCALOOSA');
insert into plants values('RADAR SHACK','PITTSBURGH');
insert into plants values('RADAR SHACK','GULF BREEZE');
insert into plants values('RADAR SHACK','SAN FRANCISCO');
insert into plants values('RADAR SHACK','HONOLULU');
insert into plants values('RADAR SHACK','BINGHAMTON');
insert into plants values('RADAR SHACK','TUSCALOOSA');
```

```
insert into plants values('PHIL$S BAKE SHOP','PITTSBURGH');
insert into plants values('PHIL$S BAKE SHOP','GULF BREEZE');
insert into plants values('PHIL$S BAKE SHOP','SAN FRANCISCO');
insert into plants values('PHIL$S BAKE SHOP','HONOLULU');
insert into plants values('PHIL$S BAKE SHOP','BINGHAMTON');
insert into plants values('PHIL$S BAKE SHOP','TUSCALOOSA');
insert into plants values('WYATT$S TOMBSTONE','PITTSBURGH');
insert into plants values('WYATT$S TOMBSTONE','GULF BREEZE');
insert into plants values('WYATT$S TOMBSTONE','SAN FRANCISCO');
insert into plants values('WYATT$S TOMBSTONE','HONOLULU');
insert into plants values('WYATT$S TOMBSTONE','BINGHAMTON');
insert into plants values('WYATT$S TOMBSTONE','TUSCALOOSA');
insert into plants values('EAST PUBLISHING','PITTSBURGH');
insert into plants values('EAST PUBLISHING','GULF BREEZE');
insert into plants values('EAST PUBLISHING','SAN FRANCISCO');
insert into plants values('EAST PUBLISHING','HONOLULU');
insert into plants values('EAST PUBLISHING','BINGHAMTON');
insert into plants values('EAST PUBLISHING','TUSCALOOSA');
insert into plants values('UTAH BOB$S','PITTSBURGH');
insert into plants values('UTAH BOB$S','GULF BREEZE');
insert into plants values('UTAH BOB$S','SAN FRANCISCO');
insert into plants values('UTAH BOB$S','HONOLULU');
insert into plants values('UTAH BOB$S','BINGHAMTON');
update plants set company = replace(company,'$','''');
insert into prereq values('ACCT3333','ACCT2220');
insert into prereq values('COSC3320','COSC1310');
insert into prereq values('COSC3380','COSC3320');
insert into prereq values('COSC3380','MATH2410');
insert into prereq values('COSC5234','COSC3320');
insert into prereq values('ENGL1011','ENGL1010');
insert into prereq values('ENGL3401','ENGL1011');
insert into prereq values('ENGL3520','ENGL1011');
insert into prereq values('MATH5501','MATH2333');
insert into prereq values('POLY2103','POLY1201');
insert into prereq values('POLY5501','POLY4103');
insert into prereq values('CHEM3001','CHEM2001');
insert into room values(13,101,85,'Y');
insert into room values(36,123,35,'N');
insert into room values(58,114,60,null);
insert into room values(79,179,35,'Y');
insert into room values(79,174,22,'Y');
insert into room values(58,112,40,null);
insert into room values(36,122,25,'N');
insert into room values(36,121,25,'N');
insert into room values(36,120,25,'N');
insert into room values(58,110,null,'Y');
insert into section values(85,'MATH2410','FALL','08',
'KING',36,123);
```

```
insert into section values(86,'MATH5501','FALL','08',
'EMERSON',36,123);
insert into section values(87,'ENGL3401','FALL','08',
'HILLARY',13,101);
insert into section values(88,'ENGL3520','FALL','09',
'HILLARY',13,101);
insert into section values(89,'ENGL3520','SPRING','09',
'HILLARY',13,101);
insert into section values(90,'COSC3380','SPRING','09',
'HARDESTY',79,179);
insert into section values(91,'COSC3701','FALL','08',
null,79,179);
insert into section values(92,'COSC1310','FALL','08',
'ANDERSON',79,179);
insert into section values(93,'COSC1310','SPRING','09',
'RAFAELT',79,179);
insert into section values(94,'ACCT3464','FALL','08',
'RODRIQUEZ',74,null);
insert into section values(95,'ACCT2220','SPRING','09',
'RODRIQUEZ',74,null);
insert into section values(96,'COSC2025','FALL','08',
'RAFAELT',79,179);
insert into section values(97,'ACCT3333','FALL','09',
'RODRIQUEZ',74,null);
insert into section values(98,'COSC3380','FALL','09',
'HARDESTY',79,179);
insert into section values(99,'ENGL3401','FALL','09',
'HILLARY',13,101);
insert into section values(102,'COSC3320','SPRING','09',
'KNUTH',79,179);
insert into section values(107,'MATH2333','SPRING','10',
'CHANG',36,123);
insert into section values(109,'MATH5501','FALL','09',
'CHANG',36,123);
insert into section values(112,'MATH2410','FALL','09',
'CHANG',36,123);
insert into section values(119,'COSC1310','FALL','09',
'ANDERSON',79,179);
insert into section values(126,'ENGL1010','FALL','08',
'HERMANO',13,101);
insert into section values(127,'ENGL1011','SPRING','09',
'HERMANO',13,101);
insert into section values(133,'ENGL1010','FALL','09',
'HERMANO',13,101);
insert into section values(134,'ENGL1011','SPRING','10',
'HERMANO',13,101);
insert into section values(135,'COSC3380','FALL','09',
'STONE',79,179);
```

```
insert into section values(145,'COSC1310','SPRING','09',
'JONES',79,179);
insert into section values(158,'MATH2410','SPRING','08',
null,36,123);
insert into section values(201,'CHEM2001','FALL','09',
null,58,114);
insert into section values(202,'CHEM3001','SPRING','10',
'CARNEAU',58,null);
insert into section values(100,'POLY1201','FALL','09',
'SCHMIDT',null,null);
insert into section values(101,'POLY2103','SPRING','10',
'SCHMIDT',null,null);
insert into section values(104,'POLY4103','SPRING','10',
'SCHMIDT',null,null);
insert into student values(2,'Lineas','ENGL','1','15-APR-90');
insert into student values(3,'Mary','COSC','4','16-JUL-88');
insert into student values(8,'Brenda','COSC','2','13-AUG-87');
insert into student values(10,'Richard','ENGL','1','13-MAY-90');
insert into student values(13,'Kelly','MATH','4','12-AUG-90');
insert into student values(14,'Lujack','COSC','1','12-FEB-87');
insert into student values(15,'Reva','MATH','2','10-JUN-90');
insert into student values(17,'Elainie','COSC','1','12-AUG-86');
insert into student values(19,'Harley','POLY','2','16-APR-91');
insert into student values(20,'Donald','ACCT','4','15-OCT-87');
insert into student values(24,'Chris','ACCT','4','12-FEB-88');
insert into student values(34,'Lynette','POLY','1','16-JUL-91');
insert into student values(49,'Susan','ENGL','3','11-MAR-90');
insert into student values(62,'Monica','MATH','3','14-OCT-90');
insert into student values(70,'Bill','POLY',null,'14-OCT-90');
insert into student values(121,'Hillary','COSC','1','16-JUL-87');
insert into student values(122,'Phoebe','ENGL','3','15-APR-90');
insert into student values(123,'Holly','POLY','4','15-JAN-91');
insert into student values(125,'Sadie','MATH','2','12-AUG-90');
insert into student values(126,'Jessica','POLY','2','16-JUL-91');
insert into student values(127,'Steve','ENGL','1','11-MAR-90');
insert into student values(128,'Brad','COSC','1','10-SEP-87');
insert into student values(129,'Cedric','ENGL','2','15-APR-90');
insert into student values(130,'Alan','COSC','2','16-JUL-87');
insert into student values(131,'Rachel','ENGL','3','15-APR-90');
insert into student values(132,'George','POLY','1','16-APR-91');
insert into student values(142,'Jerry','COSC','4','12-MAR-88');
insert into student values(143,'Cramer','ENGL','3','15-APR-90');
insert into student values(144,'Fraiser','POLY','1','16-JUL-91');
insert into student values(145,'Harrison','ACCT','4','12-FEB-87');
insert into student values(146,'Francis','ACCT','4','11-JUN-87');
insert into student values(147,'Smithly','ENGL','2','13-MAY-90');
insert into student values(148,'Sebastian','ACCT','2','14-OCT-86');
insert into student values(31,'Jake','COSC','4','12-FEB-88');
```

```
insert into student values(151,'Losmith','CHEM','3','15-JAN-91');
insert into student values(153,'Genevieve','UNKN',null,'15-OCT-89');
insert into student values(155,'Lindsay','UNKN','1','15-OCT-89');
insert into student values(157,'Stephanie','MATH',null,'16-APR-91');
insert into student values(158,'Thornton',null,null,'15-OCT-89');
insert into student values(163,'Lionel',null,null,'15-OCT-89');
insert into student values(161,'Benny','CHEM','4','10-JUN-90');
insert into student values(160,'Gus','ART ','3','15-OCT-88');
insert into student values(5,'Zelda','COSC',null,'12-FEB-88');
insert into student values(7,'Mario','MATH',null,'12-AUG-90');
insert into student values(9,'Romona','ENGL',null,'15-APR-90');
insert into student values(6,'Ken','POLY',null,'15-JUL-90');
insert into student values(88,'Smith',null,null,'15-OCT-79');
insert into student values(191,'Jake','MATH','2','10-JUN-90');
insert into dependent values(2,'Matt','Son','M',2);
insert into dependent values(2,'Mary','Daughter','F',1);
insert into dependent values(2,'Beena','Spouse','F',19);
insert into dependent values(10,'Amit','Son','M',3);
insert into dependent values(10,'Shantu','Daughter','F',2);
insert into dependent values(14,'Raju','Son','M',1);
insert into dependent values(14,'Rani',' ','F',3);
insert into dependent values(17,'Susan','Daughter','F',2);
insert into dependent values(17,'Sam','Son','M',1);
insert into dependent values(20,'Donald II','Son','M',Null);
insert into dependent values(20,'Chris','Son','M',4);
insert into dependent values(34,'Susan','Daughter','F',1);
insert into dependent values(34,'Monica','Daughter','F',1);
insert into dependent values(62,'Tom','Husband','M',25);
insert into dependent values(62,'James','Son','M',1);
insert into dependent values(62,'Hillary','Daughter','F',2);
insert into dependent values(62,'Phoebe','Daughter','F',3);
insert into dependent values(123,'James','Son','M',3);
insert into dependent values(123,'Jon','Son','M',1);
insert into dependent values(126,'Om','Son','M',2);
insert into dependent values(126,'Prakash','Son','M',1);
insert into dependent values(128,'Mithu','Son','M',1);
insert into dependent values(128,'Mita','Daughter','F',Null);
insert into dependent values(128,'Nita','Daughter','F',2);
insert into dependent values(128,'Barbara','Wife','F',18);
insert into dependent values(132,'Rekha','Daughter','F',2);
insert into dependent values(142,'Rakhi','Daughter','F',1);
insert into dependent values(143,'Mona','Daughter','F',1);
insert into dependent values(144,'Susan','Wife','F',19);
insert into dependent values(145,'Susie','Wife','F',21);
insert into dependent values(146,'Xi du','Wife','F',20);
insert into dependent values(147,'Barbara','Wife','F',20);
insert into dependent values(147,'Sebastian','Son','M',1);
insert into dependent values(147,'Jake','Son','M',2);
```

```
insert into dependent values(147,'Losmith','Son','M',Null);
insert into dependent values(153,'Madhu','Daughter','F',3);
insert into dependent values(153,'Mamta','Daughter','F',2);
insert into dependent values(153,'Mahesh','Son','M',1);
insert into dependent values(158,'Sally','wife', 'F',20);

select top 6 sname, major, class into teststu from student;
```

Glossary of Important Commands and Functions

ABS(n) Row-level function that returns an absolute value of some number, n.

ALTER COLUMN Command used to change a column's size or type in a table.

ALTER TABLE Command used to modify a table's design.

AND Binary logical operator that, when used in a WHERE clause, means that both criteria have to be met for a row to be included in the result set.

ASC Keyword in an ORDER BY clause used to put a result set in ascending order.

AVG Aggregate function used to average a group of row values.

BETWEEN An operator used to determine whether a value occurs within a given range of values (inclusive); used in a WHERE clause.

BIGINT Integer data type that can store numbers from -2^{63} to $2^{63} -1$.

BINARY Data type used to store strings of bits.

BIT Data type that consumes only a single bit of storage.

CAST   Conversion function used to change the data type of a column (row-level function).

CEILING(n)   Row-level function that returns the next larger integer above n.

CHAR($size$)   Character data type used when the column length is known and unvarying.

CHARINDEX $(a, b, [c])$ String function that returns the starting position of string a in string b. The optional third parameter, c, specifies the starting point to begin searching string b. If c is unspecified, the search begins at the first character of b.

CHECK   An integrity constraint used to create bounds for an attribute.

CONSTRAINTS   Restrictions that can be placed on values in tables to ensure integrity in the database.

CONVERT   Conversion function used to explicitly convert to a given data type.

COUNT(*)   Aggregate function used to count the number of rows in a result set.

COUNT($attribute$)   Aggregate function that counts the number of rows where $attribute$ is not NULL.

CREATE DATABASE   Command used to create a database.

CREATE INDEX   Command used to create an index.

CREATE SYNONYM   Command used to create a synonym.

CREATE TABLE   Command used to create a table.

CREATE VIEW   Command used to create a view.

CROSS JOIN   "Join" used to generate a Cartesian product.

DATE   SQL Server 2008's new data type that is commonly used to store a date without a time component.

DATEADD   Date function that adds to a specified part of a date, e.g., add n months to a date.

DATEDIFF ($date\ part,\ date1,\ date2$)   Date function that returns the difference between two parts of two dates, such as how many days between $date1$ and $date2$. For example, "SELECT DATEDIFF(day, '2/3/2008','3/4/2009') = 395."

DATEFORMAT Date function that controls how SQL Server interprets date constants that are entered.

DATEPART Date function that returns the specified part of the date requested.

DATETIME Data type that can be used for dates; mostly used in earlier versions.

DATETIME2 SQL Server 2008's new data type that can be used for dates; an extension of DATETIME.

DATETIMEOFFSET SQL Server 2008's new data type that provides time-zone awareness.

DAY Date function that extracts a day from a date.

DEC Data type; synonym for DECIMAL data type.

DECIMAL(P,[s]) Numeric data type where precision, p, specifies the maximum number of digits and the optional s (scale) specifies the number of digits after the decimal point.

DECLARE Command used to create variables within a query.

DELETE FROM Command that deletes rows in a table that satisfy a particular condition.

DESC Keyword in an ORDER BY clause used to put a result set in descending order.

DISTINCT A function that omits duplicate rows in a result set.

DROP COLUMN Command used to delete a column in a table.

DROP CONSTRAINT Command used to delete a named constraint.

DROP INDEX Command used to delete an index.

DROP SYNONYM Command used to delete a synonym.

DROP TABLE Command used to delete a table.

DROP VIEW Command used to delete a view.

EXISTS A WHERE clause keyword that returns true if the subquery following it returns at least one row.

FLOAT Numeric data type that has a precision of 15 digits and stores numbers in scientific format, e.g., 6.0221415E+23.

FLOOR(n) Row-level function that returns the next lower integer value of n, e.g., "SELECT FLOOR(3.4), FLOOR(–3.4)" returns 3 and –4.

GETDATE Date function that returns the current system date and time.

GROUP BY A SELECT statement option that generates one summary row for all selected rows that have identical values for the attributes specified in the GROUP BY.

HAVING A SELECT statement option used to determine which groups of a GROUP BY will be included in the result set.

HIERARCHYID SQL Server 2008's new data type that allows you to construct hierarchical relationships among data elements within a table.

IMAGE Large object binary data type; can be used to store pictures.

IN Logical operator for a WHERE clause that tests for inclusion in a named set.

INT Integer data type that can store numbers from -2^{31} to $2^{31} - 1$.

INNER JOIN Command used to join two tables on some common column.

INSERT Command that adds new rows to a table or view.

INSERT INTO .. SELECT A way to insert *many* rows into a table at one time.

INSERT INTO .. VALUES A way to insert values into a table *one* row at a time.

INTEGER Numeric data type that has no digits after the decimal point.

INTERSECT Set operation that combines two queries such that it returns all rows that are in both result sets. Sets have to be union compatible.

IS NOT NULL A WHERE clause option that retrieves all rows that are not nulls.

ISNULL Function that returns a substitute value if a value is null.

JOIN Command used to join two tables. *See also* INNER JOIN.

LEFT(a,b) String function that returns the left b characters from string$a$.

LEFT JOIN *See* LEFT OUTER JOIN.

LEFT OUTER JOIN A join where all the rows from the first (left) relation are retained in a result set.

LEN String function that returns the length (as an integer value) of a string.

LIKE WHERE function that matches a given pattern.

LOWER String function used to display a character string in lowercase.

LTRIM(*a*) String function that removes blanks from the beginning of string *a*.

MAX Aggregate function that returns the highest of all values from an attribute in a set of rows.

MIN Aggregate function that returns the lowest of all values from an attribute in a set of rows.

MINUS Set operation that returns only those rows from the result of the first query that are not in the result of the second query; this operation is not directly available in SQL Server, but a workaround is to use IN or NOT .. IN.

MONEY Data type used with currency data.

MONTH Date function that extracts the month from a date.

NATIONAL CHARACTER Data type; synonym for NCHAR data type.

NCHAR Fixed-length Unicode character data type.

NOT Operator that inverses the logic of a logical operator like IN, LIKE, and EXISTS.

NOT BETWEEN Operator that allows you to determine whether a value is outside of a given range of values.

NOT EXISTS Operator that returns true in a WHERE clause if the subquery following it returns no rows (i.e., is false).

NOT NULL Operator that returns true if an attribute has a nonnull value.

NOT NULL Constraint Integrity constraint that denies the insertion of a value that is null.

NULL Value that is unknown or undefined or not knowable.

NULLIF Function that returns a NULL if a certain condition is met in an expression.

NUMERIC Synonym for DECIMAL data type.

NVARCHAR Variable-length Unicode character data type.

OR Binary logical operator that returns a true value if either one of the expressions is true.

ORDER BY WHERE clause add-on that sorts the results of a query before they are displayed.

OUTER JOIN Join where rows from a table are kept in the result set even though there is no matching row in the other table used in the join.

PERCENT Display function that is used to return a certain percentage of records that fall at the top of a specified range.

PRIMARY KEY Constraint used to create a primary key in a table. Primary keys are unique to a table, and no part of a primary key can be null.

REAL Decimal data type that has a precision of seven digits.

REFERENCES Constraint that defines the table name and key used to reference another table.

RIGHT(a,b) Function that returns the right b characters from string a.

RIGHT JOIN *See* RIGHT OUTER JOIN.

RIGHT OUTER JOIN Join where all the rows from the second (right) table are kept even if the matching condition of the join is not met.

ROUND Function used to round numbers to a given number of decimal places.

ROWCOUNT n Display function that returns the first n rows in a query. When executed, this function will limit all output until SET ROWCOUNT 0 is executed.

RTRIM String function that removes blanks from the right end of a string.

SELECT Command that allows you to retrieve rows from tables (or views) in a database.

SET Command used to assign values to variables. SET is used in UPDATE commands.

SET DATEFORMAT Date function used to change the format in which SQL Server reads in dates.

SMALLDATETIME Data type that can be used to store dates from January 1, 1900, to June 2079.

SMALLINT Integer data type that can store numbers from -2^{15} to $2^{15} - 1$.

SMALLMONEY Data type that can be used with currency data.

SQL_VARIANT Data type used to store values of any data type except TEXT or IMAGE.

SQRT Row-level function that returns the square root of positive numeric values.

SQUARE Row-level function that returns the square of a number.

STR(n) Conversion function that transforms a number, n, to a character data type.

SUBSTRING(t, s, n) String function that returns part of a string, t, starting at position s for n characters; for example, SUBSTRING('abcdefg', 3, 2) = 'cd'.

SUM Group function that sums all the values for an attribute in a set of rows.

TEXT Character large object data type.

TIME SQL Server 2008's new data type used to store the time without a date component.

TINYINT Integer data type that can store numbers from 0 to 255.

TOP Display function that returns a certain number of rows.

UNION Set operation that combines two queries such that it returns all distinct rows from the result sets of both queries.

UNION ALL Set operation that combines two queries and returns all rows from both the SELECT statements (queries). A UNION ALL includes duplicate rows.

UNIQUE Integrity constraint on a table that disallows duplicate entries for an attribute even though the attribute is not a primary key.

UNIQUEIDENTIFIER   Data type that guarantees worldwide uniqueness of the identifier, even among unconnected computers.

UPDATE Command that changes values in specified columns in specified tables.

UPPER String function used to display a character string in uppercase.

VARBINARY Data type used to store variable-length binary data.

VARCHAR Character data type used when the field length is varying.

VARCHAR2 Oracle equivalent of VARCHAR.

WHERE An optional clause in a SELECT statement that acts as a row filter. The WHERE clause allows you to specify columnar criteria for rows to be selected from a table.

WITH TIES   Display function clause used with the TOP display function to retrieve rows where there are ties.

YEAR Date function that extracts the year from a date.

Index